PENGUIN BOOKS

Letters from the Bay of Islands

Caroline Fitzgerald was born in Christchurch, New Zealand. She gained an MA in Life Writing from the University of East Anglia, Norfolk, England, in 2004. Having worked in journalism and television production, she has also taught English in Germany and New Zealand. She continues to research the history of her ancestors.

The Story of Marianne Williams

Letters from the Bay of Islands

Edited by Caroline Fitzgerald

PENGUIN BOOKS

PENGUIN BOOKS

Published by the Penguin Group

Penguin Group (NZ), 67 Apollo Drive, Rosedale,
North Shore 0632, New Zealand (a division of Pearson New Zealand Ltd)
Penguin Group (USA) Inc., 375 Hudson Street,
New York, New York 10014, USA
Penguin Group (Canada), 90 Eglinton Avenue East, Suite 700, Toronto,
Ontario, M4P 2Y3, Canada (a division of Pearson Penguin Canada Inc.)
Penguin Books Ltd, 80 Strand, London, WC2R 0RL, England
Penguin Ireland, 25 St Stephen's Green,
Dublin 2, Ireland (a division of Penguin Books Ltd)
Penguin Group (Australia), 250 Camberwell Road, Camberwell,
Victoria 3124, Australia (a division of Pearson Australia Group Pty Ltd)
Penguin Books India Pvt Ltd, 11, Community Centre,
Panchsheel Park, New Delhi – 110 017, India
Penguin Books (South Africa) (Pty) Ltd, 24 Sturdee Avenue,
Rosebank, Johannesburg 2196, South Africa

Penguin Books Ltd, Registered Offices: 80 Strand, London, WC2R 0RL, England

First published by Penguin Group (NZ), 2004
This edition published in 2010

1 3 5 7 9 10 8 6 4 2

Copyright © Caroline Fitzgerald, 2004

Typesetting and origination by Sutton Publishing Limited
Printed in Australia by McPherson's Printing Group

ISBN 9780143205708

A catalogue record for this book is available
from the National Library of New Zealand.

www.penguin.co.nz

This book is dedicated to the memory of

Hilda Temple Williams
Algar Temple Williams
David Temple Williams

And to
My Mother and Father

Hauraki Gulf, New Zealand
(future site of Auckland)

On our return we were much relieved by the sight of the *Karere* standing towards the place; she anchored at sunset, and delivered letters from our wives and children, and from many of our natives, for ourselves and [Maori] boys. This was an interesting particular for the people of the place, as they were thus enabled to perceive the nature and value of written characters, by the testimony of these, their countrymen.

Our [Maori] boys seemed to look for, and read over their letters with as much pleasure as we did ours, to the delight of all around; they repeated them aloud, to the admiration of their auditors, who were struck with wonder, at hearing, as they described it, 'a book speak' – for though they expect that a European can perform any extraordinary thing, yet they cannot understand how it is that a New Zealand youth can possess the same power.

Henry Williams
8 November 1833

Contents

List of Illustrations

List of Illustrations

Foreword

The personal letters of Marianne Williams provide an important account of the interpersonal and cross-cultural relationships of Pakeha and Maori in the northern part of Aotearoa/New Zealand in the mid-nineteenth century. Marianne's letters were written during a period of early settlement and mission, and bridge the time before and during British colonisation following the signing of Treaty of Waitangi in 1840. As such, the letters were written at a time of great transition for Maori, and provide an important insight into the everyday lives of Maori and European missionaries while these changes were taking place.

On another level, the letters also give an insight into the everyday problems encountered, such as time spent away from immediate family. Henry Williams writes, 'I am paying more attention than heretofore to the children, a duty which I think has been too much overlooked, in a too ardent desire to carry on the public duties of Mission.' Similarly, one gets a sense of the danger Marianne was exposed to, especially during the early years, when intertribal conflict was a very real threat to her and her family's safety, as well as that of local Maori. These accounts also bear witness to the demands placed upon Henry and Marianne as missionaries with the Church Missionary Society, and help us understand how bonds between Maori and missionary were formed from these common experiences.

I commend the efforts of Caroline Fitzgerald to allow the testimony of Marianne and, through her, of our Maori forebears to speak again of what might have remained hidden.

The Right Reverend Waiohau Te Haara
Retired Bishop of the Bishopric of Te Tokerau of the
Anglican Church of Aotearoa, New Zealand and Polynesia
Paihia, Bay of Islands

Acknowledgements

I wish to thank all those who believed in this project over the years: my mother, Belinda, who pointed me towards the boxes of letters and my father, Gerald, who gifted me the appreciation of this history; Rod, whose memory, although faded, will continue to live through dreams once dreamt; Sandy Pepperill, who encouraged me to revisit this work; Debbie Healy, who reminded me of my dream; Elisabeth and Laura Ludbrook, who walked and talked me around Paihia; Deborah Ludbrook and family, who showed me Northland and fishing; Tom Reed, for his wisdom and insight; and, finally, Bishop Ben Te Haara for 'challenging' me to do this.

For support over many months from friends who have read and reread various drafts and listened to my never-ending discourse, in particular, Rachel Dodd, Wendy Hamilton-Gates, Barbara Tan, Ken and Yvonne Hall, Nicola Nolet, Debbie Spencer Johnson, Allan Matson and Pauline Donovan. With enormous thanks to the following for their hospitality while in England, Tom and Jo Hudson, Simon and Emma Bruce, Miss Emma Bruce, Richard Rowley; and in Germany, Ann and Claus Heidekrueger and Cathy Kos. I would also like to thank the numerous people who kindly gave me their time both in my research and by freely discussing the early history.

With thanks beyond measure to my literary agent Caroline Dawnay and Alex Elam at PFD, London; Margaret Sweet, for her editing and advice in New Zealand. I would like to thank all those at Sutton Publishing, Stroud, England, in particular Jaqueline Mitchell, Senior Commissioning Editor, for believing in this project and Hilary Walford for her thorough and constructive copy editing. Also Ann Hall for her excellent job of indexing and Stephanie Erlich, who braved the Cornish rain for her photograph. Finally, I remember the kindness of the late Archdeacon Sam and Mrs Sybil Woods for the hours of interviewing and their lunches at Waikanae.

Editor's Note

Original letters can be important but not interesting; the letters reproduced in this book are both important and interesting, and their publication will provide some fresh insights into the early associations between the European and Maori in New Zealand during the 1820s and 1830s. *The Dictionary of New Zealand Biography* acknowledges Marianne Williams as 'the first substantial witness to record, from a woman's point of view, early domestic interaction among Maori and Pakeha (European)'. The surviving letters reproduced in this book cover the period from 1822 to 1838, documenting her life, and that of her close relatives and companions, before the British colonisation of New Zealand.

In the light of these letters, I believe we must revisit the story of the British involvement with New Zealand before the Treaty of Waitangi in 1840. For many years Marianne and Henry had, with Maori chiefs, voiced their concerns about the behaviour of seamen, runaway convicts and land speculators from Australia, French colonial interest and the attitudes of some visiting American whalers. Several northern chiefs had asked Henry and other missionaries to request the British Government's assistance in establishing law and order. In 1840, without warning, the British Government's representative, Captain William Hobson, arrived in the Bay of Islands. He brought with him the Treaty of Waitangi. He asked Henry Williams and his eldest son Edward to translate, overnight, the Treaty into Maori. Both of them, after the original signing, took copies of the Treaty to different parts of New Zealand to be signed by Maori chiefs. The differences of opinion that lay between the Church Missionary Society, with whom Marianne and Henry were allied, and the New Zealand Land Company, which became the dominant colonising force in the country, have caused some distortion to the early history.

Since the late 1980s I have sought out and interviewed a number of elderly historians in the family, descended from Marianne and Henry; most of them have since died. I have spoken to descendants of the Maori and European families who lived and met Marianne and Henry from the 1820s to the late 1870s. One Maori Ngapuhi elder, Toru Puriri, based at Waitangi, told me at the end of the three-hour interview: 'You must do this work; so many of the younger generations do not listen nor believe what we elders tell them of the past.'

Toru Puriri died in 2002. He was a direct descendant of the warrior chief Hone Heke and had been a manager of the Waitangi Te Ti Marae trust land. Toru and others had produced a brochure for the tourists, which explained how Henry Williams returned to the Waitangi tribe some eighty-two acres of land he had been given by a chief. These eighty-two acres are all the land on which the Marae and surrounding houses stand, now the home to most of the Waitangi Maori. On the Te Ti Marae, Toru's ancestors carved a statue of Henry into one of the supporting pillars in the meeting house, which became the focus of debate a few years ago when some protestors wanted to destroy the carved effigy.

Since the 1870s a small number of history books have been written about Henry Williams, but Marianne's letters have remained unpublished. A limited edition two-volume *Life of Henry Williams* was produced in 1874 and 1877 by Henry's son-in-law, Hugh Carleton, giving Henry's account of recent history; however, these are now out of print. In 1961 *The Early Journals of Henry Williams, New Zealand, 1826–1840* was edited by Lawrence M. Rogers, but this work does not include Henry's intimate letters written to his family in England. This book is also out of print. Later, in 1973, Rogers wrote Henry's biography, *Te Wiremu: A Biography of Henry Williams*, which was recently reprinted for a family reunion.

There have also been a small number of books written about the early settlers in the 1820s and 1830s, the most recent and notable being Patricia Bawden's *The Years before Waitangi*, self-published in 1987, detailing the history of the interaction between the CMS and the Maori before 1840.

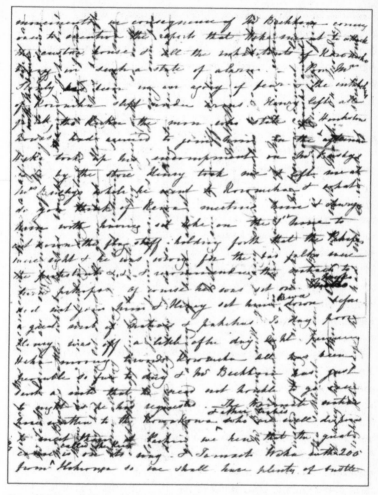

One of Marianne's letters, showing the hatched effect produced by turning the page horizontally. *(Auckland War Memorial Museum, NZ, MS91/75, Item 764)*

In 1977 Sybil Woods wrote *Marianne Williams: A Study of Life in the Bay of Islands New Zealand 1823–1879*, which she published herself. This very limited-edition booklet, written for schoolchildren, is now out of print. There is no doubt a new appraisal about Henry will be written in the future; in my opinion, however, Marianne must come first.

My great-great-grandmother wrote these letters five generations ago in the Bay of Islands, New Zealand, to her family in Nottingham, England, and since that time they have not been read by anyone except my immediate family. For the first ten years Marianne wrote to her mother-in-law, Mary Williams, who passed the letters around the family before they were bundled up for safe keeping. Until, that is, 1832, when through an incidental mention in a letter, Marianne discovered Mary's death. Subsequently, she wrote regularly to her sister-in-law Lydia Marsh, Henry's elder sister. One hundred years later, during the First World War, Marianne's granddaughter, Hilda Williams, was staying in England with her cousin Hal Williams and was shown the boxes of letters written by Marianne and Henry and sent to the family from 1822 until Marianne's death in 1879.

At the end of the war, she brought these back to New Zealand with the aim of having some of them published. Her mission was very personal: the vindication of her grandfather, Henry Williams. Accused of being a 'traitor', 'land-grabber' and 'deceiver' by influential and powerful colonising forces in the 1840s, he was later dismissed from his Paihia mission station. By publishing the letters, Hilda hoped to restore his reputation. She was unsuccessful in her mission and, upon her death in 1939, she left the letters to her brother Algar, who then spent almost twenty years transcribing the handwritten records, which were typed out and bound for safe keeping. In 1961 *The Early Journals of Henry Williams* was published but the family letters remained in their boxes. Algar died in 1965, leaving the original letters to the temperature-controlled Auckland Museum Library and the boxes of typed copies to his daughter.

Owing to wear and tear, they are now almost impossible to read. Paper was a precious commodity in the 1820s, both husband and wife vying for each sheet; to economise, words were written across the page as normal, and, when it was filled, the page was turned horizontally and written across, creating a hatched effect. In some cases, the quality of the thin paper was similar to blotting paper and the ink writing became visible on both sides of the sheet. In regard to the limited supply of paper allocated on leaving England, Henry wrote on Tuesday, 19 November 1822: 'All the paper which was put up for me was two quires; and, as Marianne scribbles as well as myself, she expends her part. My journal also will require all the long paper. The remainder is therefore for writing letters and sermons.' Two quires are the equivalent of fifty sheets of A4 paper. Henry also wrote regular reports to the CMS headquarters in London.

The letters in this book are taken from the typed copies, showing, in most cases, the original spelling and punctuation. However, as Marianne could not speak the Maori language when she first arrived in New Zealand, many names and places that were spelt in the old missionary form have been changed for the purpose of this publication to the modern spelling. For example, Kerikeri (Kiddee Kiddee), Kawakawa (Cowa Cowa), Waimate (Wymate), Hongi Hika (Shunghi), Rangihoua (Rangeehoo), pakeha (packaha).

I have made a decision not to attempt to interpret the material, but simply to present in their entirety these letters as they were originally written in the 1800s. Among the letters I have included some accounts by her husband Henry, his brother William and his wife Jane, Charles Darwin and a Pakeha Maori, as well as entries from young children. Material written by Marianne, by others and by myself is differentiated typographically.

At the close of the letters I provide a short account in the Afterword of the lives of Marianne and Henry Williams after 1838, leading up to the time of the Treaty of Waitangi, Henry's dismissal and subsequent reinstatement.

This collection of letters, written to her family, provides a window into a vanished world. As the wife of the leading missionary, Marianne had access to the important comings and goings around the Bay of Islands, as she witnessed historical events from her Paihia beach home. She also recorded daily events of Maori visitors and the arrival of British explorers to one of the most remote European outposts. During her lifetime Marianne never returned to England but managed regularly to correspond with her often-concerned family, while attending to her ever-growing family and schools in New Zealand. There are large time gaps in the available letters; it seems many never reached their destination, as ships were often lost at sea, or they were misplaced and rotted during the nine-month sea journey. Many more have been damaged and destroyed over the decades, and no doubt some are still in the private hands of her numerous descendants. But those that reached the family were lovingly read and replied to.

Marianne writes of her 'widowhood' when Henry sailed off for months at a time in his role as peacemaker amongst warring tribes, and the anxiety of awaiting his return. During these times she would become the mission leader, totally dependent on the local Maori tribe for protection and food. She writes about her frustration at the lack of supplies from the closest colony, Sydney, and her appreciation for receiving boxes of clothes from family and friends in England. In 1828 she wrote: 'In gratitude to you all for the kind assistance you have given me in presenting us with so many stitches I would willingly send you as many words in return.' For the first few years of their new life in the Bay of Islands, they were often short of food. Limited quantities of flour, sugar, salt, tea, whale oil and soap were allocated quarterly from the Mission Store at Kerikeri, but supplies from Sydney were irregular and frequently insufficient. The local Maori were happy to sell their pigs and potatoes, but usually in exchange for muskets, which was strictly forbidden.

All Marianne's letters were written when the mission stations in the Bay of Islands were the only permanent European settlements in the country and they document the interaction between these two cultures with intimate detail and courageous humour. But above all, they record the thoughts and feelings of a young wife and mother, whose life's work bears testament to her sense of responsibility and duty as a missionary.

Caroline Fitzgerald, 2003

Introduction

Marianne's adventure began the day she left England by sea in 1822, landing a year later on a small beach in the remote Bay of Islands in the north of New Zealand. Marianne, with her husband Henry and three small children, named their new, one-house settlement, Paihia. Under the watchful eye of the local Maori chief Te Koki and his tribe, this remained their home for the next thirty years. At the time of Marianne's arrival there was a small handful of Europeans living in the country, virtually all based at the two nearby Church Mission Society (CMS) mission stations, Kerikeri and Rangihoua, also in the Bay of Islands. Her closest shop was over 1,100 miles away in the Australian colony of Sydney, and her family and friends were 12,000 miles by sea in her native England. All communication was by sailing ship, and, with services irregular, it took eighteen months to obtain a response to a letter. This is her story.

Marianne, known as *Mata Wiremu* (Mother Williams) by the local Maori, was the wife of New Zealand's leading CMS missionary, the Revd Henry Williams. The isolation, poor communications and lack of resources would demand a life of self-sufficiency, versatility and pioneering resourcefulness.

Both husband and wife were continually frustrated by the tyranny of isolation. With all supplies and instructions coming from England and Australia, problems often arose from the inability of others to comprehend the many difficulties they faced daily in the Bay of Islands. For Henry, the fact that the CMS headquarters were based in London made effective leadership a constant challenge.

For Marianne her trials took another form. On any given day she could be expected to face a variety of roles in addition to being a wife and a mother. These would include being a cook, seamstress,

1

hostess, nurse, pharmacist, midwife, schoolteacher, counsellor, domestic science teacher, missionary, community leader, correspondent and historian.

Over the decades, Marianne would be left to run the mission station for long periods of time while Henry travelled by land and sea around New Zealand. Isolation once again added to her stress; with no communication available, it was impossible to know when, or even if, her husband would return from his perilous journeys.

This is a book of letters; a testament to this forgotten era of history, capturing in detail the years between 1822 and 1838, and documenting the harsh realities faced by a handful of English missionaries in pre-European New Zealand. During this time, Marianne found solace in writing, both journals and letters; they were her only link with the world she had known and left behind. They became her sanity and sanctity, her lifeline and wish list. Amidst the clamour of activities, duties and uncertainties, her writing time was sacred and reassuring.

MARIANNE'S ENGLAND

Marianne was born in Yorkshire on 12 December 1793, during the reign of King George III, and was the oldest child of Wright and Anne Coldham. In 1796 they all moved south to Nottingham, where her father hoped to make his fortune in the lace-making industry. During her childhood Marianne witnessed seven small coffins leave the house for the burial of three baby brothers, all christened George, then her infant sisters Frances, Caroline, Fanny and Emily.

When she was sixteen, her father had become the Mayor of Nottingham and her mother was pregnant for the eleventh time. The future looked bright as they celebrated the New Year of 1810, but their joys were short lived. By that summer her mother was dead. Six days after giving birth to a baby daughter named Anne, Marianne's mother died of complications.

There was little time for Marianne to grieve over the loss of her young mother, for she now faced a huge task. Placed in charge of three little sisters, Sarah, Maria and Anne, her blind grandmother

Mrs Temple and the daily running of the three-storeyed mayoral household plus its domestic staff, Marianne also acted as de facto Lady Mayoress for her father at civic functions.

In September 1815 her father died, making her the senior family member remaining for her three younger sisters. Marianne was twenty-two years old and that same year she fell in love with her future husband, Henry Williams.

Henry was born in Nottingham on 11 February 1792, and knew Marianne in childhood, as their fathers had shared the public roles of Sheriffs of Nottingham; both families were also involved in the lucrative lace industry at the height of the Industrial Revolution.

Until, that is, in 1804, Henry's father Thomas Williams died suddenly of typhus fever, leaving behind his widow Mary and their eight young children. Mary eventually sold the family business and opened a boarding school for young ladies in Southwell, just north of Nottingham. Two years later, at the age of fourteen, Henry, with an inherited love of the sea, joined the Royal Navy and served continuously for the next nine years. In January 1815 he fought in the last naval battle against the Americans off New York, which resulted in the capture of the warship USS *President*. With the signing of the peace treaty, they returned to Britain.

In the same year war against France ended with the battle of Waterloo. The Royal Navy decommissioned hundreds of ships, and Henry, now twenty-three years old, retired as a lieutenant on half-pay, returning home with war wounds and a pacifist mindset. Once back on land he took a job as a drawing master at a girls' school not far from Nottingham and soon became a regular visitor to the Coldham household.

Marianne's daughter Marianne Davies later wrote that her mother was described at this time as being:

Tall, about 5 feet 9 inches, slender, very fair, with large blue eyes and a dazzling complexion. Hers was a very gracious personality, but under an apparent sweet gentleness there was an unbending will.

She was a very accomplished young woman, her education far above the average, she had a clear, logical brain, an inexhaustible fund of humour, a very strong sense of the dramatic and would express it in writing and painting. She was an excellent letter writer.

On a winter's day in January 1818, Marianne and Henry were married by his cousin and brother-in-law, the Revd Edward Marsh, who at the wedding reception passed them a copy of the Missionary Register, a magazine produced by the Church Mission Society (CMS). During their honeymoon they read about the newly established mission settlement, Kerikeri, in the Bay of Islands, New Zealand, and plans to provide the missionaries with a supply ship. As a result, Mr and Mrs Henry Williams were soon dreaming about the possibility of moving to the South Pacific and working for the CMS.

Not only did Marianne and Henry share childhood memories and a sense of adventure; they also shared a strong Christian faith, which they had inherited from their parents. Marianne had grown up around her father's interest in the Church of England's Evangelical Movement, some of whose members had been involved in the abolition of slavery in Britain and also in founding the CMS.

Henry's religious education had been hugely influenced by Edward Marsh, who had taken on an almost fatherly role during Henry's years in the Navy. Edward was an active member of the CMS and kept Henry closely informed on the progress of their first New Zealand settlement at Rangihoua in the Bay of Islands. It had been established in 1814 by the Revd Samuel Marsden, the chaplain to the prison colony in New South Wales since 1793. Based in Sydney, Marsden had developed strong friendships with visiting Maori chiefs from the Bay of Islands and at their request had sent three lay-missionary families to New Zealand to help introduce European farming skills and establish a school for Maori pupils.

Not long after their honeymoon, Henry volunteered his naval expertise to the CMS. His offer was declined. The situation the CMS now faced was the possibility of ending missionary work in New Zealand and recalling the families to the safety of Sydney because of the threat of attack and the escalating intertribal wars. However, the CMS suggested another course of action. Would Henry consider moving to New Zealand as an ordained missionary? With Marianne's total backing and support, he accepted. Over the next three years they prepared themselves for their new lives ahead: Henry studied medicine and surgery while gaining practical skills in boat building.

During this time news arrived that the mission stations in New Zealand were being attacked and plundered. The Society, expecting reports at any moment that the lay settlers had been expelled from the country, advised Henry and Marianne that all their arrangements could be cancelled. But they were not discouraged.

Marianne was under no illusion about the enormous challenge that lay ahead for her and had been busy training in midwifery, nursing, teaching and organisational skills. Learning to cook with the aid of her book *Domestic Cookery by a Lady*, she also gained instructions on how to build a vegetable garden and even learnt the art of building a fire in a river bank.

Friends and family showed a supportive interest in the future missionary work that lay ahead for the young couple. However, many were concerned about the realities they would face in New Zealand without doctors, churches, shops, tea houses, schools or other conveniences so taken for granted in England. Before her marriage, Marianne's position had provided her with a full social life and comfortable home, but she soon discovered her taste for fashion was not totally approved of by some members of the Williams's family. Not long before leaving England, Marianne was given a gift of a pretty, frilly parasol, a necessary accessory against the hot sun of the South Pacific. However, she was soon reprimanded by Henry's sister Lydia Marsh, who told her to return it, as it was of 'imputed extravagance' for the wife of a missionary. To keep the peace, Marianne exchanged it for one less elegant.

At the beginning of 1822, with Marianne expecting her third child, the family moved to Hampstead to be closer to the Revd Edward Marsh, who was preparing Henry for ordination. On the night of 16 January, Marianne faced one of her worst fears, and for the next sixteen hours she laboured with a breech birth. When finally, with the help of the doctor, the baby boy was delivered, all thought he was dead. Although Marianne wished to name him Henry, he was called Samuel and, like his biblical namesake, was offered as a servant to God. As an adult, he was their only child to become a missionary.

In June that year, Henry was ordained a priest by the Bishop of London. The departure date was set and last-minute preparations and final farewells were made. As he was on half-pay as a retired naval officer, he refused to accept a salary from the CMS. So keen was he to begin missionary work immediately, Henry had arranged a passage out as chaplain on a women's convict ship. To prepare for this unique position, he spent a few days discussing with Mrs Elizabeth Fry practical ways to help the women during the nine-month journey at sea. She was known for her humanitarian work at Newgate Prison, where she had recently set up a school for female prisoners and their children.

With all preparations complete, Henry and Marianne received their final orders at a special farewell meeting at the CMS head-quarters in London. Addressing the governing committee as the newly appointed missionary leader to New Zealand, Henry spoke of his belief in Marianne as his equal and of the challenges that lay ahead:

> I am not ignorant of your great anxiety in reference to this Mission. I feel anxiety myself. . . . With regard to Mrs Williams, I beg to say that she does not accompany me merely as my wife, but as a fellow helper in the work. Though it will be, for some time, her chief care to watch over those tender plants which are committed to her immediate charge, yet she will, I trust, be performing therein no inconsiderable duty to the Mission.

THE CMS IN NEW ZEALAND

As a young boy Henry had read the accounts of Captain James Cook's expeditions to map the coastlines of New Zealand and

Australia. Aboard that 1776 expedition was the botanist Joseph Banks, who had recorded in his journals his impressions of the land and peoples in the far north of New Zealand: 'It is more thickly populated than those parts further south, the people more elaborately tattooed, some of their canoes more elaborately carved; the bay itself beautiful, with many good anchorages, the hills and valleys round it, forests and cultivations beautiful also. Cook called it the Bay of Islands.' Ten years later, Joseph Banks suggested to the British government that Botany Bay on the eastern coast of Australia could be a suitable location for penal settlements, to replace the lost colonies of North America, where convicts had been sent in the past.

In 1788, with the arrival of the first fleet of prisoners from England to New South Wales, the penal colony of Port Jackson was established. Soon many captains of convict ships, on returning to England, reported seeing large numbers of whales in the Tasman Sea between Australia and New Zealand. This led to innumerable European and American ships sailing into these southern waters in pursuit of valuable whale oil, which was fetching high prices in Britain, where it was used for lighting street lamps and greasing the wheels of the Industrial Revolution. Vast numbers of seals on New Zealand's south-west coast were then reported and another industry sprang up. Sealskins were traded for tea in China and goods in Europe. The oceans of the South Pacific were soon seen as a South Seas emporium.

As a result, whaling and sealing traders became frequent visitors to New Zealand's shores, buying flax, wood, fresh water and food, which they exchanged for axes, tools and fish hooks. Many New Zealand Maori served as crew on the whaling vessels, and soon the Bay of Islands in the far north of New Zealand became the main port of call for these ships.

In 1805 a Bay of Islands chief, Te Pahi, took his five sons to visit the New South Wales's Governor King in Port Jackson (Sydney), where they were introduced to life at the colony, observed European farming procedures and attended church services at Parramatta. There they met the colonial chaplain, the Revd Samuel Marsden, who took a keen interest in the visiting New Zealanders.

During his visit Te Pahi discussed with Governor King the problems arising from the aggression shown by many visiting ships' captains towards the New Zealanders and their lack of respect for the local customs and laws.

One day while visiting court he observed the trial of two male convicts accused of stealing pork from the colony's stores. One of the men was sentenced to death, which shocked Te Pahi. It so happened the following Sunday he recognised them in church and, returning to their jail cell with them, he agreed to present their petition to Governor King. But no amount of reasoning worked with the Governor, and finally, begging for their forgiveness, Te Pahi threw himself to the floor, sobbing bitterly.

John Nicholas recorded the conversation that took place later that evening. During dinner Te Pahi again tried to reason his point that execution was excessive for stealing food, and, in his bid to save the men, he offered an American captain, also sitting at the table, payment of potatoes, if he would ship these two convicts home to New Zealand with him. Unmoved, King again told Te Pahi that these men had violated the laws that were designed to protect the property of others in the colony.

'In that case,' demanded Te Pahi pointing to a ship's captain sitting opposite, 'why not hang up Captain ——? He come to New Zealand, he come ashore and he stole all my potatoes. You hang up Captain —— too !' As a result, the two convicts were eventually pardoned.

Not long after Te Pahi had returned to the Bay of Islands, his nephew, the young chief Ruatara, set off with two friends aboard a sealing ship heading to London to meet the 'Chief of England' King George. Four gruelling years later and after much hardship, he finally reached London, but, unable to arrange a meeting with the King, he was placed aboard the only Pacific-bound transport, a male convict ship heading to Sydney.

Marsden was also aboard with his family returning to Parramatta and found the 22-year-old Ruatara friendless, poor and dangerously ill with tuberculosis. They had met previously in Sydney not long after Te Pahi's visit, but now Marsden found him wrapped up in an old great coat coughing blood. He was rescued from the convicts' quarters and nursed back to health in the safety of the Marsden family cabin. Also aboard were two young lay settlers whom Marsden was taking to Sydney with the hope of eventually sending them to New Zealand. One was William Hall, a carpenter and his family; the other was John King, shoe- and ropemaker and flax dresser, who became good friends with Ruatara, as he had learnt English from sailors during his years at sea.

Upon reaching Sydney shocking news met them. The *Boyd*, an English ship that had visited Whangaroa Harbour just north of the Bay of Islands to purchase timber, had been attacked and all but four of the ship's seventy occupants had been killed and many eaten. This massacre was an act of reprisal or revenge (*utu*) for previous harassment by Europeans. Any plans Marsden might have had of sending missionaries to New Zealand came to an immediate halt.

Although every voice in the colony was raised against the New Zealanders, Ruatara went on to spend seven months on Marsden's Parramatta farm, gaining knowledge in growing wheat and in agriculture and seeing how the British settlement worked. During this time he had discussions with Marsden about taking some of these techniques and skills home to his tribe in the Bay of Islands. Ruatara believed New Zealand could become a great South Pacific nation by growing and exporting wheat to Sydney in exchange for tools and food.

At the same time Marsden also had three other New Zealanders living with him, one being a son of his friend, Chief Te Pahi. Tragically, Te Pahi had been wrongfully blamed for taking part in the massacre of the *Boyd*; subsequently English whalers attacked his island, killing him and a large number of villagers. Later news arrived that it was not Te Pahi, but Te Puhi and his son Te Ara who were the culprits.

Marsden wrote, 'I believe it will be found that we have treated the New Zealanders with the greatest injustice. It is much to be lamented that English men should be the savages they often are. No doubt various reports will be spread in England against the New Zealanders, but it should be remembered that they have no one to tell their side of the story.'

Ruatara eventually returned home after an absence of five years, taking with him the bags of wheat seed that Mr Marsden had given him. Explaining that wheat made the biscuits some of them had eaten on board the European ships, he divided up the seed between six chiefs, his uncle Hongi Hika, his own people and himself.

The wheat was planted, growing well in the Bay of Islands soil, as he had known it would, but, long before it was ripe, some chiefs pulled out a few plants too early, expecting to find the wheat at the roots, like a potato. Initially Ruatara was ridiculed, but before long he harvested his wheat, proving the grain did grow at the top of the plants. He sent word to Sydney for a flourmill, and Marsden put the required equipment and bags of seed onto a ship heading towards New Zealand, but the ship ended up in Tahiti.

Three years after the attack on the *Boyd*, many European vessels still stayed away from New Zealand, making it difficult for Marsden to send out supplies to Ruatara. He decided the only option open to him was to buy a ship himself, and then he could deliver the three lay settlers, Hall, King and the newly arrived Kendall, a London schoolteacher, who were all employed in Sydney awaiting their departure for New Zealand.

Marsden organised for Kendall and Hall to visit Ruatara in the *Active* and deliver a letter informing him of progress for their planned mission station in Ruatara's village Rangihoua. When the *Active* eventually sailed into the Bay of Islands that June, Ruatara left his wheat and potato farm twenty-six kilometres inland and returned to Rangihoua to welcome the visitors. Once on board, he was handed Marsden's letter:

Parramatta, 9 March 1814
Duaterra King (Ruatara)
I have sent the Brig *Active* to the Bay of Islands to see what you are doing; and Mr Hall and Mr Kendall from England. Mr Kendall will teach the Boys and Girls to read and write. I told you when you were in Parramatta I would send you a gentleman to teach your Tamoneeke's [children] and Cocteedo [young girl] to read.

You will be very good to Mr Hall and Mr Kendall. They will come to live in New Zealand if you will not hurt them; and teach you how to grow corn, wheat and make houses and everything. Charles [Marsden's son] has sent you a cock and Mrs Marsden a shirt and jacket. I have sent you some wheat for seeds and you must put it in the ground as soon as you can. I have sent you a mill to grind your corn.

Marsden also invited Ruatara to make the return trip to Sydney on the *Active*; however, if he was unable to do so, he was to advise Hall and Kendall of anything he might need and it would be sent to him. The letter ended with greetings from Marsden's six children and Mrs Marsden.

With the new flourmill and sieve, Ruatara returned to shore and ground some of his wheat. Making it into a cake, he placed it in a frying pan and baked it, finally proving bread and biscuits could be made from wheat.

For six weeks Hall and Kendall stayed with Ruatara, examining his village on the northern shores of the Bay of Islands, where they planned the first CMS mission station, at Rangihoua, and in August the same year the *Active* sailed back to Sydney. Aboard were the chiefs Ruatara, Hongi Hika (with his eight-year-old son, Ripiro), and Korokoro from Paroa Bay. During their crossing of the Tasman Sea, the chiefs and Ripiro became very keen students of the English language, but Kendall believed the New Zealanders would be better taught in their own language and that schoolbooks would need to be prepared.

Upon arriving in the colony, the three chiefs together with their relatives and attendants lived with Marsden for three months on his farm at Parramatta, getting to know the three lay missionaries and their families. The year was 1814.

ESTABLISHING THE FIRST PERMANENT EUROPEAN SETTLEMENT IN NEW ZEALAND

A few months before Henry and Marianne left London in 1822, Henry bought New Zealand's only travel guide of the time, the two-volume set of *Nicholas's New Zealand*, which gave the eyewitness account of the historical 1814 voyage to New Zealand to establish the first permanent European settlement in the Bay of Islands. Accompanying Marsden, the chiefs and the lay missionaries, was John Nicholas, a young settler farmer from New South Wales. During the excursion he kept a daily journal of events, which was later published in London in 1818, in which he described many places and people Henry and Marianne would soon be seeing for themselves.

Ruatara was described by Nicholas as

a man in the full bloom of youth, of tall and commanding stature, great muscular strength, and a marked expression of countenance: his deportment, which I will not hesitate to call dignified and noble, while the fire and animation of his eye might betray, even to the ordinary beholder, the elevated rank he held among his countrymen. His face formed an agreeable contrast to those of his fellow chiefs, for it was not disfigured with the disgusting marks of the tattoo. His complexion was not darker than that of the natives of Spain or Portugal, and in general his countenance assumed the European character.

Hongi is a chief of superior rank and more extensive power than Ruatara. He is not as robust as Ruatara, but his countenance is much more placid and I think more handsome in spite of the tattooing. . . . As the mind of Ruatara was chiefly concerned with agriculture, Hongi was bent on mechanics of which he gave some extraordinary proofs of his skill and ingenuity. I have seen the gun he brought with him stocked in so complete a manner that even the most expert and finished mechanic could not possibly have done it better with the same implements. . . . Although Hongi had the reputation of being one of the greatest warriors in his country, his natural disposition seemed to be mild and inoffensive. He appeared to be much more inclined to peaceful habits than to strife.

Governor Macquarie had taken a keen interest in the settlers' plans, as it was hoped that establishing a settlement in the Bay of

Islands, both whaling and trading ships, would contribute towards the upkeep of a permanent and safe supply base. To provide the New Zealanders with protection against aggressive ship captains, Kendall had been sworn in as New Zealand's first magistrate. He took with him a New South Wales Government proclamation, which now covered the coastal waters of the islands of New Zealand. It stated that any ship belonging to any British port or any of its colonies would have to adhere to British laws of conduct. Any reports of mistreatment, insult or taking New Zealanders against their will by any ships' captains or crews would be punishable in New South Wales and England.

On the day of their departure Nicholas wrote:

19 November 1814. Port Jackson.
The time now arrived when we were to proceed on our destination, and the chiefs, who appeared highly gratified with their visit to the colony, received at their departure a variety of presents. The Governor gave them several articles of very great value, in addition to handsome uniforms which he ordered for them, and three cows, one for each of them. Ruatara was given a gift of a fine mare; and Mr Marsden shipped another, together with a stallion, for the use of the settlers.

Aboard the 110-ton *Active* under the command of Captain Hansen were thirty-five people, including the crew and the lay settlers' wives, Jane Kendall, Dinah Hall and Hannah King, and their children. Nicholas recorded:

It will easily be supposed that with such a number of persons crowded on board a small vessel, our situation was not very comfortable; yet, besides human beings, we had also cattle, together with sheep and pigs for our live stock, and an immense quantity of poultry, belonging to the missionaries. In short, with the addition of goats, cats and dogs, and a variety of other animals, our ship contained such a heterogeneous collection, that it might be said to bear a perfect resemblance to Noah's ark.

13

Owing to a strong easterly headwind, the *Active* was delayed for a week in Watson's Bay, and it was during this time they discovered the chiefs, 'on whose good faith the safety and success of the expedition were to depend, gloomy, sullen and reserved'. When Marsden asked the chiefs what had caused their change of heart, they said they had been told by some unknown gentleman in the Colony that, if the missionaries came to New Zealand, the New Zealanders would lose the independence of their country, their influence, liberties and possibly even their lives. This person had also told Ruatara as proof to his statement, he need only 'look at the conduct of our countrymen in New South Wales, where, on their first arrival, they despoiled the inhabitants of all their possessions, and shot the greater number of them with a merciless cruelty; while, in some few years, the whole race of that once happy people would be entirely extinct'.

The entire expedition was on the brink of collapse; without the promised support and protection from Ruatara and the other chiefs, Marsden could not expect his missionaries and their families to head off to New Zealand without guaranteed security. To reassure Ruatara that the missionaries were interested only in the well-being and happiness of the New Zealanders, Marsden suggested the vessel should return to Sydney Cove, where the missionaries and their families would unload and 'never more think of holding any intercourse with his country'.

It was discovered that the chiefs had been told in Sydney of a plan to form a company that planned to build settlements in New Zealand. These rumours had created such speculation in the colony that now the chiefs feared a possible tidal wave of settlers. However, the chiefs agreed that the *Active* should continue on to New Zealand.

After almost three weeks at sea they reached the North Cape of New Zealand, where Marsden sent a party with Ruatara on shore so they could invite some northern chiefs aboard and explain the planned settlement in the Bay of Islands. Showing them the Government Proclamation, he told the chiefs that any future trouble with aggressive European ships' captains should be reported to Kendall, who in turn would ensure the guilty parties would be dealt with severely in Sydney.

Three days later they anchored off the Cavelli Islands, opposite Matauri Bay, just north of the Bay of Islands, where Ruatara discovered his enemies Te Puhi and Te Ara, camped with 100 Whangaroa warriors a short distance from the village.

Upon seeing Ruatara, they ran off, with Ruatara in hot pursuit. Drawing a pistol from his belt, Ruatara told Te Ara (also known as George) that, if he moved, he would shoot him. He then expressed his wish to live in peace in the future and for them to visit the ship and see Marsden. He told George of Marsden's intentions to establish a mission and teach the New Zealanders the many skills seen in the colony. Nicholas described the scene at Matauri Bay:

It was certainly a grand and interesting spectacle. These savage warriors, amounting to about a hundred and fifty of as fine men as ever took the field in any country, were encamped on a hill which rose in a conical shape to a considerable height. . . . Few of these men were under six feet in height, and their brawny limbs, their determined countenances, and their firm and martial pace, entitled them very justly to the appropriate designation of warriors. . . .

With the exception of the chiefs, there were very few of them tattooed, and all had their hair neatly combed and collected in a knot upon the top of the head, where it was ornamented with the long white feathers of the gannet.

Nicholas continued:

When we got back to the village, Ruatara, with Mr Kendall and Mr King, returned to the vessel, and Hongi, who had ordered his people to prepare some fish and potatoes for our dinner, had them now brought before us, and we sat down with a good appetite.

Men, women and children, flocked in upon us so that to keep ourselves from being suffocated, we were obliged to form a circle, which none was allowed to pass, and seating themselves all round the verge of it, they watched our motions with the most eager curiosity. . . .

They kept their eyes steadfastly fixed on us all the time and they frequently called to those around them to look at the wonders we presented. Many of them expressed their astonishment in silent attention, and others bursting out into fits of laughter at every bit we ate, were exceedingly amused by the spectacle. We distributed biscuit and sugar-candy among several of them, which they liked so well that they appeared eagerly desirous to get more, smacking their lips with an exquisite relish for these unknown luxuries.

Nicholas observed among the crowd some 'venerable looking old men, who regarded us with silent contemplation', who appeared more curious as to what the Europeans were doing there than showing any interest in 'the distribution of the biscuits and sugar-candy. These mute sages were wrapped in profound meditation and looking on us with an air of dignified gravity and serious reflection, they never uttered a word.'

On 22 December they entered the Bay of Islands and with Ruatara at the helm they sailed towards Rangihoua, anchoring in four fathoms of water. Nicholas described the site for the new settlement:

We landed at the opening of a narrow valley, through which a small meandering stream found its way to the sea; the hills on each side were very steep, in some places almost perpendicular, and covered with fern and trees. On the top of a hill that rose to the left of us with a rugged ascent, and overlooking the harbour, was built the town of Rangihoua, now the residence of Ruatara, and lately that of Te Pahi.

Around this town (if it may be so called) were several plantations of potatoes, kumeras, and other vegetables, with an appearance of neatness and regularity. Each plantation was carefully fenced in, and hanging down from the sides of steep hills, reminding one of Chinese cultivation.

With the unloading of the animals from their 'Noah's Ark' and the arrival of the boats with the cattle, the villagers 'appeared perfectly bewildered with amazement towards such extraordinary looking animals'. They had never seen cows or horses before, but their astonishment soon turned into alarm and confusion. One of the cows that was wild and unmanageable, upon landing, rushed in among them, and caused 'such violent terror through the whole assemblage that, imagining some preternatural monster had been let loose to destroy them, they all immediately betook themselves to flight'.

However, they soon returned to watch Marsden mount a horse and ride up and down the beach, creating even more excitement. They had all heard Ruatara's stories of the horse after his previous visit to Sydney, but they had never believed his 'preposterous' accounts. Having no word in his language for this animal, Ruatara thought that *kuri*, a native dog, would be the closest in description; but struggling to imagine such a creature could exist, they never believed a single word he said. (The native dog had been brought by the early Polynesians in the first fleets to reach New Zealand.) To make matters worse, 'when he told them that he had seen large kuri carry men and women about in land canoes [horse-drawn carriages], they would put their fingers in their ears to prevent themselves from listening to him, and desire him very indignantly not to tell so many lies'.

Ruatara then introduced his three wives. His head wife, Miki, considered by the tribe as queen, was presented by Marsden with a cotton gown and petticoat, a gift from Mrs Marsden, which she put on. 'The curiosity of the natives to see us brought crowds of them round the hut of their chief, and there were many old men, who, like those at the Cavallis, regarded all our actions in profound silence.' Over the following days, Marsden's party were entertained to a mock Maori battle and shown around the settlement by Ruatara.

On Christmas morning, all on board were up at an early hour, with the English party making their way onto the Rangihoua beach. They found Ruatara had arranged an enclosure and constructed the first New Zealand pulpit with planks and an old canoe. In front of it were long planks for the Europeans to sit on. Nicholas described the day:

> As soon as we landed, [Chief] Korokoro drew up all his men and marched them rank and file into the enclosure, where the whole population of Rangihoua had assembled in expectation of our arrival. The chiefs were dressed in their regimentals, with their swords by their sides, and keeping their people in good order, awaited, with becoming silence, the commencement of the service.
>
> When we were all seated, Mr Marsden, dressed in his surplice, ascended the place designed for him, which was covered in a black cloth manufactured in the country, and began in solemn and impressive manner the service for the day.
>
> The natives, being ranged in a circle at a convenient distance within the enclosure, were directed by Korokoro, with a flourish of a cane which he held in his hand, to rise and sit down as we did; and he was not more exact in giving the signal than they were in attending to it. If he saw any of them inclined to talk, he tapped them on the head with his cane, and immediately commanded silence.

Ruatara interpreted the service for the congregation, explaining to them the importance of what they had heard, and that they should all be anxious to know and worship this God. He also advised them that they should all do everything they could to understand the religion that was being introduced to them. Any difficult questions asked were momentarily sidelined and all were told that all would be made clear to them at a future time.

> The service ended, we left the enclosure; and as soon as we had got out, the natives, to the number of three or four hundred, surrounding Mr Marsden and myself, commenced their war dance, yelling and shouting in their usual style, which they did, I suppose, from the idea that this furious demonstration of their joy would be the most grateful return they could make us for the solemn spectacle they had witnessed.

It was not, however, without feelings of sincere pleasure at the promise afforded by this day, of the future success of the mission, that we stepped into the boat to return to the ship; and the chiefs, with their people, gave us every reason to hope that they might, at no distant period, become as civilized as they were brave, and as enlightened as they were hospitable.

After the Christmas service, Marsden and Nicholas travelled to many places in Northland and as far south as the Hauraki Gulf, today the city of Auckland. They took with them Ruatara and Korokoro, plus twenty-six other New Zealanders and seven Europeans. During the voyage they bought extensive supplies of flax and timber for subsequent sale in New South Wales, and visited many tribes in the Thames area, exchanging gifts of nails, fish hooks, wheat seed and feather adornments.

Just before he left on 26 February, Marsden bought for twelve axes more than 200 acres of land at Rangihoua. This was the first European land transaction in New Zealand. It was signed by Kendall and Nicholas, while Hongi suggested that Gunnah and his brother Whare, neither of whom could write English, should use the drawing of their moko, or facial tattoos, as their signature. These two chiefs were cousins of Ruatara and owners of the land.

Rangihoua was the first attempt by Europeans to live in a permanent relationship with the New Zealand people, and, with the land transactions in order, the area was now made tapu (sacred) by Gunnah for the settlers. Marsden hoped Rangihoua would be considered neutral territory, where people from tribes and cultures would always be welcome to buy supplies and tools, and meet in peace and harmony. As the New Zealander always respected the tapu as sacred, the European settlement was to continue in safety in the years to come.

When Marsden sailed out of the Bay on 26 February 1815, he left behind the three lay settlers and their families in one of the most isolated settlements imaginable. The total number of Europeans at

Rangihoua, including a blacksmith, sawyers and their families, was twenty-five. Without the means to leave the island, these families would be totally reliant on the goodwill of Ruatara and his tribe, and dependent on visiting whaling ships for incoming supplies. The regular arrival of ships from Port Jackson was unpredictable and the lack of communication and instructions from Marsden added to an already demanding situation.

Marsden had taken back to Sydney with him a number of chiefs and chiefs' sons, and he set up a farming school on the northern banks of the Parramatta River. The plan was to provide a safe place where the sons of chiefs of rival tribes could live and work together, build friendships and gain a greater understanding of each other, away from the tribal tensions of everyday life at home.

However, no sooner had he returned home, than Marsden received the news that Ruatara had died of tuberculosis within days of the *Active* sailing out of the Bay of Islands. His dying wish included that his cow and new calf, gifted to him by Governor Macquarie, should be given to his aunt, Te Pahi's widow. He also asked for his young son to be sent to Sydney to be educated at Marsden's school. Finally, he asked his head wife, Miki, to remind Gunnah and Whare to continue being kind to the settlers.

In response to Ruatara's death, Miki hung herself the following day. Marsden later wrote to the CMS headquarters in London:

Parramatta, 28 October 1815

His death has been a subject of much pain and regret to me. On my arrival with him at New Zealand with the rest of the settlers, he appeared to have accomplished the grand object of all his toils, an object which was the constant subject of his conversation, namely, the means of civilizing his countrymen.

He thus observed to me, with much triumph and joy, 'I have now introduced the cultivation of wheat in New Zealand; New Zealand will become a great country in two years more; I shall be able to export wheat to Port Jackson, to exchange hoes, axes, spades, tea, sugar,' etc. Under this impression he made arrangements with his people for a very extensive cultivation, and formed his plan for building a new town with regular streets, after the European mode, on a beautiful situation which commanded a view of the mouth of the harbour and adjacent country. . . .

He was a man of clear comprehension, quick perception, and of a sound judgement, and a mind void of fear; at the same time he was mild, affable and pleasing in his manners. His body was strong and robust, and promised a long and useful life. At the time of his death, he was in the prime and vigour of manhood, extremely active and industrious. I judge his age to be about twenty-eight years.

The relationship between Marsden and Ruatara had been critical to establishing the Rangihoua mission station. Hugh Carleton, Henry's biographer, wrote in 1877: 'but for the determined support which Ruatara, as a high chief, was able to afford, Marsden could never have gained a footing in the land.'

However, from Sydney in June 1815, Marsden had also written: 'I am happy to say I left all the settlers satisfied, and I think they will do well.' This confidence soon proved misguided. Although Hongi and others had promised him protection of the European settlers, Marsden had failed to appoint a European leader, and this led to a split in the small settlers' community. King, Hall and Kendall were struggling to get along; they had to live in a single hut on the low-lying piece of land, which flooded when it rained. Described by John King, the hut was sixty feet long by fourteen wide, with no window and it could 'neither keep wind nor rain out'. Marsden's plans for communal living in the absence of mutually acceptable leadership proved whimsical.

As Kendall had been appointed a magistrate before leaving Sydney, he believed these credentials gave him the indisputable right of authority over King the shoemaker and Hall the carpenter – a power both men refused to accept. In January 1816 King wrote to the CMS: 'We are endeavouring to live in peace with all men, but meet with great opposition from Mr Kendall. He tries to set the natives against us by telling them I am nothing but a servant, that he is a great gentleman, he goes aboard ships that come in, and gives us a bad name to the Captain . . .'. The men resented Kendall's attitude. They were disturbed by the implication that they were considered labourers whereas Kendall was regarded as their intellectual superior with the easy job of running the school and studying the Maori language. Despite all this, a schoolroom was built and opened in 1816 with thirty-three young pupils, mostly girls.

In 1819 Marsden returned to establish a second settlement in the Bay of Islands at Kerikeri on land brought from Hongi Hika, where they built homes and a stone store supply depot for the mission workers. He brought with him the first ordained missionary, the Revd John Butler, his wife and child, plus the Kemp family. A year later Mr Marsden made his third visit to New Zealand with a cargo of stores, cattle and horses.

Since his previous visit, the question of leadership amongst the two mission stations had caused more disharmony. Butler's appointment as superintendent had not been the hoped-for success; he had offended both Maori and other settlers, and now Kendall secretly planned to sail to England with the chiefs Hongi Hika and Waikato (Hongi's brother-in-law and Ruatara's brother). Kendall resented Butler as the new leader, and this had motivated him to return to England to become an ordained missionary 'in order to perform full divine service and to ensure his independence from Butler'.

In March 1820 Kendall sailed to London taking the two chiefs with him, where the CMS leaders received them with much respect and kindness. Soon after their arrival, they spent two months working with Professor Lee at Cambridge University on the construction of the first Maori Grammar. This work had been one of Kendall's objectives, but the major purpose of his voyage was his ordination. Although he had left New Zealand without the permission of Marsden or Butler, authority was finally granted to him by the CMS and Kendall was ordained.

While in England, they also visited King George IV, who, like many others, gave to Hongi and Waikato valuable gifts, including a suit of armour. Hongi's chief objective in visiting England was the purchasing of guns and he became furious with the CMS in London when they encouraged him to give up fighting and cultivate peace.

On their return to Sydney in May 1821, the royal gifts were exchanged for a large supply of muskets and ammunition, which led to a bitter dispute between Marsden and Kendall, with Marsden accusing him of trafficking in arms. Meanwhile, Hongi Hika, while staying with Marsden in Parramatta, met a party of four enemy chiefs from the River Thames, who were also planning to visit King George. Hongi talked them out of it, telling them they would not like the English weather, but suggested they might be better off returning to New Zealand in preparation for war and to await his imminent arrival.

Once back in the Bay of Islands, Hongi threw aside the peaceful support of the missionaries and embarked upon war. With 2,000 men in fifty war canoes (*waka*), they swept down the island, killing thousands of men, women and children, and taking about 2,000 prisoners, the majority being children. On returning to the Bay of Islands, Hongi paraded his captives at Kerikeri, in front of the horrified missionaries, who witnessed dozens of executions. Following Hongi's contempt towards the missionaries, lesser chiefs began to enter the missionaries' homes, stealing food and goods.

Added to this, within the two stations, Rangihoua and Kerikeri, there was now a total breakdown in leadership. Kendall and young Samuel Butler (the son of John Butler) were dismissed for their part in trading guns and Butler was having drinking problems. Marsden, forced to implement clear and very specific regulations and to re-establish order, would soon appoint Henry Williams as the new mission leader.

THE LETTERS

1822

Marianne (28) and Henry (30) left England on a September summer's evening in 1822 aboard the Lord Sidmouth, *a ship chartered to carry women convicts to the Australian penal colony of New South Wales. Aboard were their three children, Edward (Teddy), almost four, Marianne (Totty), a two-and-a-half-year-old and Samuel, only nine months, in the cramped, stark cabin that would be their home for the next half year.*

Sailing slowly away from Woolwich, down the River Thames towards the open sea, the convict women and children were confined below in the ship's hold, out of the way of the crew working on the deck. In all there were ninety-seven prisoners with twenty-two children, plus nineteen free women and their forty-four children, who were travelling out to meet their husbands in Australia. Of the ninety-seven convicts facing 'Transportation to Parts Beyond the Seas', fifty-nine had been sentenced to seven years, eighteen to fourteen years and twenty to life.

As the Lord Sidmouth *began its journey, most of the cargo was suffering from nervous stomach upsets and within days this turned to seasickness, for no one aboard except Henry and the crew had ever been on an ocean voyage; some had never seen the sea before.*

15 September 1822, the date on which our voyage commenced. We passed a dismal Sunday, worked round the north foreland, and sent our letters on shore by the pilot.

Henry

16 September 1822. The wind for the last three days has been blowing strong from the east. We did not see the downs till yesterday evening, and dismissed the pilot at eight o'clock. During the rough weather all the women and children were very sick. Marianne braved the first day remarkably well, and was able to attend to poor Teddy and Totty, who were in much distress. But Saturday and yesterday they were all ill together. We obtained assistance from one of the women [Frances, a convict woman].

Poor Teddy asked if we could not get to New Zealand in a coach, for he did not like to be pulled up and down so much. Little Samuel was quite uncomfortable at the tossing of the ship. I feel much delight amidst all this, that no one has wished to be back in Camden town. The children have behaved exceedingly well, and appear quite at home; and Marianne, their mother, has not shown any signs of fear, though she has suffered very much.

Yesterday was a sad Sunday. Being tossed to and fro, there was but little appetite for reading. We are this morning riding on a smooth sea, Dover on one side of us, and Calais on the other, and the weather remarkably fine. This is a great treat to Marianne. There is a light air, but it is contrary.

Wednesday, 18 September 1822. Henry called me on deck late in the afternoon to take my last view of dear England off Plymouth. At midnight the Lizard lights were abreast of us. The easterly breeze freshened as the night advanced.

Thursday, 19 September 1822. The wind roared, and the waves dashed against the ship's side the whole night, and though I was disposed to sleep, relieved from all the side-ache and headache of the former night, yet I was continually awaked by the loud rattling and banging of various articles of cabin furniture, which the heavy rolls of the vessel occasioned. The little French lamp would not burn, as the heavy motion of the ship buried the wick in the oil; and, to obtain light to attend upon the children, we were obliged to have the door open into the steerage, where thirty of the crew sleep and mess, and where a lamp swung violently, and glared partially upon the strange scene.

Hearing in the morning that the sea-sickness had commenced in the prison, I had the precaution to remain in my cot till after breakfast. Frances was able to attend, as usual, and except little Teddy being sick when first he arose, our little family escaped this distressing attendant upon the rough weather, which made havoc among the women and children.

While I was dressing, the captain sent the carpenter to lash down the lea dead light, a sort of outside closely fitted window shutter, to save us from shipping a sea, as one had come on board just after the children's dinner. The daylight was now totally excluded, and a candle, lashed tight to my little work table; Totty and Teddy laid fast asleep, upon the sofa bed; and little Samuel, heedless of the storm, gambolled upon my knee while Frances read a portion of the scripture.

When summoned to dinner at two o'clock, the scene exceeded all my ideas and all the descriptions I had read. I had thought it very grand when I sat on the quarterdeck with the children in the morning, watching the sea as it broke over the head of the vessel. But now the continuance of wind had increased the sea and we were in the words of the psalmist 'mounted up to the heavens, and cast down into the depths'. The whole arrangements of the dinner table were extraordinary to me. At tea, seven o'clock, the night was dark, the sound and motion increased, and during our meal a most vivid flash of lightning made us all start, and the thunder instantly broke over our heads.

Friday, 20 September 1822. This day was dismal from the rain, which fell in the morning and the motion became more unpleasant from the wind being contrary. Even Henry was sick. Frances, though still weak from her illness the first few days, was able to attend and stagger about to our assistance. The children were both sick, and the daylight again excluded except that it was partly admitted for an hour or two when we rose in the morning. I felt so much supported, that about noon, a storm being apprehended, I left our little family, comfortably seated by candle light, in the cabin, and went to comfort the poor prisoners, by reading the 71st, 91st and 116th psalms. Soon the sun broke, the tarpaulin was removed from off the hatchway, and the women, those who were able, to their great relief admitted on deck.

Sunday, 22 September 1822. A much calmer day, though with contrary wind. At breakfast the captain proposed the service being on deck, and as I sat with the children upon the quarter-deck, I was amused by seeing the sailors, one by one, showing their humanizing faces and forms above the hatchway. The spruce jacket, the clean straw hat, the shoes, the change in their whole appearance, gave some indications of a Sunday and a cessation from work. The boys of some of the most respectable of the free women appeared, walking about with gloves on; and from distant whispering groups I caught the sound of 'Church! Dressing for Church!' and saw many a facetious look I could not fathom. The service was, however, owing to the dampness and variableness of the weather, performed in the prison.

23 September 1822. Atlantic. At dinner this day the motion of the vessel was so great, that the captain said that he did not expect to have seen me; and the passing remarks at the table convinced me that they did really consider this a tremendous sea, and also that the captain was preparing for bad weather or a squall. The captain continually called to the man at the wheel as we were pitching against a head-sea, as it is called, 'Ease the helm! Ease the helm! Down with it!'

The sea dashed over the vessel, each time she seemed to dive her nose into the deep. Then a sudden lurch would send the plates and dishes against the puddings, which are narrow cloth rollers filled with peas, and strapped lengthwise and crosswise on the table. The fiddlestrings are four long strings passed through four holes in a small square piece of wood at each end, and then tied across the table, one at the top and another at the bottom, just above the space left for the plates. In these the glasses are set, and though thus confined we were obliged to empty them each draught to preserve the contents from spilling. Our chairs were lashed to the table; and we held our soup plates in our hands, and they reeled with us and thus were preserved from spilling. It was with great difficulty that the steward who waited upon us kept his legs.

Returning to our cabin, I found the three darlings lying on the couch, and Frances, securely jammed in between the couch and the drawers, holding Samuel, and keeping watch. Teddy explained he had been sitting again from breakfast to dinner, and could not stand a bit.

Henry

23 September 1822. For many days after our departure what with the illness of one and the other, little communication was held with the women by me; for every part of the ship below was so offensive that I was always glad and almost obliged to keep the deck.

Marianne was the first who ventured there for the purpose of reading the scriptures. I felt quite unable at that time, but on the week after our departure, being Sunday, we had service below.

The captain read the prayers of the church on deck to his own crew. In the evening I read to the prisoners part of the psalm for that morning and gave them a few words upon it, particularly pointing out that, when men cry unto the Lord, he is ever ready to deliver them out of their distress. As it was the psalm for the day, and applicable to the present state of the persons on board, I called their attention to it rather than any other. We afterwards had the evening hymn and closed with a short prayer.

The poor women appeared to feel a degree of pleasure, and on taking my leave, expressed themselves thankful. They afterwards sang many hymns and psalms by themselves. I then visited the free women, and invited them.

On Monday the school was to commence on deck, but the weather proving cold, with a fresh breeze, nothing was accomplished. In the evening I visited the prison, and read to them the passage of Christ stilling the tempest, with a few remarks, the hymn and prayer, as before. I did not observe the free women. I have since entered into conversation with one or more at a time, and observe great quietness and order amongst them.

Tuesday, 24 September 1822. I rose this morning with my usual feeling of fatigue, for although I had the benefit of a good and quiet sleep before twelve o'clock, yet the tremendous pitching of the vessel about that time, from a squall, and the incessant and heavy rolling and banging from the succeeding calm occasioned us a disturbed and anxious night. Little Edward was sick again. It was wet and dirty.

At breakfast the captain greatly rejoiced to perceive a gleam of sunshine; for his men (he said) had been soaking wet through the night. He himself was twice wet through, and between one and two this morning it rained so fast that the scupper holes would not let it out fast enough, and it was over the shoe-tops. By the time we had got our cabin in order, and finished, not without much staggering to and fro, our morning operations, Henry came down to say it was fair, and we might go on deck, and the wind was abaft the beam. I staid with the children some time on deck, though we were obliged to sit very steadily. The sun shone and the captain seemed in spirits. The swell continued, and now as I am writing at the cabin window while Frances is feeding the children as they sit upon the sofa bed, the sound of the vessel passing through the water resembles a large water mill.

We are, however, again bounding over the foaming deep, no longer delayed by contrary winds; and we should do well to sit down, and consider how much we have to be grateful for. Even now the pitching of the vessel is great. We are still mounted up to the heavens and down into the deep, and should be at our wits end, were it not that we have become accustomed to the scene.

At teatime when I ascended the hatchway, the ship by moonlight afforded a striking sight, and the portentous clouds were beautifully feathered off by the moonbeams, which illuminated the foamy billow and the sails. We have every cause for thankfulness. Our temporal comforts are many, but most of all we have cause to praise that redeemer, through whom we have access to the throne of grace, that our minds have been kept staid and even cheerful amidst such distress.

For myself, unable as I was to separate the idea of constant danger from a continuation of fatiguing and very rough weather, I have increased cause for joy, that when watching for the morning, as the psalmist so faithfully describes, through a long night season of apprehension and fatiguing watchfulness, the overwhelming billows and the yawning gulf have alike seemed divested of their terrors.

Strength and sweetness I have found in those words,

> Jesus thou our guardian be!
> Sweet it is to trust in thee!

Wednesday, 25 September 1822. I was too fatigued and too much overcome with extreme lassitude to write a line, even while the children were asleep this morning; and I believe everyone on board felt overcome by the tremendous motion of the vessel last night. I had slept for the last two or three nights in the standing bed, feeling that the swinging of the cot made me giddy; and now I was obliged to hold firm by a bolt in the side of the cabin, fearful that with my babe I should be rolled out of bed.

Little Teddy woke more frequently than usual, alarmed by the swinging of his cot, and exclaiming that he should fall out of the ship. Even the captain said he had not had half an hour's sleep. This morning there was still a heavy cross-sea, but just as the children had finished their dinner, Henry came to fetch us upon deck, when we found that the captain was in high spirits, the weather fine, the wind fair. It is impossible to express how easy the rolling and pitching of the ship becomes under these inspiriting circumstances. The wind being with us gradually drives us down the sea, and it is not so much of a swell as it was. Still we roll very much.

Thursday, 26 September 1822. Lat.38, Long.14, west. We rose, very much refreshed by the first night of sleep since quitting the channel, the weather fine and moderate, an inexpressible relief to all on board, and, as the surgeon said at dinner, might be the saving of the lives of some of the women.

Still there is much motion in the ship, though easy by comparison. We have great cause for gratitude that through the rough weather the children met with no accident, and that no heavy things got loose in the cabin to endanger our legs or our necks. Of late to walk or to stand has been almost impossible, and to sit or lie down very fatiguing. I myself am covered with bruises. The two eldest children are grown thinner, but little Samuel has thrived exceedingly, and is as fat, merry and hearty as possible. He cut his fifth tooth this day.

Teddy has not missed one day begging me to write either to his little cousins or his grandmamma, and is continually thinking of somebody in England he should like to see again.

'Do mamma, tell them Teddy has been very sick.' His plaintive and affectionate remarks are very moving. Poor boy, his uncomfortable feelings have rather tried his temper, but the moment calm weather returns he is as happy as ever. He is greatly distressed to see the poor sailor boys without shoes and stockings, and one day when the carpenter came into our cabin to lash the dead lights in (for we have several days sat by candle light) little Teddy exclaimed – 'O Mamma, look at that poor man without shoes and stockings!' Henry put his hand before his mouth, fearful that the carpenter, who is a great man here, should be offended. Dear little Samuel gambols about, and has gained as much fat as the others have lost.

We have seen a good deal of the women considering the distressing state they have been in; and Henry has read and prayed with them several evenings. I have only been once down into the prison to read to them, and that was last Sunday.

The occasion, the scene, and the stormy wind so excited me that I spoke more words of exhortation than I ever did in my whole life. Afterwards I staggered and stumbled into the place occupied by the free women. There the scene was ten times more distressing than in the prison. The number of the children and the sick was much greater. The cockroaches were swarming in some of the berths where the poor creatures lay, too ill to regard them, and the water was so bad, that those who were frantic with thirst could scarcely bear to taste it. Never had I regretted that I came, but nothing short of our undertaking could support me. I am very happy, and I wish I had time to tell you of our many comforts. It is impossible to express how I enjoy the present quiet moments.

Henry adds: 'We have a most destructive animal on board, the cockroach. Innumerable hoards of them attack all before them. They are something in the nature of the locust, and have committed dreadful havoc amongst the bread, cheeses, hams, potatoes, books, but none of ours, boots, shoes, paper parcels, musket stocks etc., and nearly tapped the gooseberry wine by eating away the cork. The mate, going down, observed it dropping. We therefore just saved it in time. The destruction is considered worse than with rats. When we first come down in the evening to the cabin, it always occupies me some time to slay these monsters with the heel of the shoe; which they understand as a summons to beat the retreat, and scamper off as fast as possible.

They sometimes visit us in vast numbers (I may say) multitudes at an instant from all quarters, and run over everything. This is termed a wedding, and is a most extraordinary evolution that with one consent at the same instant of time thousands of these creatures should leave their habitations and go abroad not from one place, but from all sides of the vessel.'

Friday, 27 September 1822. The inexpressible relief which the cabin and quiet of yesterday and today has afforded me the refreshment of two nights of sleep, the first I had had since leaving the channel, and the hopes which the first mate gave us yesterday that the captain would probably call at Madeira and thus give us an opportunity of sending letters home, have excited in us the greatest thankfulness and joy. The pleasure of writing to all with the prospect of soon sending our communications is so great that not even a headache, which the close warm air and gradual change of climate with long continued fatigue has occasioned, can unfit me for it.

Edward is always begging me to write to his cousins or his grandmamma, and whenever Henry takes his station by the cabin window, little Totty begs to see Papa write to Uncle Marsh. The day before yesterday just after being very sick Teddy exclaimed – 'Mamma I do not want all my little dear cousins to leave me. I should like to see them all again.'

Saturday, 28 September 1822. Lat.35, Long.14. I still suffer much from head-ache, for which the doctor administered some medicine. Henry distributed prayer books.

Sunday, 29 September 1822. It blew a gale all night and through the whole of this day. Service on deck or below was alike impossible. We were driving off Madeira, and prevented touching. My indisposition increased, and I took more medicine. Sea sickness returned in the prison, and Henry felt unwell. A dismal Sunday, so great a sea that the spray broke over the children on the quarter deck to little Samuel's great delight, and we retreated just in time to escape a complete drenching.

2 October 1822. Moderate and fine wind, south-west. At daylight we saw the Island of Canary. I engaged Kitty Jones, one of the convict girls, to assist in taking care of the children. I talked seriously of weaning little Samuel.

Henry
3 October 1822. Marianne has taken very unwell with feverish symptoms, and has suffered much from a severe head-ache, the fever increasing. We were obliged to separate little Samuel from her. He has borne his privation like a philosopher. We have received hitherto the utmost civility from the doctor and captain, who have not failed in providing anything which might tend to the comfort of Marianne.

I read the funeral service over a little child, one of the twins.

4 October 1822. Lat.25. Yesterday the doctor said the pressure upon the head and the fullness of pulse was relieved, and after many days of stupour and inactivity I have this day, by the blessing of God, been able to take a little charge of my children and even set a few stitches of work as I sat with them under the awning on the quarter deck. I still have some head-ache and quickness of pulse. But may I be saved from ingratitude, for all these mercies, and patiently await my recovery in the Lord's own way!

These letters dance, and I am not able to write much. Yesterday we caught the trade wind. Our dear infant may be said to have had a providential escape to-day. Kitty, coming down to the cabin, fell into the hold, which is just outside the door and was carelessly left open. Had the babe been in her arms, which was the case just before, I tremble to think of the consequences.

9 October 1822. To-day for the first time I saw some flying fish, although they have been seen by many on board for more than a fortnight. Two of them flew on board. Their light transparent wings are very beautiful.

The island of St Anthony has been in sight all day. At first it appeared like a light cloud. Just now I saw the divisions of the high barren land. Two days ago a ship passed us, homeward bound, without speaking. My head and eyes are too weak for writing.

Sunday, 13 October 1822. Another fine Sunday, the second time of Henry's performing service to the whole ship's company. I was sorry that Henry had so disturbed a night from dear little Samuel being restless and feverish with his teeth, the heat is intense.

Monday, 14 October 1822. The thermometer in our cabin, with doors and windows open constantly night and day 84. It has been 90 in the night. Henry had again a disturbed night with little Samuel. The remaining twin died about eleven a.m. on deck. Henry read the service over it at three in the afternoon. He began this morning his adult school on deck. It lightened much in the evening.

Tuesday, 29 October 1822. Lat.4.44. I have graciously been permitted steadily to gain appetite and strength notwithstanding the excessive heat and disturbed nights with dear Samuel, cutting his teeth. I had lost so much flesh that I had resolution to wean Samuel. The goat still gives milk; and another goat is daily expected to kid. For this we are very thankful. Samuel is Henry's care in the night only, that now I help little. We have been more than a fortnight becalmed in this hot and trying climate, and all on board have suffered much. Yet have there been very few sick, and our own children are in good health.

To-day we have got a breeze which (they hope) is the trade, to carry us to the coast of Brazil. You cannot imagine the relief it is to know that we are now proceeding, besides the coolness. The ample supply of under-linen is a great comfort to us, for here linen becomes unpleasant from the constant and profuse perspiration, before it is soiled. This breeze makes me cry for joy.

I hope I never look back according to scripture meaning of the word upon my dearest friends, though during my late illness I was obliged strictly to watch my thoughts, English comforts, and English friends were becoming too dear to me. I was happy to find that as I decidedly began to recover, the interest and energy returned, which illness had benumbed, and New Zealand became again the leading object.

Henry

29 October 1822. Atlantic. We were unable to call at Madeira, but were driven close to Grand Canary, and also to the Cape-Verd islands. They were not in the least inviting, for they appeared dry parched up spots. The sight of them almost melted us, and brought to our remembrance our brethren, going to Sierra Leone.

> *The first wave of CMS missionaries leaving Britain went to Sierra Leone, in West Africa, which was founded as a colony for liberated slaves in 1787. They took their belongings out in custom-built coffins, as they were usually in need of them within a year of arrival. CMS missionary death records show: 'died of fever – five months; died of fever – one month; died of fever – three days.'*

30 October 1822. Lat.3.34. Henry has kept a constant journal. I hope his labours among the women will not be in vain, although the bad, the dissolute and the careless seem very far to exceed the quiet, the attentive, and the serious.

The church on deck on the late fine Sundays has been an interesting scene. The whole ship's company as well as the women assembled on the quarter deck, and Henry is mounted upon the poop at the top of the roundabout house. The only uncomfortable feeling to me is their all sitting during the whole service; and the officers who certainly have sea legs, sit too. The men stand the whole service for want of room.

An American captain, outward bound, dined on board of us on Monday. He requested Henry's name to show to the missionary society at home.

Samuel has had a bowel complaint. I can joyfully say he is getting well. We have made a degree since yesterday. The day before we went four miles. A ship homeward bound is nearing us fast. It puts me quite in a flutter and heat. The captain has no letters prepared himself, and does not intend to board her, only to speak to her, and tell her to put him in the papers. I get out the letters we this morning finished for the chance.

Thursday, 31 October 1822. Lat.2.28. You cannot imagine how keenly I felt yesterday when the vessel passed round our stern within a stone's throw of us, and I had not the power to send our letters home. All were on deck and all were silent, while the captain conversed through the speaking trumpet. She also had female passengers, and was bound from the Cape to England. I felt as if I had passed you all without being able to speak to you. Our breeze carries us too much to the westward. We have not yet got the right trade wind, and expect some trouble.

BRAZIL

On 7 September 1822, Brazil had gained independence from Portugal.

Rio Janeiro. Friday, 22 November 1822. Cool breezes relieved all suffering from the intense heat, from the time we caught the trade wind, and although we were gradually reaching the centre of heat and did not pass under the sun's destination till latitude 17.42 south in the night of November 11th, we have never since felt anything like the heat, when we were becalmed for three weeks north of the line!

And now anchored in this harbour within the tropics in the season of their spring, we are so much relieved by the sea and land breezes, that it is comparatively cool. Yet, to show how necessary it is not to expose ourselves to the sun, on the tenth of November one of the convicts was raving all night from being sun-struck, and did not recover without copious bleedings.

Little Samuel has, to my no small fatigue, obliged me to move him all day, and his nurse has great part of the time, stood looking on, and he scolding her, and waving his little hand for her to go. I cannot hear his piteous cries without taking him; and the captain, not rendered at all more agreeable by a sudden attack of gout, would soon be in arms. They have never yet, one of the children, been admitted into his cabin. But while they are peaceable, he is civil to them upon quarter deck, which is during the fine weather the nursery and eating room.

Mr Burney, surgeon of the *Conway*, our kind conductor through the town on Wednesday morning, carefully suggested a handkerchief to be tied round little Marianne's neck to save it from blistering, and umbrellas to be held over us. Europeans (he said) are not sufficiently cautious. He mentioned some ladies he accompanied on a picnic party up the bay, who to their great surprise the following day found one the neck blistering, the other the skin peeled off, and he had known instances of persons in full health being in a state of decomposition in a few hours.

Henry notes: 'One great motive for my going on shore to-day was to attend the slave market. The slave trade is carried on here to a great extent. Very many vessels are employed in it. To-day there were four close to us, laden principally with children.'

Thursday, 28 November 1822. In seeking after Henry, to give our letters for England by the *Conway* to the captain on Saturday afternoon, I met with an accident in getting over a chest, and the irritation of the sprain has caused a little trifling cut on the skin which I received from tumbling over a bucket a few days before, to fester.

On Monday I was not able to accompany Henry to dine. The surgeon of the HMS *Dorne* breakfasted on board. I scrambled down the ladder and limped with some difficulty and pain to my bed, where I applied cold water till dinner, when upon being summoned I found only the captain and doctor, the others being on shore; and the captain asked the doctor if he had delivered his message to me. It was, that if I would like to go into the country, and stay while the ship remained in harbour, I was to get ready to go with all the children at seven o'clock the following morning, as the vessel would be detained till Sunday.

My bustle to get out garments for the purpose, some from trunks in the hold, some from the chest which was fixed under the bed place, was (you may imagine) not a little. That, and the exertion of the following day did not improve my knee, and yesterday a surgeon came to see Mr Thornton, and prescribed for me.

Imagine us with the whole of our little family, enjoying true English hospitality, in the house of an English merchant, in a romantic situation on the shore of a beautiful bay on the south side of this magnificent harbour! The children are delighted. The run of large, lofty rooms, the green trees, the walk on the beach, the shells, a play-fellow, the privilege of sitting at table, a garden to play in when the sea-breeze sets in towards evening, are all unbounded sources of delight; and it is impossible to describe to you how much we enjoy English hospitality and Christian society amidst the natural beauties of a foreign land.

The only drawback to my enjoyment is a sprained knee which confines me to a sofa or on the bed, instead of exploring the shore or ascending some way up the hills, which are behind us, to enjoy the prospect, or taking a moonlight walk.

From what I could understand, our friends here are chiefly of the Church of Scotland. Yet they met Henry as a brother. They speak with affectionate regard of Mr Boyce, an evangelical clergyman, many years chaplain of St Helena, who visited this place, and from the circumstances of his wife's confinement remained five months on his return from a visit to England. He had a school, to instruct black slaves, and seems to have exerted himself in everything laudable.

Mr Macray gave us some intelligence of the *Heroine* in which Mr and Mrs Clarke sailed for New Zealand. It was here in June. Mr Macray, hearing there was a missionary, called upon Mr Clarke, who was on shore in company with a pious captain. He was told that he was out in the country shooting, and afterwards heard that this was a mistake in the person, and that the Mr Clarke sought after was in the house, and quite dispirited that he could find no person with who he could associate.

We are shocked to find that New Zealanders' heads are becoming quite an object of traffic. They are eagerly bought here, and many sold very high in England. Not a ship arrives without some on board.

There are (it is supposed) full a hundred English families residing in Rio Janeiro. Many of them are very dissipated; and among the merchants' wives is all the jealousy, ambition, and love of display of high life. Some pride themselves upon their superior education, some for their high connections, some for their wealth, but those who give the best parties bear the prominence.

The Portuguese are imitating the English in many respects. But the old Portuguese were five years ago, and are now quite barbarous, in some of their customs. The ladies appear at Church full-dressed, and very gay, with bare heads and necks. Whenever they go out, their attire is rich, the infants' robes of white satin, their attendant slaves dressed also. But as soon as they go home they take all this off, and the ladies are clothed all day in nothing more than a chemise.

A mosquito just now alighted upon my paper, the first I have seen. The situation is particularly free from them, being not at all damp, and open to the sea. But in the city, they are very annoying. The black slaves here are very numerous. If a white servant is sent to market, he always hires a black, to carry home his purchases. Even a black who is a household servant is too proud to carry a basket home.

Mrs Thornton has a little black girl with her, four years old, given her by an English family, before they returned to England, upon condition that she would have her freedom when she was thought to be of a proper age. She was born in a Portuguese family, and speaks that language, is remarkably quick, and takes away the plates and carries them as steadily as a grown person. She sews them neatly, and is very tractable. But this little creature will go into the kitchen at home and give her orders with all the consequences imaginable.

30 November 1822. We took leave of our kind friends with great regret yesterday evening, and as wind and tide were against us, we were not on board till eight o'clock. The elder children awoke out of their sleep, and cried to go on shore again. We are now all business to collect our linen from the wash on board and on shore, to arrange our trunks and prepare for sea. For the last few days we have been in England. My knee is easier, and not so much swelled. The ship is unmoored. Best love to all.

1823

*On 3 December, they sailed out of the humid port and headed
south into the Atlantic Ocean, where the women and children
were soon suffering from seasickness and the cold.*

20 January 1823. Long.27. Off St Paul's Island. Indian Ocean. Our
wedding day. I have possession of the captain's cuddy, while the
party are on shore. The cold and wet confines us all much to our
little cabin, and it requires no little ingenuity to stow us all in so
small a space, sometimes by candle light at mid-day, and never with
more than one window unclosed. Added to this, my knee, which I
sprained at Rio, and twice since we left it, has frequently laid me on
the sofa bed. Several seasons lately recurring, such as Christmas day,
New Year's day, dear Lydia's and our little Samuel's birthday have
brought you before our mind's eye with peculiar interest. There are
besides little incidents constantly recurring, which bring such a
sudden sensation of home as cannot be described.

The party consisting of the captain, surgeon, and Henry, with the
boat's crew, have been gone about two hours. They took with them
guns, pistols and fishing tackle, expecting to bring back wild pigs
and fish. We have been standing off and on, continually putting the
ship about, waiting for them.

*Although the island was uninhabited, Henry mentioned that
they came across three huts and lying nearby 'a letter was
found in a bottle, directed for any friend containing another for
some person in the United States, with a request to forward it'.
They returned to the boat with a 'tolerable quantity' of fish.*

During the crossing to Vandieman's Land, now known as Tasmania, Henry wrote:

24 January 1823. Long.86.
The dear children have braved it nobly. Teddy and Totty have long had their sea legs, and can run with any of the children on board. You may perhaps be curious to know how many there are. Sixty-nine is the present number, two having died on the passage; and one fine boy, about ten years old, fell overboard. Our two elder ones have required great care to preserve them from this last disaster. They are two dear, quick little ones, and are surrounded by evil, oaths and curses flying in all directions.

Dear little Samuel is well, but does not thrive as the other two. His flesh is slack on his bones; for it is not everything he will eat. There is but very little milk, and no potatoes now. Soup he is very fond of. Totty and Teddy are quite fat and full of fun; for they will eat everything.

We are upon the high expectation of seeing Vandieman's land in less than three weeks, and the joy is great.

Saturday, 8 February 1823. In the morning we spoke to a vessel which had left Hobart town on Thursday morning. By this vessel we learned that the *Morley* had sailed from Vandieman's land for Sydney ten days since.

We seemed to hear of the *Morley*, as an old acquaintance; the surgeon had been a voyage in her, with convicts. Mr Reed's first voyage was in her. Henry had been with her under convoy at the Isle of France; and last, but not least, all our goods and chattels are in her, and we have the comfort of knowing Mr Marsden would be expecting us.

We made the land before dinner, and in the afternoon and evening proceeded along the south of Vandieman's high rocky shore. Those only who have been long at sea can imagine how interesting is the sight of the most rugged shore. I sat upon the top of the round house with Henry and the children, watching the different headlands, islands and rocks, as they appeared through the haze.

Sunday, 9 February 1823. It was so ordered that the quietness of the Sabbath was not broken into as we expected. The morning was almost calm, though what wind we had was favourable. After service we ascended the poop, where the captain, Henry, and the surgeon with the glasses and chart examined the shore. We sailed smoothly and slowly. The day was warm, and fine, the women all on deck. We sailed up Dentrecastres channel. Just at the entrance we saw a wreck of a vessel about two miles from us. Only the head of the vessel, supposed to be more than 250 tons, was seen, sticking up right on the beach of a small island. It made us shudder and feel thankful.

The shore on either side was steep and woody, and the rocks in some places divided regularly, like buildings. We saw no signs of inhabitants till after dinner, when a quantity of smoke proceeded (we imagined) from some persons clearing land. The trees, the surgeon said, were of three kinds, the cherry, the native oak and the gum tree. The naked slender stems of the gum tree, just crowned with green, intermixed with the more bushy trees, resembled leafless trees among the evergreens.

We anchored about nine o'clock, and many fires (I was told) were seen on the shore. The ship has never been so steady since she left Woolwich. I wish I could have heard Henry's sermon. Several of the women appeared affected, when he considered his drawing near the end of the time, when he was to close the commission he opened to them from Ezekiel. He then dwelt upon the principal object of the text, 'The end of all things is at hand.'

Monday, 10 February 1823. Awoke by heaving the anchor. I rose early. From the cabin window we saw a pretty farm on Bruny island upon a gently slope down to the water's edge. In clearing the land they had left some trees close to the water, which appeared like an English hedgerow, behind which the corn which was in stock cast a bright yellow gleam through the mist, the first corn-land we had seen since we left dear England.

The pilot came on board immediately after breakfast. The rain prevented my watching the shores of the Derwent until we were off Hobart town, when it cleared up, and gave us a view of this young capital, which after leaving Rio appeared diminutive, but in contrast with our expected destination a very pretty town and exceedingly promising. We particularly admired the church and the government house.

Henry learned from the pilot that Mr Marsden was here on a visitation, the first time of his visiting the island. Immediately upon our anchoring he came on board with Mr Bedford, the new clergyman. They staid but a few minutes, and I did not see them. Henry, after we had got out the dispatches from the Church Missionary Society, went on shore with the surgeon and dined at Mr Bedford's, the new clergyman. By this meeting with Mr Marsden our anxiety is unexpectedly relieved, and much information obtained.

He took Henry to call upon the lieutenant governor. From Mr Marsden we learned that Mr Kendall is suspended, Mr and Mrs Clarke in New South Wales and in charge of the native institution. He gave Henry a letter to his agent here, and another at Sydney, to get what money he wanted, and told him he expected us to stay at his own house at Parramatta.

During Henry's absence on shore I was much interested in the situation of the free women. No boat was allowed to come on board, but that of the water bailiff, a convict, and round him they all flocked to obtain news of their husbands. Several of them were from time to time fetched away by this person; and their husbands, convicts, waited for them, on the jetty. Our convicts were all gazing over the ship's side, and many persons on the beach. The first woman, for whom a note was sent, was a young, pretty looking, and well behaved woman with three children, dressed so sprucely, I could not recognise my old bare-footed acquaintances. A little boy about three years old was first handed down; and the father immediately jumped off the landing place on to the stones beneath; and this sign of impatience created no small interest on board. Some of the poor women could gain no tidings of their husbands, and were in great anxiety and distress.

Tuesday, 11 February 1823. About eleven o'clock we went on shore taking Kitty, and the three little ones in the boat with the surgeon and captain. The surgeon introduced us to his brother, who lives in a small, neat looking wooden cottage, one storey high, in the centre of a square allotment of land, which might be made a beautiful garden. Here we found his two sisters and seven nephews and nieces. One brother was at a farm in the country. A settler of gentlemanly appearance called in just after us, a German officer in the English service, who with indefatigable perseverance had travelled over the island with his gun on his shoulder to examine for himself the best spot to take his two thousand acres of land. He told us he had several children who could speak several languages. Some were born in the Great islands, some in different places in the Mediterranean.

We were surprised to see such excellent stone and brick houses, and the streets all laid out in parallel squares. When completely built on, and the wide vacancies filled up, it will form a large and handsome town. We returned to the ship a little before 8. It was Henry's birthday, as I remembered just after dinner. We thought of our dear brother and sisters at Hampstead, and refreshing seasons of prayer and praise we had enjoyed together upon this occasion.

13 February 1823. We experienced one of the hot winds which blow here occasionally during the summer. It was very trying, more so than the heat of the tropics. The surgeon told us it seldom occurred more than four days during the summer. It was a wind that blew over the hot plains of New South Wales, and was always attended with a great deal of dust. The mosquitoes became very troublesome.

SYDNEY (PORT JACKSON), AUSTRALIA

Henry wrote: 'On Feb. 27, we entered the heads of Port Jackson. The barren appearance of the coast is sufficient to strike the beholder with terror. But directly upon opening the harbour, it is most beautiful. Several islands are scattered about, and the water instantly loses its roughness. I had been up nearly all night, having too much on my mind to allow of my sleeping, and we came to an anchor by eight o'clock.' At the time Sydney was a bustling town of some 10,000 inhabitants.

17 March 1823. On Thursday I dined at Government House with Henry, and received marked attention from Lady Brisbane. The Revd Mr Hill of Sydney received us the day we landed into his house and brought us to Parramatta.

17 April 1823. On Monday, 30 March, Henry took me with little Marianne over to Blacktown to take my station as nurse. We found poor Mrs Clarke [a New Zealand missionary's wife] suffering with inflammation on her chest. She was affected by convulsive fainting fits, and in this state expecting her confinement [delivery date of her baby]. She remained in this distressing situation the first week. In the second she gradually regained appetite and strength and lost her fits and pains in the chest. Being myself very unwell, I suffered Henry to bring me back on Tuesday, but expect to resume my office in the bush on Monday. Mrs Clarke has no female attendants but the little black girls, and occasionally an old English woman.

The weather still continued warm, between the heavy rains, which are attended by thunderstorms and sudden high winds. The oranges and lemons are beginning to succeed the peaches, and the mosquitoes are upon the decline. The peaches are so plentiful that they feed the pigs with them. The frogs are of a bright grapy green. The snake is the terror of the unfrequented parts of the country and is sometimes brought into the towns with the loads of firewood. Several were killed in summer in Mr Marsden's grounds, and in the government domain, but we have never seen one yet. In New Zealand there are neither snakes nor mosquitoes.

We are very anxious to go but fear we must wait two months. We may then have four months to get there and build a house before my confinement. I have not had an anxious or rather a fearful thought respecting, and have not the least of that dread I once anticipated, on leaving this Colony for New Zealand.

We have two New Zealanders now domesticated with us – they sleep at Mr Marsden's; and one or both of them are here in the day-time. They constantly attend church, and do not arrive here on Sundays. They are very anxious to learn. Walter (Watu) learned his letters with Mr Clarke. Bushy is beginning. As Henry was out this morning they were with me an hour. One learned to say his letters, the other to write them on a slate. They counted to ten in New Zealand and English just as it was set down in the grammar. They showed great perseverance, and laughed very much at my teaching the children to count in New Zealand.

I wish to mention a circumstance Mr Hill told me, Mrs Kemp [in New Zealand] was providentially succoured by a ship accidentally touching at the island with a surgeon on board, after she had been two days in a state of suffering. This does indeed urge William's coming [Henry's younger brother, a surgeon also planning to come out to New Zealand], but it also shows that God can always raise up help in the hour of need, and forbids us under any circumstances to fear.

We are at present situated upon a steep slope on the bank of the river, nearly opposite to a water mill and Mr Marsden's residence. Mrs Marsden is very kind in sending us daily a large jug of milk, and other things frequently, Mr Marsden rode over to see Mrs Clarke last Saturday. He delights me with his zeal for New Zealand. He said, he had been afraid the Society would give up the mission, and if so, he would have gone there himself.

I have had much conversation with Mrs Clarke and admire her faith and fortitude. She seems to have experienced the truths which she is anxious to convey to others and to rest on the only true source of strength. I hope we may be useful to one another. In attending upon her I feel I am upon missionary work.

Henry

22 April 1823. Parramatta. I must confess for several reasons, I am anxious to be set down in some spot, which we may consider as our home. I have spoken to Mr Marsden upon the necessity of our not losing time; but he does not enter exactly into my feelings upon the subject. He is very independent himself, but forgets that women and children are not so. Marianne is now in the best of health and able to exert herself. This we must not expect long, and the care of the children is very considerable.

14 May 1823. I have quite given up the idea of landing in New Zealand for many months, for Mr Marsden is determined not to move till Mrs Clarke is recovered, which time must render it imprudent and improper for Marianne. I shall endeavour to make as much use of the time as possible, hoping God may yet cause all things to work together for our good. We have hitherto been living in a room and a half for all purposes, with the use of a cookhouse, not a kitchen – and not even a nook for myself to retire into.

3 June 1823. We have been feasting on despatches from England, dated September – and although our hearts were gladdened, our appetites have ever since craved for more. Your letters were most exhilarating, and come at a time when we wanted a little cordial. We were enabled to remove poor suffering Mrs Clarke to our own abode just the day before the return of the heavy rains; and ever since she has occupied all my care and attention.

I told you (I fear I almost boasted) I had not an anxious thought about going to New Zealand; I have ever since been made to learn a lesson of humility and acknowledge my lack of unshaken reliance and faith.

The two New Zealanders, who have lived here ever since I wrote last, are a real comfort to us. They are very affectionate, intelligent, willing and active. They are attentive at church and family worship. But it is very little we can explain to them about God or Namu Atui until we know more of the language. Mrs Trimmer's sacred prints delight them and even those in the children's spelling books. They say, 'Mr Williams soon talk New Zealand' and sometimes when he is out and I keep school, Watu will say – 'You say England. Me tell you New Zealand. You "make a write".'

They were very much pleased when we made them spell tangate = man, wahine = woman, wari = house etc. Bushy says he will live with us. Watu says, he will live with Mr Williams two moons and then come back to Parramatta. Bushy is the most active and useful servant of the two. He is an inferior chief of Hongi's tribe and is tattooed.

Henry

16 June 1823. Parramatta. My fears respecting our departure are removed, Mr Marsden having determined that we should proceed by ourselves, not even waiting for him. The station he wishes us to take is Wangarua [Whangaroa], about 30 miles north of the Bay of Islands.

10 July 1823. Our attention has been greatly occupied lately in making preparations for our voyage and intended settlement. Mrs Clarke was confined on Sunday week. The infant is remarkably small but healthy, and both it and its mother surprisingly well. But as this is the depth of winter, there is imprudence in removing her to a new settlement; besides Mr Clarke is engaged to remain another quarter. It is therefore determined to proceed without delay.

We shall move a tolerably large company. We take a little girl [Betsey] to attend entirely to the little ones. There is also a carpenter [Mr Fairburn] with his wife and children going with us, who were stationed in Newzealand for some time, but owing to some unpleasant affairs, they retired. They appear very quiet people and (I could hope) under some concern for the welfare of their souls.

It is Mr Marsden's wish that a small vessel should be built in process of time, at which the natives might work. This would be a strong inducement for many to reside round about, and give a turn to their present savage and wandering disposition, besides the benefit of it to the mission in ensuring constant communications between the colony and the island. A school, however, will be the first thing to which our attention will be turned.

18 July 1823. We are to embark tomorrow and sail on Sunday, the general day for sailing from this port. On Monday last we left Parramatta amidst abundance of rain, and were 4 hours on the water. But part of our tent being with us, we rigged one over the aft part of the boat and escaped well and free from colds.

NEW ZEALAND

It took Marianne and Henry just under two weeks to sail to New Zealand aboard the Brampton. *This was Mr Marsden's fourth visit to the Bay of Islands and he accompanied the young Williams family to their new home. Also on board was the carpenter, William Fairburn, his wife and family. Henry was thirty-one years old and Marianne twenty-nine and six months pregnant. They brought with them from Sydney a young convict girl, Betsey, to help with the children.*

Map of New Zealand with a detailed inset of the Bay of Islands.
(Designed by Gail Williams, MG Publications, Christchurch, NZ)

2 August 1823. Bay of Islands – Newzealand. I am anxious to embrace a little space, afforded me, of ease from toothache, relief from seasickness, and quiet after three days tossing in a tremendous gale. The wind, though it has subsided, is still contrary. It wafted us speedily to the shores of New Zealand, of which we had the first view on Thursday, a little after noon, but is quite against our getting into the bay. So we and our voyage end, as we began it more than ten months since, working against the wind.

7 August 1823. Kerikeri. Events crowd so rapidly upon one another, I long to stop the revolving hours to recount them. Sunday we were working against a strong wind and passed the settlement of Rangihoua. It was too rough in the morning to have public service. Our missionary party met in Mr Marsden's cabin, to partake of the Lord's supper. They were precious moments. The party consisted of Mr Marsden, Mr and Mrs Turner (Wesleyans), Henry, myself, Mr Hobbs and Mrs Fairburn. Just as the table was spread and we were about to engage, a canoe full of natives was seen through the port holes, cheering the ship, and endeavouring to get alongside. The sight affected us all, and moved our hearts in prayers for that time speedily to come when these strangers should come in to partake.

We anchored about six o'clock about half way between Rangihoua and Kerikeri, when we sat down to dinner, after which, though dark, some natives came on board, from whom Mr Marsden gained intelligence that the chiefs were all gone to the east cape to fight. We were too much excited to sleep. Next morning Mr Marsden put into our cabin a pretty little naked Newzealand boy, about 2 years old, to the no small astonishment of Samuel and Marianne.

The poor little fellow did not relish his company, for he set up a cry, and we let him go out to his father and mother who were called Mr and Mrs Gunnah – mentioned in Nicholas's voyage; to whom I was shortly afterwards introduced, and to many others in their native dress. [Marianne is referring to Henry's copies of *Nicholas's New Zealand*, recording John Nicholas's historical voyage to the Bay of Islands in 1814.] As they sat, crouching down on the deck in their mats, they reminded me of a print in Capt. Cook's voyages of the natives in Nootka Sound, except that their mats are mostly fringed and rough all over.

The animation and energetic expression of these noble natives cannot be described. We were surrounded by chiefs, as we sat at breakfast all earnestly begging to have missionaries. I could have gone with any or all of them. Both Henry and myself felt a wish to satisfy the wishes of three disconsolate chiefs from the river Thames, had Mr Marsden thought it prudent. We learned that Mr Leigh had gone with Mr White (Wesleyan) to Whangaroa and settled on the very spot intended by Mr Marsden to be our station. Mr Shepherd had accompanied them, which had occasioned much anger to the natives.

Tohitapu, a warlike looking chief stained red, told Mr Marsden they did not so much object to Mr Leigh going, because he did not belong to our party – but Mr Shepherd they seemed to look upon as their property, and had even been over with a strong party to bind him hand and foot and bring him back, and would have done so in all probability had not Mrs Shepherd been on the eve of her confinement.

Mr Marsden after breakfast proceeded with Henry, Messrs. Turner, Hobbs and Fairburn in the captain's boat to Rangihoua. Our faithful Bushy's father, a venerable looking old man, came to see him, and one interesting native in an English dress, who said Watu was his friend, sat at the table. He had been a twelve month at Mr Marsden's house at Parramatta, and his manners were quite gentlemanly. He was very urgent to have a missionary to himself.

We heard that Maki, a principal chief at the river Thames, was some time since killed and eaten by Hongi. The three chiefs present were Maki's relations. There is now peace between Hongi and them; and there were some female prisoners from the river Thames on board who set up a dismal cry, which they continued some time as they stood before the cabin window with streaming eyes, gazing upon these three chiefs seated upon the sofa.

Our three little ones were much admired. They were much pleased to distribute some raisins among the little Newzealanders and Edward rubbed noses with one or two tattooed heroes. The great cabin and the deck continued crowded with natives young and old, male and female, chiefs, kukis [slaves] and prisoners. Many seemed glad to see Mr and Mrs Fairburn returned to them; and I was pleased to hear the shout of joy with which the natives in some of the canoes both this day and the first evening, exclaimed Mr Marsden, as they came alongside and saw him leaning over the gangway.

After the party departed to Rangihoua, I was glad to retire with my children to the cabin, wishing to keep them from what I feared might be showered upon them from the mats of the natives as they stalked majestically along. I had much trouble to keep any bounds upon the wild curiosity of Betsey, who was more troublesome than any one of my little ones.

Mr Butler soon after arrived, a stout robust man, looking in hearty good humour. It was near tea-time before the party returned in Mr Hall's boat, with himself and Mr King.

The Waitangi was now thought of for our settlement, a beautiful situation in the Bay of Islands, to which Mr Hall had wished to move, but the natives had compelled him to return to Rangihoua.

Mr Butler gave us a friendly invitation to his house on the morrow, and offered to stay on board all night for the purpose of taking us in his boat in the morning. His stay afforded us an unexpected gratification; for upon going below to prayers, our hearts were cheered by hearing his boat's crew, who made a neat appearance in an English dress, sing a hymn most sweetly in the native language, written by Mr Shepherd, and also repeated a prayer in their own tongue, with much melody and harmony in their voices. It gave every one of us great delight.

I was too much fatigued to begin packing, and relinquishing an attempt to write, was glad of rest. The tall and muscular forms of the Newzealanders, flittered before my mind's eye, whenever I endeavoured to sleep. I felt a wish to convey every look and every conversation to our absent friends, and several times in the course of the day had I said to Mr Marsden – 'I wish our English friends could peep in upon us'. It indeed seemed worth all the undertaking of a voyage from England to behold with our own eyes the scenes of this day. I felt a fervent thankfulness that we had been brought and had been permitted to bring our little ones to this scene of labour.

8 August 1823. The following morning the natives were again flocking round us. Among the first was Tohitapu, who was very angry when he found the Waitangi chosen for our settlement, in preference to his place. I could hear him stamping and talking with great noise and vehemence. He was, however, satisfied by Mr Marsden telling him that Mr Shepherd should come back and live with him; and went to set to work immediately to collect raupo [bulrush] to build him a house.

Henry went after breakfast upon an exploring party, to visit our proposed residence and took Edward with him. I waited on board while Mr Butler took Mrs Turner and Mrs Fairburn to Rangihoua in his boat. Packing and preparation occupied the morning, and just as the children's dinner was placed before them Mr Butler returned for us.

We had a delightful row to Kerikeri. The river wound like a corkscrew, and the banks were in some places very pretty, fringed with low shrubs. The native huts we beheld with curiosity on the top of the rocks, and Hongi's rude palace. The men who rowed the boat were fine, intelligent, active looking lads, talking with great animation to Mr Turner; and in comparison with the sleepy, degraded and disgusting looking natives we had just left at Port Jackson, they appeared quite astonishing.

On a sudden and complete turn of the river Kerikeri opened upon us, quite in appearance a little lake with a pleasing fall of water. The situation was beautiful, but wanted wood. The native settlement was upon the hill, or rather ridge of hills, and upon the beach, the refreshing sight of Mr Butler's and Mr Kemp's English looking houses – the flag was up and we entered through a small court, enclosed by high paling, a house two stories high, and a veranda in front. At a distance it had appeared like stone or stucco. But it was built of wood, painted white, and lined with plank within.

Mrs Butler received us with a manner as kind as it was blunt. We were made quite at home, and a strapping Newzealand girl ordered to make a fire in a room which was intended for me. We had arrived (we found) at a very quiet time, when all the principal natives were away to the fight, and the missionaries not only unmolested but unvisited.

After the children were in bed I went with Mrs Butler, according to Mrs Kemp's request, to call in and see Mr Kemp. I found them, their house, their manner, everything that I had anticipated, and felt to love Mrs Kemp at the first interview. Everything around was neat as wax, and three Newzealand girls tidily dressed in English bedgowns and aprons, welcomed me with a courtesy, and 'How do you do Ma'am' in English in answer to my 'Tina raka kue'.

It was late before Henry came in. Little Edward was left on board the ship to come up with the captain and Mr Marsden on the morrow; and Marianne, half asleep, asked in vain for Teddy. Henry expressed himself delighted with the situation at Waitangi. The natives appear friendly and are of Hongi's tribe. They had caressed Edward greatly during the day.

Wednesday, 6 August 1823. [Marianne has added this entry as an afterthought.] Henry and I went to Mr Kemp's with the children, and saw all over their compact and pretty house. The boat arrived and dear little Edward quite safe. He slept alone in our cabin. In answer to my questions, who put him to bed, who dressed him etc., it was all 'Bushy, mamma, Bushy'.

Henry and the captain walked to see a waterfall, while the committee sat. At last an adjournment took place, when we sat down to soup, fish, ham, vegetables and pudding. I mention this, because it was the first dinner I tasted on the shore of Newzealand.

The weather became cold at night and we were glad to draw near a comfortable wood fire made upon the hearth. I would scarcely believe myself in New Zealand, except when the native servant came in to prayers. Mr and Mrs Butler were hospitably kind with no lack of good cheer. I saw my children comfortably asleep, our ship mattresses and bedding, being spread upon the sofa and carpet, and retired myself to rest with a full and I trust a grateful heart and prayerful spirit.

On the 6th all the settlers assembled at Kerikeri to welcome the Williams family and to discuss the crisis of leadership. A few days later a formal letter of dismissal was given to Butler and Kendall, and Henry was installed as the new leader.

Saturday, 9 August 1823. I went with Mrs Butler to gain some information respecting the management of her pigs, poultry, rabbits, etc. Goats we have none, having in vain attempted to buy a milch goat in Port Jackson. Mrs Butler offered to give us one out of her flock. She has not a cow at this time giving milk. Therefore we had goat's milk and Irish butter. Mrs Kemp from her cow, which they brought from England, has plenty of milk and makes excellent butter. I have been taking lessons also in making bread from leaven, and regret I neglected to bring a bottle of yeast from Port Jackson.

Sunday, 10 August 1823. We had divine service in one of Mrs Butler's sitting rooms. Mr Butler read prayers and Henry preached from John XIII.35.

In the afternoon we had native service in the kitchen. They sang several hymns in the native language. They repeated a prayer and the creed. They also answered questions put by Messrs Butler, Kemp and Shepherd, the purport of which I did not understand. The service was closed with a chapter and a prayer is English. There were 20 natives present, and it was to us a most interesting meeting. Mr Shepherd, having made great proficiency in the language, has written many hymns and begun to translate the scriptures. Henry and I felt great delight in perceiving so much more encouraging than we had expected.

The state of the natives is most deplorable. As an instance of their savage nature, we were told that Jane, the native girl in this house, upon the return of the fight from the river Thames, killed two prisoners herself, the instant the canoes landed at Hongi's point.

Monday, 11 August 1823. Henry and Mr Butler went down to the ship. Mrs Butler kindly insisted on our having our linen washed, and two native girls, one of who had been servant to Mrs Kemp, and the other to herself, were hired to do them under her own skilful superintendence. I was rather curious to know, what was the payment, and was told that when they had washed four times, she gave them a hoe. Her servant girls and Mrs Kemp's are paid once in three months, an axe one time, and a hoe the next.

12 August 1823. Henry began his operations in the bush [on the Paihia beach]. Mr Butler was hard at work, helping Mr Fairburn to erect a substantial store of plank and timber, while Henry fetched the stores from the ship in a large canoe and landed them. We passed a very quiet week. Mrs Butler would allow me to engage in no bustling or fatiguing work. Therefore as her eyes were bad, and her constant bustling life left her no time for the needle, I gladly stitched for her, and often took my workbasket to enjoy Mr and Mrs Kemp's society.

The children began their long neglected lessons; and to go to Mrs Kemp's to play with Henry was the reward for saying them well. I was told by everybody that I came at a happy time, for New Zealand was a paradise, when the chiefs and fighting men were absent. The missionaries could stroll out of their high paled yards and gardens in perfect quiet, and were free from angry visits of parties of naked savages. Indeed my only grief was that my gratitude was so cold for mercies so many and so striking.

I hear from Mrs Butler's many dismaying accounts of the past ferocious conduct of the natives, most of which was confirmed by Mrs Kemp's experiences, but from none of which, taking all circumstances into consideration, I gathered any cause for future personal dread, though there was the greatest need of missionary labour and earnest prayer for the outpouring of the Holy Spirit.

For the females I feel great pity. Their state is degraded indeed. Many are the evils, besides the rage for muskets and powder, which arise from the frequent arrival of European vessels; and sad indeed it is that the practice of Englishmen should be in every way opposed to the precepts and steady example of the faithful missionary. But in God's own time, the little leaven will spread; and the surrounding mass may even be in a state of preparation. The head wife of a chief, named Rivers, lately killed her child. Mrs Butler refuses on that account to admit her into her house; and she now begins to say she was ashamed.

Elisabeth Puckey the carpenter's daughter, when a child, endangered her father's life, in consequence of a conversation between her and Hongi's daughter, during the absence of that chief in England. Hongi's daughter told Elizabeth that her father was not a 'rangatira' – as hers was –. The other contended he was. Hongi's daughter said he was a Kane, and that when her father came home from England he would cut off his head and put it in a frying pan. Elizabeth replied that *her* father would cut off Hongi's head and put it in a pot. This threat of the child was conveyed to the tribe; and after Hongi's return, it was made the pretext for an outrageous attack upon Mr Puckey's at 5 o'clock in the morning, when they threatened his life, and several successive parties stripped his kitchen.

Friday, 15 August 1823. Mr Butler came home greatly fatigued, with a violent cold, having been at work all the week without the comfort of a razor – sleeping without bedding, or even a blanket, and not having had his clothes off since Monday. The accounts he brought were very comfortable, the work getting on and the natives behaving well.

Saturday, 16 August 1823. Mr Butler, having rested his weary limbs till noon, announced his intention to my no little satisfaction of taking the boat to fetch Mr Williams for a day of rest. Late in the evening Henry did arrive, greatly fatigued in body, though in excellent spirits. Indeed, it did appear, as he said, that the way for us seemed to be made too easy and we must expect and prepare for difficulties to arise. Mr Fairburn was left in charge. The stores were landed and walled in, but without a roof to a building.

The goat had been very useful in drawing up the stores in the cart from the beach to the great delight of the natives.

Goats and goat carts were also in common use at the time in the Australian outback. Goats, sometimes called the 'poor man's cow', were small, multi-purpose animals, providing meat, wool, skins and cheese; they were also very practical on the long sea voyages out for supplying milk. They would eat anything, including the washing on the line. Strong and surefooted, they pulled the small wooden two-wheeler goat carts filled with fire wood, stores and sometimes even children.

The poultry were under the care of a chief. The chief of the place Te Koki was absent at the fight, but has often expressed a wish for missionaries, and is of a mild character. His sister lends every assistance, and makes herself useful in protecting property. The beach is a fine dry sand, the situation beautiful, very near the timber districts, and with a view of the harbour and shipping. We have abundant cause for gratitude for the plain and easy way in which we have been conducted and directed and assisted to our settlement; and no doubt this is an answer to many prayers offered up for us in England.

Te Koki was the protector of the Paihia mission; his wife Hamu, however, was a woman of high rank and, in her own right, owner of Paihia. Their son had died while studying at Mr Marsden's school in Parramatta, so, to ease Hamu's grief, Mr Marsden had promised that he would send her a missionary and she was later baptised Ana. In his turn Te Koki accepted responsibility for the general safety of the mission, which meant that any tribe attacking the mission property and personnel would be regarded as attacking Te Koki and his tribe. As Te Koki was a powerful chief of great mana or respect, this gave the mission a relatively safe base.

18 August 1823. Henry again set off with Mr Butler. This week was spent in a similar manner to the last. One day this week, a chief named Warepapa brought a musket, which he desired Mr Kemp to mend. Mr Kemp mildly refused, and gave his reasons. But the chief was exceedingly violent, persisting for a length of time, urging his request with angry threats telling Mr Kemp he would kill him, and he would take away everything he had.

Mrs Kemp went in repeatedly, to call him to dinner, and found the loud and angry chief brandishing a bar of iron, which he said he would take away, and did actually do so, while Mr Kemp, quietly working at his forge, answered him with the greatest calmness, telling him that he did not expect a rangatira (gentleman) would steal: to which the chief replied he did not steal, but took it, because he would not do what was required, and he would kill Mr Kemp. Mr Kemp replied, he was not afraid of anything he could do to him, that he had refused to mend a musket for Hongi, and *he* would listen to reason.

Amongst other things the chief said, the missionaries only came because the land was good and they could live more comfortably than they did at home; and that it was not good for Mr Williams to go to Waitangi and Mr S. Butler to Nanganu, that they were spreading themselves about, to buy all the land, and then they would make it like Port Jackson.

This chief was going down to the ship with forty pigs in hope of getting for them a gun with 4 mouths, having heard that the captain had a four barrelled piece. In a few days he returned, and brought back the bar of iron.

Another native brought Mr Kemp a pig, which (he said) he should have if he mended a key, and made it fit a box, which the captain had given him, saved out of the vessel lately wrecked at Hokianga. This was done. This captain and crew had met with great kindness from the natives and came overland to the missionaries, who administered to their wants; some of them are still here.

Monday, 25 August 1823. At breakfast, Jane (Newzealander), who is a cousin of Hongi's, appeared very ill and was unable to assist in waiting upon us. On inquiry we found our maid Betsy had given her something, which we fancied must be essence of peppermint. Betsy denied it, and said she had given her some peppermint lozenges. Of these I knew she had none; and mine were all gone. Mrs Butler missed a small bottle of the essence out of the store room.

After prayers we had an investigation when Betsy brought forth the bottle which she had concealed in a glass bookcase in our room.

Betsy, it seemed, had been observed to smell of peppermint lately, so that she knew how to dilute it for her own palate. She was pert and indifferent till brought before Mr Marsden and Mr Butler, when with some solemnity, she was ordered to be locked up for the day, as a thief. A little solitary confinement made her petition on her knees, with many tears, and a manner, we disliked as much as her former pertness, but we kept her shut up all day; and as our room was taken up by the committee, I took the children over to Mrs Kemp, who was busy preparing dinners for the whole party. Poor Jane continued to feel her mouth painful, and said that if she had died, her tribe would have made a great fight and killed all the white people.

No doubt it will cure Betsy of teasing the natives. But we determined to send her back to Port Jackson, and trust to native girls. We all dined at Mrs Kemp's. Thirteen sat down to dinner besides nine children. Mrs Kemp showed her hospitality and good management and gave us excellent Norfolk fare in New Zealand. After dinner the committee returned to Mr Butler's, and sat so late that it was after ten o'clock before I could leave the room to make my bed.

Wednesday, 10 September 1823. The last committee was held at Paihia, not Waitangi, as I have called it by mistake, and Mr Marsden when he came to take leave on Tuesday morning, gave us an entertaining account of Henry's reception of them. They found him with his hands in the dough, making cakes for them, which proved excellent.

On Wednesday Mr Marsden left, and Thursday, very early, Mr and Mrs Leigh with my little maid, whom I was truly thankful to get rid of. The captain came up to dinner on Friday and said he should not sail till Sunday. In answer to my remark on sailors 'always sailing on that day', he said: 'The better the day, the better the deed, and Sunday's sail will never fail.'

Saturday Henry came up. Sunday Henry addressed us very sweetly and earnestly from the 139th Psalm. It was a dismal night. We remembered in prayer our friends lately embarked on the deep. Monday the wind still blew a gale, and the rain continued to fall in such quantities, we apprehended the river would overflow and carry away the fences and stock in Mr Butler's farm yard.

Tuesday the weather continued very unsettled and squally. During family prayers, some natives, with earnestness not to be suppressed, spoke to Mrs Butler through the back window, which they, regardless of seeing us upon our knees, persisted in opening, and upon some words, which they spoke to her, she ran out of the room. Scarcely had we risen when Tom, one of Henry's boats crew, pressed forward with uplifted hands, and native vehemence of action and expression, seemed determined that Henry should hear and understand him. Before we could ask for an interpretation, one of the domestic natives exclaimed 'the ship is broken to pieces; and Mr Marsden and Mr Leigh are come back to Mrs Kemp's!'

Henry rushed out followed by Mr Butler. It was indeed too true. Mr Leigh (who had been very ill before sailing) soon came in. I exclaimed – 'How is Mrs . . . – ' and stopping short, I trembled and reproached myself for having agitated him, fearing the worst, from seeing him enter without her. He relieved my apprehensions, however, and I met her coming in. By degrees we gathered the particulars. The captain sailed on the Sunday night though the wind was against him, and attempted to work out; and before noon the ship was upon a rock, within the Bay of Islands. Mr Marsden had just concluded social worship in Mr Leigh's cabin; and they had been conversing sweetly on divine things. Mr Leigh was going to lie down, when 3 successive shocks occasioned them to run out. The sailors trembled and said she would be lost in an hour. Mr Marsden was collected and firm.

THE BEEHIVE, PAIHIA BEACH

Monday, 6 October 1823. On Sept. 10, I laid down my pen in the midst of a history of the shipwreck: and since then we have all been as busy as bees. On Monday the 15th, leaving the children at Mrs Kemp's, I accompanied Henry in his boat, to our new home.

The day was beautiful, the only fine day in the midst of a fortnight's storms and rains. I greatly enjoyed the expedition. After rowing down the Kerikeri river, we sailed across part of the Bay of Islands. We saw the hut in which Mr Marsden and Mr and Mrs Leigh passed two nights and days, with no food except a few potatoes; near to which the captain has now landed all his stores, and erected a tent.

We then sailed to the wreck, a melancholy spectacle; for she remained quite upright, her masts all gone, and the sound of the natives' tools echoing round her sides. They had that morning begun to mutilate her. I looked up to our late cabin windows. The captain had yielded possession, and was on board waiting the return of his boat. Henry asked him for his figurehead: and we lay alongside, while they tried to get it. But from there being several bolts in it we relinquished it.

This was eight days from the wreck; and the captain had been allowed by the natives to keep possession and land all his goods, although they considered the ship their own when stranded on their rocks. The *Brampton* was wrecked the 7th of September, the very day twelve months from our embarking on board the *Lord Sidmouth* at Woolwich.

I felt much on beholding the wreck of the vessel which had so lately brought us in perfect safety to these shores, and thought lively gratitude of the night, when in a tremendous gale we were tossing off the unknown beach.

Thence we sailed to our new settlement. The beach was crowded with natives. With great glee they drew me up while I was sitting in the boat, exclaiming 'Te Wahine' [the wife], and holding out their hands saying, 'Tena ra ko koe', and 'Homai te ringaringa' (How do you do, give me your hand). I cannot describe my feelings. I trembled and cried, but joy was the predominant feeling.

The cultivated land, on which was springing up our crops of oats and barley, extended close down to the fine beach, bounded on each side by a projecting point of rock, overhung by clumps of the noble pohutukawa tree. Within an enclosure of palings stood our raupo hut, which had the appearance of a beehive. By the side stood the store, scattered about were the cart, timber carriage, goats, fowls and horse, and near the beach were the saw pits. Behind was a large garden already partially green with numerous rows of beans.

The entrance to the house was dark, and within were two rooms with no floors, and boarded and nailed up where sash-lights are to be placed. Mr Fairburn and my husband laid me a boarded floor in the bedroom before night. I never reposed more comfortably.

On Sunday Mr Williams opened another raupo hut for chapel . . . the bell was rung for a quarter of an hour. It sounded sweetly as the congregation walked along the beach. The natives carried chairs and planks for benches. The English Jack was hoisted in front of the settlement as a signal to the natives that it was a sacred day. The whole scene was delightful.

The following Thursday, Mr Marsden came to spend a week with us: by which time we had unpacked many of our comforts, and our rooms looked very pretty with good boarded floors, neatly glazed windows, ranges of books etc.

On Sunday, 8 weeks after our arrival, Mr Marsden seemed greatly to enjoy our rush chapel, and the whole scene and proceedings. On the Monday Mr Kemp came and departed with Mr Marsden last Thursday. This day Henry went soon after daylight to the committee at Kerikeri.

Mrs Fairburn is a great assistance and comfort to me. We all breakfast and dine in their room, and meet to tea in ours. After breakfast this morning we hired a chief's wife (not Te Koki's) to wash under the tuition of a native girl named Aden – Eteamo, a slave of this woman, takes care of Samuel and another girl, of Mrs Fairburn's children. That is to say, they walk after them and keep them from harm when out of doors.

About noon we were surprised to see the boat returned. Henry had gone with the captain in his boat. I set Tow, one of the boat's crew, an active native lad, to wash the rooms and scrub the floors, Aden helped me to teach him. Both laughed heartily: and the boy performed his task as well as any English housemaid. I measured off a piece of blue print to make a gown for my wash-woman, and at tea Mr Fairburn read to us the Indian Pilgrim.

How I wish you could look in upon us! We have never been more happy and comfortable since we married. We have indeed been wonderfully helped. Goodness and mercy have followed all our steps. We are in a little romantic Paradise in a barbarous land with every prospect of usefulness, every comfort, every blessing, every happiness. My heart is overflowing. May we strengthen one another in prayerful gratitude!

Friday, 21 November 1823. You will all share our joy that the Lord has given us a Henry for our Samuel. This is only the 11th day after my confinement and except my eyes, I am as well as I usually have been at the end of the month. The Lord has indeed wonderfully helped me; and never had I a stronger call to take of the cup of salvation, and call upon his name. Our little boy is quite the flower of the flock, though little Samuel stands blooming by his side in full health and as fond of him as possible. I have more cause for gratitude than I am now well able to relate.

Friday, 28 November 1823. I have been enabled to resume so many of my employments that unless I give you my history now, it will be laid aside. My three youngest, I have at length settled to sleep: Edward is gone in the boat with his papa and Mr Fairburn to fish: and though I am quite ready for bed myself, I will not lose so good an opportunity.

Our little Henry is the fourth boy born among the settlers within these four months. It is worthy of remark that nothing wrong has been permitted to befall any of the females under such circumstances during the nine years there have been settlers here; and when Mrs Kemp was in danger, a surgeon was sent by Providence into the harbour.

I must tell you, what our favourite rush cottage in this favoured spot is like. To the right of the hut, as our dwelling is called, stands the store, within the paling, and opposite to it, the carpenter's bench where Marianne and Edward delight to stray on forbidden ground. On the left of our dwelling, nearly opposite Mr Fairburn's door, stands our portable kitchen beneath a shed, not deeming it safe to have a fireplace in our raupo hut. At the back we have a large place enclosed, where we have goats, ducks, chickens, piles of boards, rafters etc., as they are brought up from the saw pits on the beach, our cart, shingles and bricks for the roof and chimney of our future house etc.

Our fowl house is half a canoe, turned bottom upward, at the end of which is a small door to get the eggs out; which until this contrivance were mostly stolen either by the natives or my wicked little maid from Port Jackson, of whom I cannot yet be relieved. Behind this yard within another paling is a large garden, well stocked at the foot of a lofty range of hills; and from our window we have a beautiful view of this extensive harbour, enlivened by three romantic rocky islands covered with foliage, one of which Henry has bought for the purpose of sending to it goats and rabbits. No ship can enter the harbour without our seeing it.

Monday, 1 December 1823. Henry went to Kerikeri on Saturday. By the time I have washed my four children and put them to bed, my head, back, and eyes ache. I have abundant excuses for gratitude to my Father in Christ. May I be saved from ingratitude!

Friday, 5 December 1823. In consequence of having done too much, I am now obliged to do too little. It grieves me to see Mrs Fairburn toiling about, running out in the hot sun, providing and cooking for the whole family. But in vain do I try to reach the standard of her exertions. Henry returned on Tuesday from Kerikeri.

1824

ATTACK BY TOHITAPU

Wednesday, 7 January 1824. The weather is so intensely hot, that I cannot summon resolution to attempt to iron linen. A cooling sea breeze has this afternoon sprung up to our great relief, I have sent the children down to the beach under Aden's care, to gather shells, that they might enjoy the air, and little Henry lies on the sofa, kicking and laughing by my side.

I have great cause of thankfulness, that I have not had any headache of any importance these 10 days, and have recovered from a variety of complaints with which I have suffered much ever since I last took up my pen brought on by getting too soon upon my legs, by over exertion and over excitement. Quiet and rest were what I needed. But these I could not have.

I feel it an imperious duty to keep the dear children indoors during the day out of the broiling sun and also to attend to their bodily and spiritual welfare with the utmost watchfulness. I am thankful that the result has been their improvement in health, manner and regularity. The circumstance of Samuel's nurse running away, which threw him entirely upon me, when I fancied myself unequal to the task, has been a blessing to the child; for thinking him too young to learn much harm, I was not aware of half his accomplishments. He is a sweet child, though so full of mischief, that I am dancing up and down, up and down after him all day long.

You can have little idea of the fatigue of being shut up all day with four little fidgety things in small close rooms, attended by native girls. For savages I think they do wonders; but still they are savages. Generally speaking, they will do what they like and when they like.

On the day of Henry's birth I drank tea with the family, and with great difficulty washed my children and put them to bed; after which I walked out into the moonlight with Henry – and soon retired to my own room. Henry summoned the family to prayers; before the close of which Mr Marsden arrived with Captain Moore in the boat of the latter, and while Henry was getting tea for them and giving grog to the boat crew, and Mrs Fairburn at the other end of the hut was putting her children to bed, and attending to her baby, I, left entirely to myself, did perhaps feel more justly my only aid to come from God, and cling more closely to the only source of strength.

As soon as the children had played themselves to sleep, I made my preparations and went to bed. I gladly heard Captain Moore depart! And a short time afterwards Mrs Fairburn arrived to my assistance just as the dear little one began to cry. I never felt so much joy before. Henry wrapped himself in his boat-cloak to watch through the night. The children awoke, and were shown the baby; but it appeared like a dream. Te Koki, our head chief, came and knocked at the gate about 12 o'clock. He perceived the fire lighted to make my gruel, and came to inquire the cause.

In the morning we were obliged to have Mrs Fairburn's baby brought to the side of ours, before the children would believe this was not Richard's [Fairburn] little brother; and now you will perceive how much cause I have for gratitude, that though I had frequently a headache, and suffered from the fatigue of noise, bustle and excitement, I was strengthened through it all, and though I caught several colds from the breezes penetrating our rush walls, notwithstanding the useful and very ornamental green lining, given us by uncle Marsh for the tent, and our white calico ceiling, which was on these occasions swelled, like a ship in full sail, yet I never suffered severely.

At the end of the week I dressed baby myself, on the eighth day left my room, and at the fortnight Henry having gone to Kerikeri for the day, I received a visit from Mr and Mrs King and 4 of their children, laid the cloth for dinner, etc. All these things were unavoidable; and it is even now extraordinary to me to look back, and see how we have been strengthened through every difficulty.

I will mention one instance to give you an idea. Five days after Mrs Fairburn's confinement, I had just finished ironing about teatime: Henry helped me to wash the children; and overcome with fatigue, I did, as I had often done before, threw myself on the bed to refresh myself by a good cry, when a boat was announced, and I was aroused anew to exertion, to receive Mr Marsden, Mr Kemp and the celebrated Hongi, to get out blankets, sheets and bedding, etc.

This evening it rained very heavily, and it will amuse you to know how many people slept in our hut. Our three visitors in the sitting room, 5 native girls in the entrance room, 4 native men of the boats crew on account of the heavy rain, in Mrs Fairburn's sitting room, all these in addition to the Fairburns, ourselves and the children, in a rush dwelling 40 feet long and 15 broad.

The meeting of the two chiefs at tea was very entertaining. Te Koki placed a chair at the table for Hongi, and sat himself on the ground beside him. Hongi was in his native dress, but made a very superior appearance. Te Koki told us to give his friend plenty to eat, and to remember that we ate very little, but the 'tangata maoris' ate a great deal. My company ate up my batch of bread, which happily held out; and the boat's crew had enough also, though this same week, the sawyers must have stopped work for want of food, had not an occasional supply of new potatoes come in, and Mr Marsden brought biscuit from the *Dragon*.

Monday, 12 January 1824. Henry is gone to Kerikeri and, freed from the wars and rumours of wars which have distracted our ears, perplexed our thoughts and put an entire stop to all business, we are enjoying a quiet afternoon.

I feel exactly as when relieved by calm weather after a succession of storms at sea. I have long been wishing to give you some home scenes, since the novelty of our situation began to wear off, the restraint which our savage friends had put upon their pilfering propensity began to relax, the continual excitement of Mr Marsden's visit subsided and we had acquired some experience of the troubles and numerous petty discouragements of the missionary life.

But to give you a week's history, which I am obliged to do by bits and scraps. On Sunday we had a fine day. Our two families met in Mrs Fairburn's room. The addition of 3 sailors from an English ship added to our congregation. After service our native girls went, some with and some without leave, off to their friends, so that I had not a moment to sit down and read, till all the children except Edward were asleep, and it was time for evening service, which is held always in our sitting room. After dinner Henry and Mr Fairburn went out among the natives in a neighbouring village and had some very interesting conversation with them. Our evening service was closed as usual with the hymn for Sunday evening, when we always think particularly of our dear Hampstead friends; and this is a season I always enjoy; for I never throughout the week sit still so long together.

Monday morning, just as Aden was beginning to wash linen, a boat from one of the ships came to look for men, eleven of their crew having left. Two of our sawyers were tempted by the irresistible offer of muskets and powder. Henry spoke to the mate, who said, if they were his servants, and it was against his approbation, he would not take them. But one of them joined the boat a little further down the beach. This event unsettled all hands.

The moment a boat arrives, down scamper all hands, men, boys and girls to the beach. If there is anything to be seen, or anything extraordinary occurs in Newzealand, the mistress must do the work, while the servants gaze abroad. She must not scold them either: for if they are rangatiras, they will run away in a pet: and if they are Kukis, they will laugh and tell her she has 'too much of the mouth'. Having been forewarned of this, I wait and work away till they choose to come back.

We were all sorry that one of our most apparently faithful and attached natives was thus tempted away. He was one of the three sawyers who had remained with us from the first, had never like others taken himself for some childish pet, and had on several occasions shown great attachment.

After dinner a most troublesome chief Tohitapu, who lives about 2 miles from us, put us all in confusion. [Tohitapu was a great chief and tohunga (priest), with the power to makutu (bewitchment). The victims of makutu would waste away and die.] Mr Fairburn, who was at work at the bench, saw him coming, and had the gate fastened. Instead of knocking in the usual manner for admittance, the chief sprang over the fence, made of tall thin poles. Mr Fairburn told him he was a tangata kina, badman, and that it was coming in like a thief, tangate tahae, and not like a gentleman, rangatira, to climb over the fence.

He immediately began to stamp and caper about like a madman, attracting all around him by his vociferous gabble, and flourishing his meri, a weapon of green stone, one of which they every one of them have concealed beneath their mats, and brandishing his spear, with which he would spring like a cat and point at Mr Fairburn apparently in real earnest.

Henry, upon joining them, told him his conduct was very bad, and refused to shake hands with him. The savage (for so he did now in every truth appear) stripped for fighting, keeping on only a plain mat similar to those worn by the girls. Henry and Mr Fairburn beheld his capers with great coolness.

At length upon leaving him he sat down to take breath, and upon their going down to the beach, he went out. Engaged with the children indoors, I did not hear all that passed. Mr Fairburn went over to the island: and Henry returned when, as he told us afterwards, he saw some mats and wearing apparel, apparently thrown in haste, which he imagined to be Tohitapu's, and putting them outside, shut the door and went to the newly erected blacksmith's shop, at the back of the shop.

Shortly after this furious man ran up from the beach and snatched up a long pole, with which he drove at the door. But it not yielding to his violence he again sprang over the fence, resumed all his wild antics, and when Henry appeared, crouched and aimed his spear at him.

Henry advanced, and the savage, trembling with rage, did not throw the spear. He said he had hurt his foot with jumping over the fence and demanded a payment for it, and a great deal more which, Mr Fairburn being absent, we did not understand. Henry told him it was very good for him to hurt his foot with jumping over the fence, but that he should have no 'utu' payment.

He walked toward the store, and having snatched up an old pot, in which pitch had been boiled for atu, was springing toward the fence. But being retarded by his unwieldy burden, he made for the door, when Henry dashed upon him, snatched the pot out of his hands, and set his own back against the door to stop his retreat, and called to someone to take away the pot, which Tohitapu made several attempts to snatch away, at the same time brandishing his meri and his spear over Henry's head with furious gestures, while Henry folded his arms, with a look of determined and cool opposition, only resisting his sudden grasp upon the contested pot, and occasionally shaking his finger, telling him to beware, or exclaiming, 'Kati, emara, heoi ano!' ('Gently, sir, that is enough!')

As I looked through the window, with no little feeling of trepidation, I thought the scene resembled a man who, attacked by a furious wild bull, steadily eyes the monster and keeps him at bay. Tom the blacksmith now came forward and snatched up the pot. Tohitapu still flourished about, and then began to prepare for fight in a way which I can hardly describe. The agility of this huge man astonished me. He would run to and fro with his spear in his hand, something like a boy playing at cricket, except that the Newzealander warrior dances sideways, slapping his sides, and stamping with a measured pace and horrid gestures, every now and then stooping or crouching down, beating his breast and panting as if trying to excite his own rage to the utmost.

Mr Fairburn came back, as he sat down, and they had much talk together. Tohi demanded his ritu and said he should stay today and tomorrow and 5 days more, and he should make a great fight, and tomorrow, ten and ten and ten and ten men, holding up his fingers as he spoke, would come and set fire to the house and burn the store. Henry and Mr Fairburn when they could edge in a word replied in Maori, 'What care I for that?' A great deal of talk. You have a great deal of making gain, etc.

During prayers he was more quiet seated at the back of the house. His wife and some other women were looking in at the window and one or two chiefs sat in the room. Te Koki was absent at Kawakawa. After prayers Tohitapu came to the window and without any ceremony put one leg in, pointed to his foot, and demanded the ritu for the little blood that was spilt. Henry told him to go away and come again tomorrow like a gentleman to knock at the gate like Te Koki and others and he would say, 'How do you do, Mr Tohitapu,' and invite him to breakfast with us.

He answered that his foot was so bad, he could not walk; repeated his intention of staying here many days, of burning the house, etc., and after talking some time again, working himself up into a terrific passion, and again stripped for fighting.

It was now eleven o'clock, and by the imperfect light he looked like some wild animal capering about in mad frolic. Our friends looking in at the window, frequently one or the other called me 'Eh moder – Arimai – Come, tomorrow you see a great fire in the house, O yes, the children dead, all dead. A great many men, plenty of muskets, a great fight!'

Henry now came in, desired me to go to bed, closed the windows and left Tom, the blacksmith, with strict orders to keep watch, and in case of any outrage being committed to give the alarms. The friendly chiefs wrapped themselves in their shaggy mats and went to sleep upon the wood and bundles of poles, while we were preparing for rest. Tohitapu began to chant or yell a horrible ditty, which Mr Fairburn said was bewitching us, and this poor victim of superstition imagined he could by this means put us to death. The natives said he had 'karakia'd' us, a term they apply to our religious worship, and said he had killed a man on board the *Active* schooner in this way.

We were awakened very early by the noise of Tohi and others, who were continually arriving until our premises were surrounded. Before breakfast Henry had been obliged to turn him out of the yard by main force, because of his having taken up in his rage a young kid. I made a cup of tea for each of our friends: and having a curiosity to see how he would act upon it, we sent a tin potful outside to Tohi, who sat on the ground in sullen majesty, surrounded by a number of his followers, who had assembled for the fight. We saw him through the palings drink his tea, and hoped it would have proved a cooling draught. But he was soon again prancing about, inside the yard with many other warriors, all hideous figures armed with spears, hatchets and some few muskets. They looked more formidable to me as I caught occasional glimpses of them and listened to their overpowering jabbers feeling that Henry was in the midst of them than if I had seen the whole.

Our native girls were all out and Mrs Fairburn and myself were close prisoners, with our windows blocked up the whole day by ranges of native heads looking in. I became soon so tired of them that I ceased to be amused by their remarks. We were excluded from pure air, on an intensely hot day, and compelled to inhale a great deal of impurity. The poor children began to pine for air and liberty, and about 5 o'clock Henry came to the bedroom window, and said things were more tranquil, and many of the people dispersing. I put on the children's things, and passed Samuel and Marianne through the window. But scarcely had Marianne's feet touched the ground, when a sudden noise was heard of loud strokes apparently against the outward end of the store which appeared like chopping a breach in the wooden walls to force an entrance.

Henry bundled the children in headfirst and ran to the spot. The noise and clamour became very great. A chief brought Edward in his arms crying and looking pale and frightened. I asked where he was hurt. The poor child exclaimed, 'No mama, I am not hurt, but they are going to shoot the house and kill papa. I saw the men. I saw the guns.'

Little Marianne immediately screamed, 'Oh papa, poor papa, they will kill papa!' As I sat in the centre of the bedroom, the infant at the breast, and the three others clinging round me, I saw through a window a man point a gun at the house, apparently making a rush to enter, and Henry step in between.

My feelings were now completely excited. Yet I felt such elevation of soul as is worth much suffering to possess even for a few moments. Oh that we did not so soon drop to earth again! The dear children, sobbing and crying, fell on their knees, and repeated after me a prayer prompted by the scene. The noise continued. They repeatedly shook our frail walls, but the house remained unbroken, and the children grew more calm.

Edward said, he liked to say, 'Jesus, thou our guardian be, Sweet it is to trust in thee.' He should like to say it for a month, and then, when the fight came again, he would pray to himself, and he would pray to the great God to make these poor creatures know him, and then they would leave off fighting. He would then repeat my words to Marianne and tell her a woman and 4 little children could do nothing, but they would pray to God and he could keep the people from hurting poor papa, and it was not the natives we ought to be afraid of (for they could not keep us out of Heaven, even if they killed us), but we should be afraid of sin.

Marianne and Samuel soon began to be troublesome, trying to get to the windows and look out. But Edward's terror continued. I told him many of the natives were our friends, who would try to save papa. 'O mama,' exclaimed the child, 'what frightful creatures our friends are!' Apo at length put up her good natured face, telling me in her own language that there would be no more fighting today and that *she* had been making a great fight for us.

Edward told me that he saw Aden take a gun out of a man's hand, which was a fact. I gladly unbolted the door for Henry to enter: who told, that it was all over, and that this second tumult was quite distinct from the first. Tohitapu had remained quiet during the whole scene, rather inclined to side with us. In compliance with the united request of our friendly chiefs, Henry had given him the disputed pot, as a reward, with which he had departed.

It seems that, in the course of the day, the son of one of the chiefs, who came as our friend, stole a blanket out of Mrs Fairburn's bedroom window. Some of our people charged him with it, unknown to us; and he took this mode of revenge for their exposure of his conduct. They were driven off from their attempt to enter the window, forced their entrance through the door of Mrs Fairburn's room, and were mastered by our people and driven out.

Silhouette of Marianne Coldham when she was nineteen years of age. *(Auckland War Memorial Museum, NZ)*

Marianne Williams when close to eighty years of age with her granddaughters, Agnes Lydia Williams (right) and Evelyn Maud Williams (left). Photographer unknown. *(Alexander Turnbull Library, Wellington, NZ, F-151366-1/2)*

The Revd Henry Williams in the 1850s.
(Auckland War Memorial Museum, NZ)

The house Marianne and Henry were married in at Nuneham Courtenay, Oxfordshire, England, in January 1818. Identified by their eldest daughter as 'Drawn by my father – the house he was married from'. *(Auckland War Memorial Museum, NZ)*

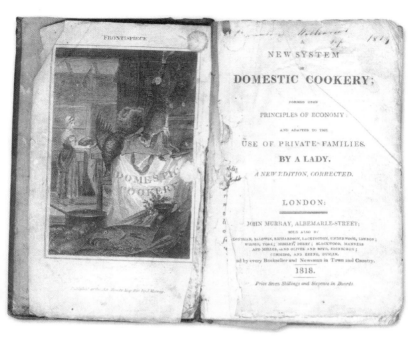

Frontispiece and title page of the recipe book Marianne took with her to New Zealand, dated 1818. *(Mrs Mary Jefford, Gisborne, NZ)*

A view of the Governor's House at Rosehill in the township of Parramatta, Australia, 1798. By David Collins. *(Auckland War Memorial Museum, NZ)*

The Revd Samuel Marsden (1765–1838). In 1800 he became the principal chaplain in New South Wales, Australia. He was the driving force behind the establishment of the first missions in the Bay of Islands. Painted between 1832 and 1838 by Joseph Backler (1815–97). *(Alexander Turnbull Library, Wellington, NZ, G-620)*

The French schooner *Astrolabe*, captained by Dumont d'Urville, during his visit of 1826–7, surrounded by canoes. Louis Auguste de Sainson, *Le Schooner entouré de pirogues Zelandaises* (1827). *(Alexander Turnbull Library, Wellington, NZ)*

Te Pahi. *(Auckland War Memorial Museum, NZ)*

Hongi Hika. *(Auckland War Memorial Museum, NZ)*

View of the home of the English missionaries at Paihia, Bay of Islands, March 1827. Louis-Auguste de Sainson, *Establissement des missionaires (Nouvelle Zelande)*. (Alexander Turnbull Library, Wellington, NZ, B-052-019)

The Beehive and storehouse in 1823. Marianne and Henry Williams's first home, constructed of raupo or bulrush. For fear of fire, all cooking was done outside, using a sailcloth as shelter. Sketch by Henry Williams. *(Auckland War Memorial Museum, NZ)*

Marianne and Henry Williams's second home, built of lath and plaster in 1830. Sketch by Henry Williams. *(Auckland War Memorial Museum, NZ)*

Tohitapu, chief and tohunga, 1823. Sketch by Henry Williams. *(Auckland War Memorial Museum, NZ)*

Rawiri Taiwhanga, a warrior chief who lived at the Paihia Mission Station. Before he himself was ready for baptism, he asked that his four children be baptised. This was the first Maori baptism celebrated in the Maori language, in 1829. Sketch by T.B. Hutton in W.C. Cotton's journal. *(Mitchell Library, State Library of New South Wales, Australia)*

Taiwhanga's cottage, built in 1831, the first European-style house to be built by Maori in Paihia. Later used by printers, including William Colenso. *(Alexander Turnbull Library, Wellington, NZ)*

Poor little Betsy Fairburn had a narrow escape. These wild creatures passed and repassed over the poor little thing as she lay on the door mat, which she had fallen over in her fright, while her mother had run to the baby. Several groups of natives sat on the ground outside the house. The little entrance room was full, and as many as room could be made for, inside the sitting room. Poor things! The worship in which they saw us engaged was nothing to them, but not so the rum and water, which Henry afterwards handed round. They all talked of the great fight which was to take place on the morrow, and expressed their determination to sleep around us for our protection, as on the former night.

In the morning, Wednesday, all seemed quiet. Our friends began to drop off, to our great relief. But just as breakfast was begun, the boys and sawyers ran up from the beach, exclaiming that the fight was coming – that a friend of Tohitapu's was coming in his war canoes, to demand an 'utu' for the injury of his friend's foot. A general scramble ensued to preserve our property from depredations like those committed on the preceding day.

The fowls (of which several had been stolen) were caught and locked up in the canoe, the pots and kettles carried into the storehouse (for we still cook out of doors). Aden brought back the fires and put the linen again in soak. No fight however arriving, things gradually reassumed their usual course. Henry went to Kerikeri; and in the afternoon we were again to our great joy in peace and quietness.

I forgot to mention that in the morning Mataoi, the hero of the blanket, brought two kits of potatoes for a present, saying he was ashamed of what his son had done. While the potatoes remained outside, and Henry had not determined whether he would accept them, news was brought that the gentleman had made off with three fowls. Upon hearing this, Henry and Mr Fairburn took the potatoes and strewed them on the ground; upon which the sawyers and boys made a feast. We expected he would come and make a fight, but we remained in peace for many days. This same person (we were told by one the chiefs assembled on this occasion) had two volumes of our 'Milner's Church History'! We missed them 3 months ago, Mr

Fairburn told us then he thought they were taken to prime their guns with.

Towards the end of Henry's career in the Royal Navy, he had been in one of the last naval battles in the war between England and the USA in January 1815. Henry's ship Endymion *had captured the larger American ship USS* President, *and Henry was one of the prize crew put aboard to sail her to Bermuda. She was badly damaged during the battle and was taking in water. During the middle of a storm, the American prisoners escaped and hand-to-hand combat followed. The Americans were finally defeated but the whole incident made a lasting impression on the young Henry. At his retirement from the Navy later that year, he swore he would never use a weapon again.*

The Revd Samuel Marsden

22 January 1824. Parramatta, New South Wales. Mrs Williams is a woman of much fortitude, faith and christian patience. I was much pleased with her amiable disposition. Her difficulties were less in number and lighter than she had anticipated. I believe she has given herself willingly to the work. Mr Williams is very anxious that his brother [William] should come to New Zealand.

DAILY DISCOMFORTS

11 February 1824. Paihia. The missionary's wife must, for the sake of cleanliness and preservation from fleas, wash and dress her children, make her own bed, her children's and her visitors'. She must be housemaid and nurse, and must superintend everything with regard to cooking. Aden is the only girl that has been able to wash the tea things for me. The best of them, if not watched, would strain the milk with the duster, wash the tea things with the knife cloth, or wipe the tables with the flannel for scouring the floor.

The very best of them will also on a hot day go (just when you are longing for someone to take the baby) and swim, after which she will go to sleep for 2 or 3 hours. Aden twice slept from dinner till after tea. If they are not in the humour to do anything you tell them, they will not understand you. It is by no means uncommon to receive such a reply as 'Ah att ati oki?' 'What care I for that?'

Etiodi, one girl I had, was always asleep and having forced her shoulders through one gown, I insisted upon her wearing a band round her waist, to preserve the others from a similar fate. Aden has run away twice. The first time was when she knocked down a bottle of brandy out of the cupboard, and started off immediately because she was ashamed. The second time was because Henry objected to her laying down [upon] his young shoot of vines. In three days she came back, as soon as it was dark, and tapped at the window of the bedroom and asked me to shake hands with her. Since that time she has been more inclined to nurse Henry occasionally. It was not until he was 2 months old that I would trust him to even her. He is a noble little fellow. The natives are very fond of him because he is a 'tangata Maori'.

About 6 weeks after I came from Kerikeri, Edward strayed round the creek and fell into the water by Jacky Watu's. This chief instantly got him out and brought him in his arms dripping wet. It was a merciful deliverance.

Our garden has turned out badly. The seeds all came up, but being a light sandy soil, most of them failed for want of depth and good earth.

The superstition of the natives is great. So is their cruelty. Mr Turner witnessed the horrid sight of a kuki [slave], partly roasted. He begged the body, and buried it. Petu, the girl who washed for me at Kerikeri, destroyed her own infant. One morning at breakfast, Te Koki, having drunk a large basin of tea, requested that his kuki (servant to Mrs Fairburn) might never be allowed to drink out of the same; and Mrs Fairburn told us that if he knew such to be the case, and were afterwards taken ill, he would immediately kill the poor girl.

The natives are all anxious to get soap: they seem to feel its value. We give tea to those who are ill, and lend them a can to drink it out of. The chiefs tell us they will bring us no pigs or potatoes, unless we sell muskets. Not long ago thirty pigs were brought down the river for muskets. The captain had so much pork that he refused to buy, and they were all taken back again. We had lived upon salt beef from the Colony [for] 3 weeks, with the exception of occasional fishing, when Captain Renneck of the *Mary* sent us a pig.

I have no time to learn the language otherwise than by conversing with my girls and every evening I read over the native prayers to Mrs Fairburn. I have promised Mr Marsden to live in our present rush dwelling till the vessel is built. He was much pleased. We are all anxious for the vessel, feeling its importance. Mr Marsden told us at Port Jackson, we could have everything made in New Zealand. Puckey would build a ship and a house and make chairs and tables. Two shoemakers were mentioned, and a blacksmith. We found when we arrived that the Society did not expect these gentlemen to work at their late employments. We in consequence send for shoes to England.

Pray for us! We need your prayers, I fear growing dead and cold from the scanty meals of spiritual food I am able to take. A short portion of scripture is all I have in a day and the only book I can open. Henry reads sometimes a little to me, and then my greatest comfort is the 'Saint's Rest'.

17 March 1824. This morning 4 of the chiefs breakfasted with us; and as we have received information that tea is become immensely dear at the Colony in consequence of the fire at Canton, and our flour is low, and the biscuit nearly exhausted, we gave them a plentiful mess of 'stirabout' made of flour and water and sugar. This they lapped up with great delight. But old Te Koki was obliged to take very small spoonsful to prevent his beard being bespattered. Amongst them was the chief Tohitapu of whose celebrated fight with us I lately wrote so fully. The last time I saw him was when he was capering about the yard with savage fury. I felt the contrast.

I have lost valuable Aden through the ill-conduct of the blacksmith. They are both dismissed our service. Bad as New Zealand females are said to be, I had hoped Aden's affectionate heart might have been worked upon by better things. I had even hoped that she might become the first fruits of our mission. So shortsighted are we. The week before she left, she had killed a kuki, a fine looking girl, who was married to a near relation of Aden's, and had gone on board the ships. I pray that I may make a proper use of this, check to my hopes, look more to Christ and less to my own endeavour and prayers.

1 April 1824. The sweet potatoes [kumera] are now getting in. Te Koki came to ask me to see them all at work. He told me, without my asking, that none of the people would work on the morrow, nor did they. When we first came here, a man from a distance came on a Sunday morning to sell a fowl. He was told it was the 'ra tapu' [sacred or holy day] and the man sat outside the whole day looking very disconsolate, with his cock perched beside him. Henry gave him a biscuit, and on Monday morning early, bought the cock.

16 April 1824. Good Friday. We have enjoyed this day a season of great refreshment. We have had all the privileges of the Sabbath. We have now established daily prayer in the native language, and singing a hymn. We do not part without some conversation to discover how much they are impressed with the truths they repeat. Mr Fairburn is principal spokesman.

One lad, coming home in the boat with Mr Fairburn the other night, said, pointing to the moon which had just risen, 'You cannot give such a garment as that!' Mr Fairburn asked if he knew who made that. 'Yes,' he replied, ' the Great God, the God of the white people did.' Mr Fairburn told him that the good men, who after death were admitted into Heaven, would be clad in shining garments like that.

Te Koki, after talking of the good Son of the great God, and of the 'utu' or payment he had made for our sins by his death, said, it would be very good for their children to understand all these things, but he was too old. The old man joined one day in singing the hymn and expressed much approbation.

Another time after a good deal of conversation, I told Te Koki, perhaps he would not be able to understand these things, but when he was dead, and I was dead, Edward and Samuel and Henry would tell them all to his children, and they would become missionaries and preach to the other natives. (They can none of them bear to be told they will die.)

The 'taorecarecas!' (slaves) exclaimed the old man, 'the children! Must they have all the good things and I nothing? Am I to be dead, laid down, not to see anything, not to speak, and the children, the taorecarecas, they to have all?' I told him, if he would know our God, it would be very good to die. His spirit would not die, etc.

Saturday, 8 May 1824. So swiftly do the days chase each other, and so little time have I to pause and note them, as they pass, much as I feel daily occurring incidents would interest you that I sometimes enjoy a pleasing contemplation of that meeting in our father's house; when we shall retrace all that is worth a thought in our journey past. This is a moment of great enjoyment. Saturday all things must be brought to a close, and Saturday night we can pause a few minutes, reflect upon the week that is past, and rejoice in the anticipation of another Sabbath. Our meetings for family worship are now very interesting. The native prayers and hymns being blended with ours, add fervency to the petition, that we may meet to mingle our praises in Heaven.

Thursday, 20 May 1824. It was a week to-day since Mr and Mrs Fairburn removed to a good substantial building of wood, intended ultimately for a carpenter's shop. It is divided into good rooms. Mrs Fairburn is quite enviable in the possession of a fireside and relieved from cooking out of doors in this cold weather. In a little time I hope to enjoy the same.

Due to the rush house being highly flammable, Marianne baked bread and cooked three meals a day outside on an open fire, under an old sailcloth, which provided some protection against the wind and rain. To make matters even more trying, Marianne's long skirts and petticoats were soon soiled from the mud and puddles.

Wednesday, 10 June 1824. During the last three weeks we have had many chiefs and parties of strangers to visit us, some of whom never before saw white people. We have been greatly favoured by the rains falling as yet only partially and so as not to stop entirely outside work. Our new kitchen and future school is roofed in and Henry and Mr Fairburn have between them built an excellent chimney. We are anxiously looking for a vessel from Port Jackson, of flour, sugar, soap, wheat, peas, etc. as we are all nearly out. Our kind friends the Wesleyans of Whangaroa lent us two casks of flour, the last of which is now begun, and we are on short allowance.

The week previous to this, Te Koki's son named Rangituki Paramata returned from an 18 month absence on an expedition to the river Thames. I was introduced to the young chief as he sat in silent majesty on a large pile of taiopi (wood for fencing) surrounded by many chiefs. Henry made presents to him and several others according to their rank, which they received in silence. Afterwards Rangituki proved his admiration of European customs and things by asking for a vast variety of things for himself, his wife and child.

He followed Henry about wherever he went, and they were so continually in and out of the house being privileged guests, that it took up all my time to answer his many questions and watch that they did not put anything slyly under their mats. In 2 or 3 days they happily took their departure. He has visited us twice since, once with another wife, who we refused to receive, acknowledging but one wife. The last time he spent a week, eating 2 meals a day with us. This, when we were all upon short allowance, was quite distressing. He attended the school and family prayers and wanted to sleep here. He wishes to possess and do everything like us. May this lead him to desire the spiritual advantages we enjoy.

3 July 1824. Yesterday, Tohitapu's son came running along the beach saying Hongi Hika was killed by a tree falling upon him. This man was going to fetch his father and mothers to go and cry. This morning Te Koki and Rangituki came from the Kawakawa to join the crying party.

I asked Te Koki where was Hongi's spirit?

'A long way off,' he answered.

I asked if it were above.

'No!' he replied, 'below, gone to his fathers.'

I said there were only 2 places for departed spirits, the one, above, the good place, the other beneath, the great fire. The old man listened but seemed to think a vast deal more about his breakfast.

8 July 1824. Hongi is not dead, tho' not quite recovered. He was felled to the ground by a tree striking him on the shoulder, and stunned. Mr Clarke bled him. As soon as he was hurt, his friends who were with him stripped him of his mats, and the numerous parties, who flocked from all quarters on the idea of his death, ate up all his potatoes.

15 July 1824. Paihia. There are times when the multiplicity of small trials attending the missionary life in a savage place require more than usual support to meet them rightly. It is a cold, rainy afternoon, and we have as yet no fireside to cheer us, and those few who cannot relish the salt pork feel weak and faint for want of animal food.

I often compare our situation to that of soldiers, who must stand to be assaulted. They advance not; they suffer every loss, yet they must stand, like those at Waterloo, to ensure future victory. Pray for us dear friends, that we may stand in this Christian warfare with the great enemy of souls! And may our children see the victory.

Henry is gone to the American ship to purchase some provisions. Yesterday he was obliged to go to Kerikeri to beg some potatoes out of the store. He brought some, and also some wheat, and took them some tea, of which they had none. It is now 11 months since stores came from the Colony except the few by the *Dragon*. We bought a twelve months' provision, but the calculation was far short of the many mouths we have to feed.

Among articles stolen lately are the pendulum of the clock, the rope by which they hoisted the colours on the Sabbath, some of the ropes of the boat, a lid of the cooking stove, a broom and a scrubbing brush. Anything their utmost ingenuity can reach disappears in an instant under their huge mats. The men are perpetually losing tools, blankets, trousers and sheets, and the girls duster, dishcloths and knives. Anything that is pewter they melt down for bullets.

14 August 1824. A vessel was in sight at dusk last night. It is a brig and is coming in. Mr Puckey came to tell me that he had seen females, and thought there were missionaries coming on shore. The rush hut intercepted my view; and I remained employed until Henry introduced me to Mrs Davis, her eldest daughter and a baby. Two daughters had gone to Rangihoua. Mr Davis followed. The excitement was quite too great, the sight of English females, the sound of English names, English news, the sight of some letters and promise of more. I was delighted, affected and confused. Mr Davis seemed full of love to the Saviour and greatly warmed our hearts.

In his journal, Richard Davis wrote: 'We are living comfortably in New Zealand. Our children are happy in their situation . . . Mrs Williams most kindly assists in the education of our daughters, who are making good progress in grammar, geography, history, cyphering, etc. They were badly off for books before the casks arrived but now they are richly supplied. We are living here with Mr and Mrs Williams who are very dear to us. Oh, how sweet is brotherly love!'

Richard Davis was a missionary farmer and there was considerable discussion as to where he should be based. It was intended by Marsden that Mr Davis should be sent inland and become Hongi's farmer, but, after spending some time at Paihia, the Davises moved to Kerikeri. In 1843 Richard's daughter, Jane Davis, married Henry and Marianne's eldest son, Edward.

MORE ATTACKS

During the journey out from England to Sydney, Henry had spent a lot of time with the ship's carpenter, who helped him design a vessel that could be used in the Bay of Islands. Upon arriving in New Zealand, Henry soon realised the urgency of reliable transportation, as the supply of food was inadequate and irregular. It was also only possible to visit other districts on foot or by canoe. With the approval of Marsden, Henry supervised the overall project, with William Hall, Maori sawyers and Maori and European carpenters assisting him. The keel was laid on 31 August 1824 on the Paihia beach, but the lack of facilities, construction difficulties and troubles with the workers created endless delays. On one occasion, work was seriously disrupted by the actions of European workmen unaware of Maori customs, which Marianne describes.

13 September 1824. Paihia. A great mob landed near Mrs Fairburn's. The horrid yell attracted me to the door of the sitting room, where for the first time I beheld at some distance their frightful gestures. They looked like something infernal. They did not annoy me much, they will not attack women when the men are about. A number of men were outside the fence. Three women were troublesome in the yard, but at length promised to go out when they had looked at me a little while.

About dinner the news flew that the natives had made a rush over Mr Fairburn's fence, broken one of his windows, beat Mr Fairburn and struck him violently with the back of a hatchet. The girls were crying and the uproar excessive. I learned afterwards that this was in consequence of an insult offered to Mrs Fairburn which he resented.

In the scuffle, after he had been repeatedly struck himself, he struck a chief. This was their 'utu'. They threatened much, and at length encamped on the beach, apparently for the night. We caught our fowls and fastened them in the store. About 10 o'clock, however, we had them haul up their canoes and they departed soon after the moon arose.

It is singular that, while these savage creatures are prowling about to seize anything that they can secretly grasp, we should be able to sleep in security on the ground floor, with no window shutters, and no other fastenings than a wooden button to glazed window frames that fasten inwards. They know that our beds are close to the windows: and blankets which they value excessively they would drag through, if only a pane were broken, nay, a crevice would suffice.

19 September 1824. I walked to meet the party returning from Waitangi. The interesting chief was beginning to ask how he could love the Saviour. He has planted some kumeras without the tapu. If they grow well, he will believe the white people have the truth.

Friday, 1 October 1824. Te Koki sat down upon the carpenter's chest, which, not being placed steady, he upset, and the carpenter, a surly old man, uttered an oath. The chief appeared angry, and did not accept Henry's invitation into the house, to talk it over, but went away, though apparently pacified.

In the course of the morning he and his son sat as usual, looking at the men who were building the vessel. The day was fine, and the girls hanging out the wash. The cloth was laid for dinner, and the men had all come in from their work, when there was, 'here comes the *taua*' (an avenging expedition, army). At first we paid no regard to it, till the cry became general, and, looking out of the door, I saw a number of these armed savages rushing towards the fence. The girls cried out, 'Mother, shut your door.'

The uproar that ensued I can faintly describe. The girls were crying, the boys shouting. Henry ran through the workshop to stop their entrance, but numbers sprang over the fence behind, and sprang back again with linen off the lines and anything they could grasp. A general scuffle ensued. The boys and girls seized each a thing for us. One brought in a frying pan, another a bucket, another a saucepan.

Of this I knew but little, nor of Jacky Watu's friendly interference, who, amongst other things, seized an iron pot which had been taken off the fire with the girls' peas in it and burned his hands as he threw it back again, and then, meeting a party who were going to smash the bedroom window, threatened to spear the first man who advanced.

My children were, except Marianne, out on the beach. Henry was outside amidst all the uproar, and my feelings were more tried than they had ever been since I left England. The girls continued sobbing and crying as they sat upon the roof. Now (it was said) Mr Williams was knocked down. Now Mr Fairburn was struck.

The children were immediately brought in: but we were inexpressibly shocked, as we stood at the door, our view entirely blocked up by the high fence and old rush hut, by beholding an Englishman come through the latter, assisted by Mr Puckey, the blood streaming from a frightful gash in the back of his leg just above the heel. He exclaimed he was done for. The poor man was very faint. Mr Puckey staunched the blood with a bandage, and we gave him something to revive him. He said he was lifting Mr Fairburn up, who was down amongst them, when a savage came behind him and inflicted the wound.

During this time the cries of the girls announced Mr Williams was down again. The sight of blood had so magnified our fears, that the worst was dreaded. I cried out 'Will no one tell me if he is killed?', but no one heard me. At last some one cried out 'No more fight, all is over.' Still there was much vociferous talking outside, and the poor wounded man was obliged to wait some minutes before a boat's crew could be summoned to fetch the doctor.

Poor little Edward was much terrified. He asked me repeatedly if we should not pray to the great God, and his mind was not tranquilized until I went with him into his bedroom. When Henry gladdened us by his appearance, his concern was very great for the wounded man. He had no idea the wound had been so serious.

The boys sang out a boat was coming, 'Perhaps it might be the doctor.' The doctor indeed it was. Our boats met half-way over. There were two doctors coming on shore to call on Henry, merely for a walk. We felt quite affected by this Providence. During several months there had not been a vessel in the harbour, and now in time of need medical assistance was sent before we could seek it. It was not until the wound was dressed, a bed made in the rush hut and the man settled quietly upon it, that all collected in the sitting room for dinner and we compared our different relations.

It appeared that, had they surprised us an hour before when all the men were away, we should have been stripped of everything. Henry told us it was not till all was over that he knew the cause of this treacherous and violent attack. He asked, for what was this violence and bloodshed. They answered, 'The carpenter swore at Te Koki!'

'What is that to me? Have I sworn at anybody?'

'No, but the carpenter had nothing to take and you had.'

'Had you come in a quiet manner, I would have obliged him to make restitution, I am ashamed of your conduct. I must note down all particulars and send them to Port Jackson. I am as angry with the carpenter as any one, as is also the great God himself, but your coming in this violent and cowardly manner to those who were sitting in peace and without a moment's notice, I shall not overlook. My heart is very sick; and I will not make peace till all the stolen property is returned and a utu for this attack and the wounded man.'

Henry immediately gave orders that all work should cease, and no one proceed with the vessel. In the afternoon our people proceeded to take down the fence of the dockyard; which appeared greatly to affect them. Te Koki and Rangituki begged and entreated they would not destroy the ship. There were told Mr Williams certainly intended to go away, unless peace was made. Henry said little, and seemed in very low spirits all the rest of the day.

While he was at Mr Fairburn's, Rangituki, who had been out and in several times without any one speaking to him, was sitting in the room. I was folding linen. Something came with force against my chest. I lifted up my eyes and saw the old chief, who had thrown two mats at me. He said, 'Your mats', and disappeared.

This is the Maori way of presenting a gift. Two of his kukis brought each a kit of potatoes. Rangituki looked anxiously at me and asked if it was good. I told him, women could give no answer, he must wait till Mr Williams came in. He then went and sat with the wounded man till Henry came, and then asked if Te Koki might come and shake hands.

Henry replied that he did not wish to see him till peace was made, that the other chiefs must also bring a payment, that he was going to Kerikeri on Monday, to a committee, when he must tell them all that happened, that on Wednesday he would return and bring some of the white people with him, and that Te Koki and the rest must come and meet them upon this business. Either they must make peace in a proper manner, or he must go to some other place. Mr Puckey and his son would return to Kerikeri on the morrow, and the building of the vessel be entirely stopped. Rangituki was admitted as a visitor, in the character of a peacemaker, but no other.

Saturday, 2 October 1824. Before I was quite dressed a general alarm was given that the fight was coming. Amo came crying to my room door. 'Here Mother, take your child! The fight! The fight!' And all was scramble and confusion. The dear children delighted me by their exclamations. 'I do not care', said Edward, 'if they take all the things, if they will not hurt my dear papa.' We were not very long in suspense. Henry soon returned.

3 October 1824. Notes were brought from Kerikeri inviting the children and myself to go and stay there till we were quiet. I immediately exclaimed, 'No! No, I will not go alone; when we all go, I will go!' Sawyer exclaimed, 'Stop here, mother! And they shall kill me if they come, before they touch you.' Rangituki said, 'If you go, they will tease you and laugh at your good place.' 'No,' we replied, 'The white people are our friends, and would not tease me.' The [Maori] boys repeatedly said, 'Do not go, mother, stop and see.'

Monday, 4 October 1824. Henry went early to Kerikeri. After breakfast Tohitapu arrived. He said Te Koki had told him to come and take care of the white people; that if they scolded him he must not mind; if they turned him out of the yard, he must not mind; if they beat him, if they swore at him, still he must stop and take care of them. He said his son was burnt. I told him to bring him here to be dressed. Rangituki said he had a kuki burnt very badly. I told him the same.

5 October 1824. Tohitapu brought his burnt son, and, before I was out of the room, David called at the door, 'Is there anything I can bring you Ma'am? There is a great talk of another fight.' This proved a false alarm, but the repetition of such rumours affect the constitution with a nervousness which tries the strongest of us. We have lost much of our confidence in the natives. May we increase in confidence and faith and trust in Him who alone can control and restrain even the savage in his fury.

We had another view of this people's character, when Rangituki's kuki crawled into the yard so dreadfully burnt that it chilled our blood to look at her. Rangituki and others all laughed at her, and when we sent them away and got her to the back of the house to dress her, not one of our girls would assist in the slightest degree because she was a kuki; and yet it seems strange that the kukis who live in the white people's houses seem to lose all these distinctions.

Tom and Dicky are both slaves of Te Koki. They eat, sleep and fare with the others, but the payments they receive all go to their mistress, Te Koki's head wife, while the others do what they like with theirs.

Te Koki's brother ran into the yard and rubbed his nose against mine before I was aware. He said he had come from the Kawakawa to make peace and tell to us not to leave our place.

A brig was seen outside the heads before dark.

Wednesday, 6 October 1824. The old carpenter came for the glass to look at the brig now at anchor. The boat went over after breakfast, and, to my unspeakable joy, Tui returned with a handful of letters. He was instantly going for Henry, part I sent and part I kept, became absorbed in their contents.

About tea-time the boat returned with Henry and Messrs Hall, Davis, Shepherd, Clarke and Puckey came for the conference. I could with difficulty gain a few moments to glance over the remaining letters.

The natives in the family crowded around us, eager to catch any word by which they might gather our intentions.

7 October 1824. At breakfast much conversation took place respecting the late events. All were of opinion that, if the natives did not come forward to make reparation, it would be necessary for the good of the mission that we should move. The prospect of toiling another year in the bush and then being no forwarder than we are at present seemed very formidable to me. Henry asked several of the chiefs if they did not think the people ought to be ashamed of coming against him armed with hatches, muskets, spears, meri, etc., when he went out to meet them with not even a stick in his hands.

He told them he did not allow one of his men to have a weapon of any description for fear they should be made angry and use it. He would not trust himself with a stick, and here one of their kukis had chopped a white man's leg almost off. 'True,' they said. 'It was all true, they were all bad people.'

Henry told them he knew how to fight, but he did not come here to fight, neither would he fight. He would sit in peace and deliver his message to them, or he would go to another place. 'Stop here,' they would answer and turning to me, 'Mother do not go away.'

After breakfast, I said to Elizabeth Puckey that nothing would trouble me so much as leaving our domestic natives. Amu asked her what I said, upon learning which she told the others, who all came crying and sobbing, saying mother's heart was sad to leave them.

A committee was assembled outside in due form; chairs, table, paper, pens and ink being carried out. The two chiefs principally concerned in the attack were on the other side of the Bay, and it was said to be too rough to cross in a canoe. Our boys asked for the boat, to fetch them. It was granted and the chiefs arrived in the afternoon. The assembly formed quite a picture outside the fence.

The natives were made to declare the cause of the attack, and were told the decision of the white people, that if within 3 days they did not bring a payment which was specified and cause the stolen property to be returned, we must leave the place.

It was thought that Mocho and Shepatahi seemed disposed to be indifferent and insolent. After it was over, Tohitapu, the high priest, who has been a staunch friend ever since his formidable attack, ran out and flourished about and made them a long harangue in favour of the white people.

Friday, 8 October 1824. The brethren departed. Before dinner Mocho and Shepetahi arrived. They sat quietly outside waiting for Henry, who went to them taking William Puckey, the better to talk to them. After some short time while we were anxiously waiting the result, the natives inside and out got up a great shout. Mr Williams had shaken hands and rubbed noses with Mocho and Shepetahi and peace was made.

A large mess of stirabout was ordered for the chiefs, and the pigs and potatoes brought in. The carpenters went to work on the vessel. Our spirits were revived, and I in particular felt an especial call for gratitude in being spared new trials and fatigue.

10 October 1824. Five boats' crew came to church. In the afternoon Henry and Mr Fairburn went to Waitangi. Mrs Shepherd and I followed with the children and native girls. I, for the first time, saw this interesting chief. He was seated in the midst of a little village on the bank of the Waitangi, surrounded by a group of natives. A red flag waved over them, the sign of the Sabbath. Several pieces of wood were laid for seats, and the man's countenance and sparkling eyes showed the deepest interest in what passed. After prayers, he asked to shake hands with me. His heart was well again, now we were going to stay. He had been very bad. He feared we should leave him, and he should forget all that the white people had taught him.

Sunday, 31 October 1824. All walked to Waitangi. A most interesting conversation took place respecting the superstitious notion of the spirits after death going to the North Cape.

'God is inviting all men to come to Heaven. If they will not come to Him while they are living, it will be too late after they are dead.'

'Maoris think of none of these things,' said the chief Rangi, 'they only think, I will eat, I will fight, I will distress some poor people, and take their children for slaves.'

'All we tell you is written in the good book and that book was written by men taught by God.'

'You are like God to us. We cannot read these things.'

'My heart would be very sad to think that after having been so long telling you these things I should not see one Maori in Heaven.'

'You must not think so; though only one man believes what you say now, by and bye many will.'

24 November 1824. November 24th. Before tea, several natives came running along the beach, armed with hatchets. One ran up to us looking very fierce. Had I been newly arrived from England I should have been much frightened. This was Matowai, whom all the natives call a bad man. He pointed to the scar on his neck, and reminded me that, when I was left alone at the settlement last year, he came very ill, and I gave him a poultice for his neck, but I told him that I would not shake hands with him till he brought back the turkeys, fowls, blankets and rum which he had stolen.

He said he would bring the turkeys but must have a great payment for them.

'No,' I replied. 'We give no payment for stolen things.'

He jumped about and flourished his hatchet, and we were glad when he walked on. . . . He turned up to the settlement. We walked home and saw him creep through a gap in the fence and sit down in the boys' yard. There he sat with several of his followers for near two hours and the sawyer, George, and Apo [the house girl] kept close watch upon him till he departed.

1825–1826

LAUNCHING OF THE HERALD

Henry

6 January 1825. Paihia. . . . I have much to say, but little opportunity, for if I sit down I am called off perpetually. We have several natives at work, some on the vessel. She is 60 feet from end to end, 15 feet wide, and will draw 7 feet of water; to be schooner-rigged, and have accommodation for passengers, and capable of bringing any supplies we may need from the colony.

The missionaries have often been at their wits' end for want of common necessaries. At this time we have not ten days' supply of flour in the island. She will also be convenient for going to other parts of the island. She will be as nice a model as we could wish, and as well built as any vessel out of London.

I shall have one seaman belonging to her. The rest will be Maori belonging to this settlement. With this will terminate the rough and bustling work of the station.

24 January 1826. Paihia. The launch of the *Herald* was to the natives a sensational event. Due notice had been given. A large fleet of boats and canoes had been assembled. Numbers had come from inland, partly in hope of payment. Upon a rough estimate, from three to four thousand persons were present.

Henry had been out the night before inspecting the ways, and taking every precaution against any risk of failure. By 7 a.m. the next morning more than 50 war canoes had arrived on Paihia beach. The natives, who had supposed that the vessel was to be moved off in Maori style by main force, had passed their time in calculating the amount of payment they were to receive, and in devising pretexts for extortion. As was the difference in size between a canoe and a fifty-ton vessel, so was the difference of payment for service. They declared they would not move a hand till their terms should have been accepted, enforcing the demand by divers weighty and ingenious reasons, in reply to each of which they had got nothing but a quiet nod of the head (from Henry).

They were already engaged by anticipation in apportioning the payment amongst themselves, when Henry announced that all was ready. Instead of going among the mob to clinch a bargain, he walked up to the vessel and named her. This was the signal for the start. The dog-shores were knocked away. The ship glided gently down the ways into the water, to the utter amazement of the natives, who rose as one man with a roar of 'ana-ra ana na-a-a-a'. The young men rushed after her into the water, throwing their spears at her as she glided along, swam off and clambered up her sides. Others crouching on their knees at the water's edge, made hideous faces, thrusting out their tongues and rolling their eyes as they would do to the enemy before battle.

The Europeans gave three hearty cheers. The natives on shore broke into a furious war dance, which was answered by those on board, to the no small risk of upsetting the light craft, as she lay unballasted, high in the water. As the vessel was getting into deep water, she touched a sandbank and stuck fast for a few minutes. A line was carried out to the moorings which had been laid for the purpose, the end being brought ashore to haul upon.

No demur, no talk of payment now. The natives rushed down with one accord, bent on the line, and easily had her over the bank. All seemed now delighted, Europeans and Maoris vying with one another in congratulations at the success of the launch.

The natives were intensely gratified and amazed, deeming themselves amply rewarded by having witnessed the wonderful genius. . . . Who by only knocking away a wedge, could launch such a huge canoe. They were calculating how many fat pigs and kits of potatoes would have been consumed over a toanga waka (launch of a war canoe).

The wives of the missionaries, who witnessed the proceedings from a stage which had been erected for them, while sharing the gratification of their husbands, could not suppress a feeling of tremor at the sight of so huge a mass of wild and excited savages, considering how feeble and powerless they were, at the mercy of such a host.

20 February 1826. Marsden Vale [the missionaries name for Paihia]. I write immediately upon the departure of dear Henry in his schooner to Port Jackson. Had I written upon the arrival of Captain Stewart from the Colony ten days since with a dozen letters new, from William and Jane, letters from them from Port Jackson which spoke of soon seeing us face to face, I should perhaps have gladdened you with the reflection of the joy which elated us so much.

But just now they are all diminished into perspective, and I can see nothing in the foreground but Henry's little barque labouring in a gale of wind attended with tremendous rain, which had continued since morning. On Thursday they worked out of the bay, I cannot preserve my mind so free from trembling anxiety as I feel it my duty to do.

I seem to have (been) startled out of a dowry of eight years' happiness. And my heart has been assailed with a feeling of desolation, it knew not before the depth of, and shall not now I am resolved (trusting in that strength which has ever yet supported me in my duty) sink under. In my better moments I have no fears or anxieties but everything to excite gratitude and love to our dear Saviour, who has permitted us to work together with and for him, and under the shadow of whose wings we alike abide on land or on sea, in the night watch in drenching rain or beneath the sheltering roof.

It is very interesting to myself to retrace the gradual improvement of the circumstances of the mission. For in everything we are so much improved that it appears quite necessary to trace the development of the increase of hope vouchsafed to us. Little Thomas is very restless, in consequence of his sixth tooth having made its appearance.

6 March 1826. Paihia. Since the *Herald* sailed February 16th, we have been in perfect peace from the natives, all the neighbouring chiefs have kept their promise of not coming near me or Mrs Fairburn during our husbands' absence. Our domestic natives have behaved remarkably well, and the school goes on just the same.

I have had Marianne and Henry ill with the mumps and Thomas with his teeth. The unexpected pleasure of a visit from Mrs Clarke who kindly came during my widowhood. Last night the wives of Te Koki and Rangituki brought me twelve baskets of potatoes as a present, seeming rather offended when Mrs Davis, who makes up purchases for me in Henry's absence, asked the price.

Though short of every kind of native food, when the schooner sailed, the natives belonging to Te Koki brought Henry an abundant stock of potatoes and pork for the voyage, and though he left me without, we were immediately and abundantly supplied. Peaches also, which we never used to see except presents from the other settlements, we have brought an abundance half ripe and I am busy preserving them for Jane and William's winter pies. We have also a few of the first produce of our own garden. I do not this year so much fear their being stolen.

May our dear brother and sister reap with us the first fruits of a spiritual harvest. Now I firmly believe in budding in some and preparing we know not in how many. I think we are not too sanguine. We cannot be as to the event though we may be as to the time. Henry had incessant fatigue and little sleep during the last of his stay. His vessel was ready to the day.

I wish I could describe the launch of the *Herald*, I think a thousand natives were present all in peace no disturbance whatever, several boats from the vessel were present, and the captain dined with us after. You I am sure will pray that she may be the 'Herald of redeeming grace'.

ALL FOUR WILLIAMSES IN PAIHIA

3 April 1826. In the midst of so much joy I feel it difficult to collect a few out of many causes of rejoicing, and to express some measure of our happiness to you. I gave you a picture of my widowhood, the last part of which was a trying season, as all my children were ill with the native fever, which (owing to a wet summer) has been universally prevalent. Edward and Samuel were the worst, and for them I suffered considerable alarm. Neither did I like to be left to dose them with calomel at my own directions. The great Physician restored them and supported me.

On Wednesday, March 3rd, we received intelligence by the *Rolla* from Port Jackson of William and Jane's near approach, and the probability, which I thought it too much joy to expect, of Henry's coming with them.

The vessel which was coming out of Sydney Harbour as our little vessel went in was just able to inform us of Henry's safe arrival, as our anxiety would have been extreme. For we had imagined him in Port Jackson when he had scarcely lost sight of our shores. Mercy and goodness have indeed followed, staid and supported us, individually and collectively.

They had a wonderfully quick passage, brought the first westerly wind, that has blown for many months, and entered the harbour early in the evening, just as the wind which seemed to have performed its office died away into a calm, which was so beautiful that the bright moonbeams seem to reflect nothing but joy and peace on its bosom.

We had all been so possessed with the idea of their being here before Easter Sunday that I had been making preparations for them, and they were just completed as the vessel appeared in sight just before dark, answering the given description and hoisting the signal previously agreed upon. The evening was closed in prayer and praise.

Easter Sunday was a day long to be remembered by us. We had a large congregation of missionaries and two boats from the ships. William's address, which was appropriate to the day, filled my heart with such powerful and varied emotions I cannot describe them. All the missionary party partook of the sacrament with feelings deeply wrought up. It was a season that well might animate us to the love of Christ.

And surely few, very few, if any, missionary families can be found so blessed in the union of family with family on this side of the grave to cheer and strengthen them on their pilgrimage. Most appropriate is Edward's advice not to rest upon an arm of flesh.

I had determined not to expect Henry, that I might not chill the joy of William and Jane's arrival, by a feeling of disappointment, yet you may imagine how anxiously I awaited the return of Mr Davis's boat and how nervous I felt as little Marianne kept exclaiming, as she stood at the window watching the boys making large fires at the landing place, 'I want to see my papa, I do want to see my papa.'

Boat oars soon were heard, before the boat could possibly have returned. The native girls came running and shouting in exclaiming, 'Mr Williams is come, your Mr Williams, your husband, I saw his eyes.' It was indeed Henry, and Henry was soon after followed by William and Jane.

And when we had composed ourselves and warmed Jane by a cheerful fire, we were joined by Mr and Mrs Hamlin, Mr and Mrs Shepherd, Mr and Mrs Davis, etc. Our room was quite filled. Mr and Mrs Davis principally presided at our table, and glad I was it was previously provided, for I was so beside myself with joy, I ran about without method and scarce knew what I did. The Evening was closed with prayer and praise.

Our joy has been shaded by dear Jane's indisposition, which though much abated still continues. I believe it is dysentery. She is very cheerful and patient, and has been able during it all to unpack her things, arrange her drawers, etc.

Perhaps excitement and exertion may have increased it. But as she has only one month to look forward to, previous to her confinement, *I as an old nurse* am glad to see her placed where she may quietly await it without any more movement. We are all together in our mud cottage, which I assure you looks much prettier now than ever did our rush hut. And the new rush hut will make William's study, library and surgery.

On Monday evening after the boats to Kerikeri, Rangihoua and Whangaroa had departed, William began to unpack his treasures.

And if our hearts had not been too full of the joy of the personal presence of some of our relations we should have been in danger of being intoxicated with the bountiful remembrances of others. The children were very much in want of frocks, and I of gowns, and yours are so pretty, so neatly made, and so exactly fit me, that I am only too well provided.

I am very thankful for the stitches more than for the things themselves. We are thankful for all the garments, and should be sorry to omit any benefactor. We received out of a cask of Mr Davis' given up for lost, some letters, one of which from you and William dropped to pieces and could not be read.

Henry and William are gone up to the quarterly meeting at Kerikeri, Jane is lying on the sofa, the children in bed, and baby on my knee. We none of us can write this time to dear mother. The meeting of so many of the old Southwell inmates reminds me so forcibly and constantly of her that we have sometimes in the evenings even expected to hear her call us.

I hope as dear Jane is on the mend she will soon be restored to health and strength. Our children though I think are now quite recovered. Your bonnets I would not forget. The children were in great want of them. Everything that has been sent for Henry fits Thomas. They are two fat little sturdy fellows. Samuel the thin is tall and in jacket and trousers.

Before Henry had left England, it had been agreed that his brother William, eight years his junior, should follow out to New Zealand. As a qualified doctor and surgeon, he then gained a BA in Latin and Greek at Oxford University before offering his services to the CMS. It was feared they might send him to India, believing his university education would be wasted in New Zealand, but in 1824 he was ordained before embarking with his wife Jane on the voyage out.

William had met Jane Nelson when she taught at his mother's girls school at Southwell. They were married in July 1825 and sailed for New Zealand a month later aboard the Sir George Osborne. *She was eight months pregnant when she arrived in the Bay of Islands.*

William

12 April 1826. We anchored in the Bay of Islands on Saturday, March 25th, after a pleasant voyage of seven days. Our comfort was increased by having Henry in our party. We are for the present living with him at this settlement.

The house we inhabit is meant for a girls' school. It consists of one good room 18 feet long and surrounded on three sides by skillons or smaller rooms in which the girls are to sleep.

The vessel is to bring provisions enough from the Southern part of the island, the want of which has been one reason why children could not be received by the Missionaries. The natives live in small villages seldom more than twenty families together. These villages are in some districts very numerous. The natives will send their children from a great distance if they are fed and clothed by the Missionaries. But without food and clothes they will not send them at all.

I have been at several places where the people have enquired whether we could receive their children. So satisfied are they that at least they will receive no injury among us. The people are upon the whole much more peaceable than when Henry came. Some chiefs who were then troublesome are now warm friends. The number of natives also is increasing. A large village has been formed about a mile from us and up the Kawakawa, the capital of our chief, the number is more than doubled.

Hongi has been considered the scourge of the land. And so indeed he is. For as the people tell us he is the only chief who has such an eager desire for war. Yet in consequence of his expeditions people have been induced to leave their own places and fix themselves in our immediate neighbourhood. The people under the protection of our chief have been more than doubled since Henry's arrival.

21 April 1826. At ten minutes past seven in the evening Jane was delivered of a girl, and both mother and child are remarkably well.

Henry
27 May 1826. We are now sitting very comfortably in view of our bright fire. William, Jane, Marianne and myself with Edward and some of the native girls who are working here. We have but little time for talking. This is an exercise limited to the time of meals.

William
27 May 1826. The study of the language occupies a large portion of time, and when that has been attended to, little is left for any other business, except those secular employments which cannot be dispensed with.

Jane is now perfectly recovered, and our little girl who we have named Mary after her grandmamma [Williams] at Southwell is a very healthy child, though not so large as Henry's which are the largest children I have ever seen.

After three months, William began work on translating parts of the Bible into Maori. Henry had always insisted the missionaries become proficient in the Maori language as school lessons and church services were conducted in Maori.

1 July 1826. Paihia. I am again a widow. Henry is gone in the vessel to Tauranga. He has been absent about ten days. The natives have teased him to go ever since the schooner was first laid down, and promised him plenty of potatoes and pigs. Just at this time we are all short of native food, and as the schools are increasing, especially at Marsden Vale, it was thought necessary to go, although Henry would greatly have preferred the summer.

They sailed on the 20th June, Mr Charles Davis, Mr Clarke and Mr Shepherd, Te Koki and Rangituke with them. The latter is married to the daughter of a principal chief of that place, and three of the native crew, our domestics, have relations there.

We are now looking for their return every day. William went in the afternoon to visit a sailor who is dying at Kororareka, and Jane and I have been sitting alone talking of Southwell etc., as we often do.

Kororareka, known today as Russell, was considered the 'hell hole of the Pacific'. Directly across the Bay from Paihia, the lawless port was regularly visited by the South Sea whaling fleets, which could find there fresh supplies, spars, alcohol and women. In exchange, the Maori received muskets, iron tools, alcohol and European curiosities and contracted European diseases.

5 July 1826. On Saturday night, William arrived between ten and eleven and said that the little schooner the *Herald* was outside. That he and Mr Davis hearing at Kororareka that schooner was in sight ascended the hill and having satisfied themselves that it was she, rowed quite out to sea; when, it coming on very dark, they were obliged to return. At that moment she hoisted a light, but Mr Davis had so severe a headache that they did not put back. This was very invigorating intelligence to me.

We called the boys up to make a fire on the beach, which they did and plied it well with fresh fuel till I closed my eyes about two o'clock, notwithstanding it had come on to rain heavily.

The next morning Sunday, the Bay was involved in an impenetrable fog, through which I anxiously longed to perceive the *Herald*. We delayed the usual very early service an hour and when we concluded at eleven o'clock, the mist had cleared off, but no vessel was to be seen. It was a calm. We were very unpleasantly on the tiptoe of expectation and unable to confine our thoughts.

William and the other friends went as usual to visit the natives at the different villages. And just as the bell had rung for the girls' school and I was beginning to assemble them, the schooner appeared towed by two boats round Tapeka Point. She appeared to us too high, and I ran by Jane's suggestion with the glass in my hand to Mr Fairburn, and called Mr Tuckwell out of the boys' school; he came from the Colony in her, and we were quite satisfied when he said it was she, and taking the boys with him in a canoe, went to the vessel to bring Mr Williams on shore.

After school Jane and I walked down to the beach to give him the meeting, when we were told the schooner was the *Prince of Denmark*. You may imagine my disappointment.

Monday night William received a sudden summons to Kerikeri to attend Mr Clarke's youngest child who was very ill with its teeth. Jane and I were very sorry to lose him, just as we had got the younger ones to bed, the hearth swept up, and sat down to comfort ourselves with work and talk of olden times. (The native domestic girls who sit with us to sew of an Evening, and Edward and Marianne were our party.)

A knock at the door caused me to open it, when the sight of Henry made me start back with a sudden exclamation. The girls were vociferous in their satisfaction. The boys collected to ascertain the cause of the uproar, and we had quite a scene.

Our neighbours quickly assembled, and the girls being told, that the way to show their love to white people was to leave off crying, whining and shouting and help to get tea ready. All was speedily arranged, and I could scarcely believe that I saw Henry by his own fireside, relating his adventures.

He had left the vessel in a calm off Cape Brett, and Messrs Shepherd and Clarke at Rangihoua, and had met William's boat just by his own beach. Nobody had heard boat oars but Mr Fairburn. Their voyage had been pleasant. The natives had behaved well. They had interesting communications with them, and had filled the vessel with potatoes in three days. But the pigs Rangituki told them to keep back, till he brought a vessel to trade for muskets and powder. They heard of the devastation of war in every direction.

Pomare, the principal chief at Kororareka just opposite to us, had lately been cut off with great slaughter at the river Thames, and they heard of nothing but wars and rumours of wars. They brought two boys for our school. The harbour was only fit for small vessels. They had been aground but were got off without any harm.

Monday, 10 July 1826. Henry and William are at Kerikeri at the quarterly committee. I have no time to look over my drawers of treasures where my English letters are hoarded. I am anxious to tell you how opportunely you and Lydia administered to my necessities, by sending frocks and gowns ready made. I really do not know what would have become of us without them.

As it was we were quite overwhelmed with good things. The frocks for the children were particularly acceptable, though two of them were a little too smart for Henry's eye, till Jane suggested covering them with a pinafore. The gown was very pretty only it required some of the trimming to be taken off, and was a little too long and wide. It will be a great treasure in the summer. Mrs Bury, though quite unknown to me, sent most useful things in the pinafores.

Such a variety of incidents have occurred within these last six months that I scarcely know what I have communicated and what I have not. Jane and I are just about to open a boarding school for

New Zealand young ladies, in a rush hut until a house can be built, to enable us to turn out of this and give it up to them.

Jane seems to fit most admirably well into her work. I cannot be sufficiently thankful that there appears a prospect of their remaining here. William is as much at home as if he had been here twelve months. He and Henry began their plans forthwith upon their arrival and have very steadily followed them up.

But the longer I write the more I find I have to say. Pray for us that we may be saved from ingratitude for all the rich mercies temporal and spiritual that we are now enjoying. Few, very few missionaries are so blessed with kindred and friends. We thought we had left all, but our Lord and Master has brought to us some of the nearest and dearest. May we be strengthened in the love of the Lord, Master and Saviour, to run with renewed strength the race set before us. I am sure you are with us in spirit, and sometimes Jane and I could talk till we almost fancied you would in bodily presence sooner or later come to join us.

Henry

12 July 1826. Paihia. We can scarcely tell how the days and weeks roll over heads. Our little vessel has returned from the colony in safety with abundance of stores. We have since been two hundred miles southwards in quest of potatoes for the schools. She was filled on the third day of trading.

The natives behaved remarkably well, Te Koki and Rangituke were on board. As we passed along the coast great desolation appeared. Scarcely any inhabitants were living between this place and Tauranga, which is due south of Mayor Island. At that place there was a vast population. But the Bay of Islanders had even there committed dreadful havoc.

Close to where our vessel lay was a mount which had formerly been a pa. But the people belonging to it had most of them been killed and eaten. The remains of old fortifications had been seen in many places, which had been deserted.

We assembled the natives on the Sabbath, and delivered our message to them. They listened with great attention and asked for some of us to remain with them. We told them when the wars were over some missionaries would reside with them. But at present we were afraid. The majority of these people had never seen a European. The children ran before us wherever we moved, and all appeared delighted.

The weather was much against us, and being winter it was needful to return as soon as possible to the Bay of Islands. It was grievous to see such numbers of men, women and children without any means of instruction. We brought back two boys for the school, sons of principal chiefs.

We had two boys on board who were slaves, part of the crew taken from thence. Their fathers, mothers and other relations came alongside to see them, and I gave them permission to return with them on shore specifying a time when I expected to see them back. I was a little surprised to see them according to promise. They told me their friends had endeavoured to persuade them to remain behind, but they would not.

A considerable number of the Bay of Islanders have been cut off lately, who were on a fighting expedition, amongst whom were Pomare and Tohi, Mr Shepherd's adversary. The natives have been and still are in a most unsettled state.

Our two families here are well. Since my return from Port Jackson I have experienced a very great change, having little comparatively to call off my attention to one thing needful, from the share William has taken in all that is requisite. He makes rapid progress in the language. We meet generally from nine to twelve each day. Our schools are on the increase.

We have opened a school fund amongst ourselves, if you can collect something for us we shall be thankful. It is exclusively for the girls, as their condition is far more degraded than that of the males. We are under some concern for our children as they advance in years. Your numberless presents have been received. Edward's clothes fitted him exactly, the only decent ones he has to wear.

Many letters, papers, etc. from you and others had been lying in Mr Campbell's store in Sydney and brought here, were quite rotten. One little book, the *Plough Boy*, was very much injured. For your remembrances we are thankful and hope you will not cease to remember us before the Lord. We need all aid.

Jane

11 August 1826. About a month ago two letters were sent to the colony on their way to England. From them you would hear of the birth of my little Mary on the 21st April, and also of the probability of our being permanently fixed at this station. Every member of the mission considers this to be the most proper place for us.

In a week or two we hope to remove to a rush house which is now preparing for our reception, and will be our habitation, till a chapel and three houses are erected for Henry, Mr Davis and Mr Fairburn at Marsden Vale. We are permitted to enjoy numberless privileges which would be denied us at a new station, particularly that of Christian society which is a blessing we cannot estimate too highly in this waste howling wilderness.

Our forces here are now tolerably strong. Besides Mr Davis and Mr Fairburn and their families, Mr Charles Davis, Mr Tuckwell, Mrs Fairburn's brother resides here, and one of our inmates is William Puckey. His parents left the island some time ago. But he has returned for twelve months to assist us in acquiring the language. In other respects he is no acquisition. But in that he is very useful, for having lived in the island nearly all his life, and been accustomed to associate almost exclusively with the natives, he acquired a very correct knowledge of the language.

14 August 1826. Twelve eventful months have now passed away since we quitted our native land, each of which has been marked by mercies too numerous to recount. On this day last year we sailed from Gravesend.

Our merciful Father has been pleased to guide us in safety across the mighty deep, and to preserve us through many perils both by sea and land. Those who go down to the sea in ships do indeed see the wonders of the Lord.

William

21 September 1826. Another vessel has arrived from England. The *Sisters*, Captain Duke, by which we have received a parcel from Mary, which I took for a parcel of letters, containing twelve copies of a book by Mr Irons. They would have been more acceptable if accompanied with a letter.

We have lately entered our rush house and are beginning to taste the comforts of our fireside. The ground on which the house stands is planted with a number of native shrubs, which will in a little time mean a very pretty appearance.

We have now passed through the winter season, but the cold has never been greater than in the early part of April, with occasional frosts not severe enough to produce snow or ice.

You would be much pleased with the beautiful woods which in many places line the rivers. Though the character of the country would prevent any English female from walking very far. The whole country, so far as we are acquainted with it, being for the most part a continued succession of hills with very narrow valleys between them.

Of the beauty of this part of the island I cannot say much, for these hills almost universally wear a most barren aspect being covered only with fern. Though here and there, there is a spot which is picturesque and beautiful.

NEW ZEALAND COMPANY SHIPS

Jane

25 September 1826. Paihia. I have now the privilege of addressing you from our own fireside. We have been inmates of our new habitation almost a fortnight, and although it is constructed of raupo or rushes, we have the great comfort of a brick chimney.

This day three weeks was the monthly prayer meeting, and Paihia was the place of rendezvous. Our friends from the other two stations generally arrive to dinner, which is provided at Henry's house. They drink tea with Mrs Fairburn. This time it was William's turn to address them, which he did from 1st Cor. 9th.16.

The following Saturday our attention was excited by the appearance of a ship entering the bay. It was ascertained that she had three masts and was an English vessel. But our hopes and expectations were greatly disappointed to find that she was only from Port Jackson and had no letter for us from dear old England.

She brought us nevertheless a visitor in the person of Mr Cunningham, the King's Botanist in these Southern regions, with whom we became acquainted in this colony. On this side of the globe a slight acquaintance is soon converted into intimacy, and he soon agreed to become our inmate, on condition that we treated him as one of the family and not as a stranger.

The next day during morning service another ship was discerned at some small distance, and our thirsty spirits again led to hope that she might bring us glad tidings from a far country. But not till Monday morning did we know for a certainty to our great mortification that it was the *Emily*, Captain Brind, neither from nor to England.

On that day we removed into our new abode in order to receive Mr Cunningham. A house consisting of two small rooms is about to be erected for him close to ours. The object of his visit will lead him to explore the interior. But his stores, plants, etc. are to be deposited here. And when he is at home he is to have his meals with us. He is an interesting character.

Our supplies of food for the natives is become so alarmingly scanty that the committee three weeks ago deemed it advisable to send an expedition to the Hokianga, to purchase pigs, potatoes, etc. Accordingly on Tuesday last the *Herald* quitted the Bay of Islands intending to sail round the North Cape to the mouth of the river, and the same day a party consisting of Henry, Mr Davis, Mr Cunningham and Mr Hamlin set out overland to meet the vessel.

The following morning soon after breakfast a third vessel sailed rapidly into the harbour, and the discharge of six guns informed us that she had letters on board for the missionaries. The thrill of joy and thankfulness caused by the successive reports you may easily imagine. The boat was immediately dispatched. It proved to be the *Sisters*, Captain Duke, from England.

Your little granddaughter is now five months old, rather a small child for her age but very plump and healthy.

Henry

16 October 1826. Paihia. When alone, which is not very often, we (that is the members of the two families) talk over old affairs. And of all whom we have left behind. Through the day it is generally hurry scurry with us all.

You will wish to hear how William and Jane proceed in their new sphere of action. It did not require long for them to get into place, more particularly as their places were before prepared. They took a cell in our hive till lately. They have now enlarged their borders and inhabit a rush house adjoining our garden fence and dine with us.

We are looking forward to assembling a school of little girls, under the joint charge of Jane and Marianne. But in this as in everything else much patience will be called into exercise. Their little Mary is a fine little creature full of life.

27 October 1826. Yesterday arrived the New Zealand Company in their two vessels from the Southward. They have been exploring the coast with great care for the last seven or eight months. I went on board on their arrival and found Mr Lechmere, a relation of Mrs Cole's at Hampstead. He brought four letters of introduction to William and myself from different persons. He appears a gentlemanly young man though he has been disposed to be wild. This voyage will tend to sober him considerably. Captain Herd, who has charge of the expedition, seems to despair of success. His account is very interesting. But they have not landed to remain any time. As the natives behaved with hostility towards them, and felt disposed to take the vessels or to attack them at Whangaroa.

The New Zealand Company had been established in England by a group of private businessmen with the aim of setting up trading posts while colonising New Zealand. It was first formed in 1825 under the chairmanship of J.G. Lambton, afterwards Lord Durham. At the head of the expedition was Captain Herd, who had visited Stewart Island and the site of Wellington Harbour before pulling into the Bay of Islands. Aboard the Rosanna *and the* Lambton *were sixty settlers, who then went on to buy land in the Hokianga harbour on the west coast. However, because of unfriendly encounters with the local Maori, they abandoned their plans and returned to Sydney.*

HOLIDAY IN WHANGAROA

Henry

3 November 1826. Whangaroa. Marianne, the children and myself arrived here last night as it became dark, overland from Kerikeri (30 miles north of Paihia). We came a goodly company, in all twenty-three persons. The two Mariannes rode in a chair twelve miles having four natives to carry them. After which they had to scramble through woods, ditches and bogs with great difficulty and fatigue.

The variety of scenery to that which is near us is very great. We entered the Mission house about eight o'clock with great delight and relief to body and spirits. Mrs Turner has been long wishing for Marianne to pay her a visit, but really New Zealand is not much of a land for that. There is so much preparation requisite that no one ought to move above once in three years.

Thus it is that the females here do not see each other above once in three or four years, and as Mrs Turner has been alone nearly from her arrival in the island, we thought it well to come at this time besides the desirableness of giving Marianne a short respite.

The journey was formidable in prospect. On Wednesday we shut up our little box at Paihia, and proceeded to Kerikeri, where we remained one night. Thursday we commenced our journey before eight. Marianne was a good deal fatigued on her arrival, but I hope upon the whole she will find considerable relief, as here she is exempt from kitchen duty.

4 November 1826. Edward is now eight years old and an active lad. As a small proof he walked the whole distance from Kerikeri to this place (Whangaroa), not less than 20 miles, through woods and bogs without once complaining. He is advancing a little in knowledge, but as I fear the attention required can never be given to him here, concluded to send him to England four years hence. Perhaps some other boys may accompany him. The little ones speak the language nearly as well as their own and Edward can talk to the natives a great deal better than I can.

Marianne grows in stature and is acquiring some little stability, but she requires great attention. She is a dear little creature and fond of reading and learning. Samuel is a little thin fellow and curious in many respects and in great need of attention. Henry is a stout, sturdy little fellow, lively and the pet of most; he is learning his letters but much more fond of play.

Thomas is equal to the others in value but can only just run about. He is attracting notice and can say a few words. All of them except Marianne may in their turn go to England to school. We think the best age for them to go is twelve years.

William has proposed to instruct the boys in the Mission himself, but I do not think it practicable in connexion with other matters. Children under such circumstances must be obliged to learn their lessons as well as say them. Our hopes are fixed on them. We may learn the language so as to converse with the natives but they will thoroughly understand it. And we hope by the grace of the Lord to see them engaged in his work.

Marianne the elder will, I think, feel herself much refreshed by her visit here. Our brethren here go on very well. The situation of the settlement is beautiful, and they appear to have whatever they want within reach, which greatly facilitates their work.

Monday, 5 November 1826. I have lately commenced holding service at Kororareka, the anchorage for the shipping. The sailors here are a bad set. It is with pain we see them coming near us. Three Sundays since we assembled about 70 on board the *Rosanne*, Captain Herd. On these occasions the people were very attentive. I felt much pleasure in going, and do think good will result therefrom. I was happy to see the Captain did not intrude upon us, in consequence of our going to them. Immediately at the close of the service I withdrew. I shall continue going to see them through the season.

The formidable New Zealand Company's vessels have at length arrived from exploring the coast southwards and I was much surprised to find that no landing had been accomplished. They were frightened at the behaviour of the natives about the River Thames. Captain Herd appears to have made up his mind to relinquish the idea of settling.

They give a good report of the convenience of this part of the island, which has several rivers running through a great extent of country, East and West, North and South. But the natives appeared hostile and had formed more than one plan for taking the vessels. They were on one occasion in the act of firing on a great party of the natives. It was with great difficulty that Captain Herd could keep his men back. They did not attempt to land.

They have charged the Missionaries with prejudicing the natives against them, forgetting that those natives were at war with our people; consequently out of our reach, even had we been that way disposed. They visited an island that was covered with brimstone; about 220 miles to the Southward.

It appears to me one of the most ridiculous schemes that could enter the imagination of man, and certainly to have been formed without counting the cost. The information by which the Company was guided must have been very bad. However, they have had their trial, and the result is that ten thousand pounds are now expended, which will not benefit anyone. Captain Herd appears very desirous to cast considerable blame on Mr Marsden.

William

6 November 1826. Paihia. Some of the customs of this people are very peculiar and nothing can be more curious than the manner in which a person is treated who has lost a relation. I have mentioned one instance to Mr Bickersteth in which Hongi was a principal actor.

A relation of his died, a chief of some consequence, and Hongi went to remove the bones to his own residence. But he and his attendants not only took away the body, but all the pigs and potatoes upon which they could lay their hands.

There was lately another instance in which one of Hongi's wives behaved very improperly. His friends immediately paid him a visit from all quarters and seized everything they could find, and all this to show their respect for him.

I was a witness to one of these acts. Hongi has a complaint in his knee which he wished me to see. I was accompanied in my walk by a chief from the neighbourhood, who, as soon as we came to Hongi's residence, seized one of his slaves as a satisfaction for his wife's misconduct. When some people expostulated with him, the chief with a great deal of gesture spoke in defence of Hongi's honour, while the latter said nothing at the loss of his slave, but only smiled at the arguments of the men.

In our school at Paihia there are about 45 men, boys and girls, who behave well, and are in general very desirous to be instructed. The natives around us are much under our influence while they remain at home. We never see human heads exhibited as formerly, nor do they I believe so frequently kill their slaves, on the death of their relations, though we have had some most shocking instances of late. But when they are out at war I believe they are as barbarous as ever, killing and devouring those they subdue without any feeling of compassion.

A chief died lately at Rangihoua, brother to the principal man there, who has behaved very well towards the Europeans of late. I was at Rangihoua the same day the chief Tuma died, and I went to see the corpse after it was laid out, according to the native superstition. The deceased was placed in a sitting posture, the whole of his body being concealed except the upper part of his face by different garments, and over all was a sergeant's coat, almost new. Behind was placed two muskets which had belonged to the deceased. Some of the relatives were hard at work making the house which is to receive his remains, while the rest were seated around uttering most lamentable ditties, which I understand are songs in general use on such occasions.

Wareporka, the surviving brother, had not tasted food since his brother died, nor does he intend to eat until the funeral ceremony is over. It is supposed that the spirit of the departed hovers around within a certain distance for three days, after which the corpse is deposited with great ceremony, in the place where it is to continue when the mourning ceases.

It is common on these occasions to kill one or more slaves, as companions for the departed on his way to Reinga, the place of departed spirits, and it was proposed to kill one now, but Wareporka and the chief's father opposed it. Two days before Tuma died it was supposed that his spirit had fled (probably he had fainted) when the friends made a shout which they thought was the means of his revival.

He related that he had been to the North Cape, while apparently dead, but that a little girl, a relation who died some years ago, met him on the ladder by which they descend into the Reinga, and told him to return in a few days when she would meet him again.

The next day being Sunday, I accompanied Mr King to the same spots, to assemble what natives we could for service. We could meet with none, however, but those who were occupied with preparations for the deceased. The same scene was continued that we had seen the day before. I felt much pity for the poor creatures, whose grief was apparently great, but who sorrowed as those without hope.

Tuma had been a great savage, and some years ago, on the death of a relation, he killed a female slave with a bill hook while washing clothes at the door of one of the Europeans, though Mr Kendall and Mr King interfered for her rescue.

We find enough to do within ten miles of home. But I have paid a very interesting visit lately to the river Hokianga in company with Mr Clarke. One object we had was to purchase food for our school, which was conveyed to our bay in the schooner built at Paihia.

Our journey from Kerikeri to the mouth of the river was only about sixty miles, this being the narrowest part of the island. The inhabitants are much better behaved than our neighbours, and a missionary field is there open which we hope to occupy as soon as our strength will allow us.

Our Wesleyan friends at Whangaroa are very pleasant sensible people, and we are glad to have intercourse with them whenever an opportunity offers. One of them comes over occasionally at our monthly meetings for the study of the language. At the present time Henry and Marianne with three of the children are gone over to stay a few days, and I expect to go myself on a professional visit in a short time.

We have of late commenced an English service on board the vessels in the harbour. There are now five lying at anchor. We have found two objections against receiving the crews on shore, but a small number continue to come, and those few generally arrive towards the conclusion of the service. Henry's first congregation amounted to a hundred and thirty, a number which renders this duty the more important. The state in which these vessels are while in the bay is most deplorable. They are for the most part wholly given up to iniquity from the Captain to the cabin boy.

Jane

14 November 1826. Paihia. We are almost inundated with pin cushions and needle books for our girls but we are without pins and needles. A few work bags and housewifes [hussif: a pocket sewing outfit] furnished with a small quantity of cotton and a few common needles and pins would be useful, but what would be far more acceptable to us are roundabouts for our native girls made of coarse dark coloured print with short sleeves.

Some common scissors and knives, coloured cotton handkerchiefs, blue check aprons, coarse broad tape are all most useful articles, pictures also are very acceptable, particularly those relating to scripture history, or representing the common occurrences of civilized life.

Henry is much stouter and Marianne looks a little older. She has been a good deal teased lately with a pain in her side which is probably occasioned by her situation. She is looking forward to a confinement in March or April.

Edward, no longer little Teddy, is growing very tall and very much resembles his cousin Edward at Hampstead in appearance. He is very quick, but owing to the great disadvantage of not having had anybody that could attend to the instruction of the children he is very backward. This evil, however, is in a fair way to be remedied, as both his father and mother are taking pains to bring him on.

Marianne is a very sweet looking little girl, of an affectionate disposition and a more industrious turn than her brother.

Little Samuel is quite a Coldham. Henry and Thomas are remarkably stout healthy children, very engaging and considering the numerous disadvantages under which the poor children labour they are wonders. The majority of the English children on the island are boys, and if society send out a person properly qualified to instruct and keep them under his eye, it will obviate many evils which now exist.

Henry and family are paying Mr and Mrs Turner a visit at Whangaroa. We are quite lonely without them. Though I have been eight months on the island, I have never yet had an opportunity of seeing the renowned Hongi, who is now lying at Kororareka, just opposite Paihia, very ill with a large swelling in his knee.

2 December 1826. Almost a fortnight has elapsed since our return to our own cottage. We left our kind friends at Whangaroa on the 17th of last month, and had a favourable day for our journey overland at Kerikeri, which place we reached by a quarter before six with much less fatigue that I had felt on going.

At Kerikeri we staid till the Monday. Our friends were exceedingly kind. The weather remarkably fine and the joy of meeting Samuel and Henry (junior) again very great. But here our dear little Thomas met with a serious accident. His native nurse let him sit too near the steps of Mr Clarke's verandah, he rolled off and broke his collar bone. Henry bound it and sent overland for William, who came with the boat the following day, as soon as his two services at home and at the ships were over.

The dear child did much better than we could possibly have hoped and his father had proved a very good surgeon. We all returned home on Monday to dinner, which Jane had ready for us on the table, when the boat landed. Our meeting was indeed a joyful one. We rejoiced to be at home, and had great reason to be thankful that our little invalid was not worse. He has, however, been suffering much from a feverish cold, with which most of the children and natives have been affected. He has been much reduced, and I have suffered also from disturbed nights. But today I am happy to say he is decidedly better. The dear little boy had out sixteen teeth and I hope will soon regain his former robust looks.

On Saturday last, Henry went to Rangihoua to bury Mr King's little boy, who has long been a sufferer. These events cause us to look at our little flock with trembling gratitude. Mrs Turner has lost hers the age of our Thomas, but these are the only two except one prematurely born of the 15 births among the missionaries since we arrived on the island.

When Henry returned on Monday, Mr King and Mr Hobbs came with him. From the latter we learnt that the natives of Whangaroa have been attacked by a party of natives of whom they had sometime been in expectation and dread, to revenge a murder. They had killed three natives, destroyed their young kumera plantations and had even molested the white people, which had not been anticipated, had trod down Mr Turner's wheat, taken away all his potatoes and the best native girl in Mrs Turner's service, who was a redeemed slave from these people.

Henry and Mr Davis sailed for Tauranga in our little vessel in search of food for the schools (that brought from Hokianga being nearly exhausted) on Tuesday morning about 9 o'clock and Mr Cunningham the colonial botanist returned from Whangaroa that same day just in time to accompany him.

So I am again left a widow, but under far more favourable circumstances. Indeed I cannot help comparing my present comforts, and the kind assistants I have in William and Jane, to my former lonely state with six children and no help. Jane and I begin to find we make a great deal of time by eating together. We dine now alternately together at each other's houses. We have each of us three working mornings in a week which are not employed in cooking and household affairs.

I am not now obliged to leave so many necessary things undone, and we have good hopes of our school, of which we have just made a beginning, and intend to take the superintendence daily in turn. Indeed we have in every way bright prospects before us, and our former difficulties must still remain to the end. Our little ones were all looking remarkably well before they got these colds.

Henry

14 December 1826. Paihia. The day before yesterday I returned from a short voyage to the Southward to Tauranga 200 miles, an interesting place with a considerable number of natives. Our first object was to procure provisions for the support of the school, as we have a number of children assembled together, but little to give them. We were too early for potatoes.

Our communication with the natives was very pleasing, though they showed their great desire for muskets and powder. They wish for someone to live among them, and we should gladly have done it had it been practicable. There is much work here for a hundred missionaries. Our situation here is peaceable though we have no certainty of its duration.

At Rangihoua the school has lately been entered by a mob, and a number of blankets, jackets, etc. cleared off because a native near the Europeans had married a wife.

At Kerikeri, a party behaved extremely ill a week ago, and showed every disposition to enter the house, but were kept in check by Hongi. They, however, did much mischief at the stock yard and outhouses. Hongi's people fell upon them and broke up four of their canoes. Thus each of the settlements has had a recent disturbance, which might have proved of serious consequence.

We must look out next. The natives are in a singular state of mind at this time, very unsettled. Several of the principal men of this bay have been killed lately, and in about two months we expect a general assembly for the Southward, when multitudes will undoubtedly be murdered.

At the settlement we visit for religious instruction, the people pay tolerable attention, and we hope it in some measure influences their conduct. There is great difficulty in conducting the schools as the natives are independent of us, and some will frequently leave us, after they have received much instruction. This is very discouraging but more particularly when it relates to the girls.

This last week Marianne lost her most useful girl which has been taken away to go on board the ships. This is a common case. As soon as the girls become useful they are carried off. For the last fortnight the natives around have been very ill, and today I have been told it is in consequence of the white people. I should not be surprised if they were to create a disturbance with us in consequence, so very superstitious are they. But these ideas do not occupy much of our attention. We trust we are acting in obedience to His command who has said that He will never leave us nor forsake us.

William and Jane are well with their little one. There is little doubt they will remain by us. It has lately been thought that it would be a considerable advantage were all the members of the Mission at one station, from which they might issue during the week. The study of the language occupies a great portion of time.

Marianne and our little ones are all well, they contribute greatly to our comfort and also to our care, especially as we have no green fields or trusty servants. I have some more curiosities for you, but as some of them are long, such as spears, I must wait for a good opportunity.

Your attention to our wants greatly contributes to our comfort. Indeed I do not know what we should do but for the trouble and interest you all take in our affairs. We cannot obtain anything from Port Jackson under any circumstances.

1827

MUTINY ON A CONVICT SHIP

17 January 1827. Paihia. It is our Samuel and his aunt Lydia's birthday. We are all in health after a late period of sickness and have had our spirits supported under much continued anxiety, excitement and fatigue, as well as commiseration for our Whangaroa friends, who are all, namely Mrs and Mr Turner with their three children, Mr Hobbs, Mr Stack, Luke Wade and his wife, with us at this station, and have taken their passage on board the *Sisters* for the Colony. On board of which vessel we have every one of us sent all our property that we could possibly do without, in order that the natives may have less temptation to strip us, and that in case of being to Port Jackson, we may find some necessaries there.

The natives of the Bay of Islands are immersed in the horrors of a New Zealand civil war. And the fate of Whangaroa shows that, as the natives themselves do not scruple to say, the persons and property of the Missionaries are exposed to every straggling party of an enemy. Kerikeri is at this time particularly exposed. So much so that we daily expect the Missionaries here.

But at this station our natives give us assurance of protection, which at the others their chiefs say they cannot afford. We are besides in view of the shipping, which at this time of the year frequents the harbour. And we may anticipate that our own little vessel on her return from the Colony, whither she is gone for food and supplies, may afford an ark for safety or for flight in case of extremity.

19 January 1827. Ever since I wrote a hasty letter to Lydia in the beginning of December we have had a succession of events to occupy our minds. And Jane and I have always had more than we could well get through. When Henry and Mr Davis returned to us in the little vessel from Tauranga on the twelfth, they found the universal sickness amongst us somewhat abated. They had had an interesting voyage, had visited a volcanic island of terrific appearance; whence walking over a hot bed of brimstone enveloped in smoke. They had brought us some beautiful specimens.

But nobody has had their minds sufficiently at ease from other matters to write any descriptions. Immediately after their return, our little vessel had to be got ready for sea to go to Port Jackson, to fetch us food and supplies. And we had to consider our commissions, to prepare some necessaries and comforts for Mr Cunningham who went in her and for whom we had all formed a great regard, and to receive the brethren from the other station, who came down to hold a committee of supplies.

Just at this time Mrs Davis was taken ill, one evening when William was at Kerikeri, and had a mishap. I was obliged to resume my doctorship, and Jane and I between us cooked her little niceties, provided for her husband and received her share of visitors in addition to our own.

Mrs Fairburn was ill a little before this. But Doctor Williams' laudanum which I went to see administered had the desired affect and we kept matters all safe. A few days after Henry's return William paid a visit to Whangaroa. Mrs Turner had managed her confinement rather sooner than was expected and was doing well. William returned before Christmas Day. The *Herald*, having been detained by contrary winds, sailed on the 28th.

This was all that occurred during the month of December except that I had little Henry Kemp in addition to my family. But at the end of ten days he cried to go home to his mother, and was sent, when they went up to the quarterly committee at Kerikeri the first week in January. It was a grief to me that I could not secure more time to wash, iron and prepare my little baby wardrobe. On the first we heard that Hongi's army had been troublesome at Rangihoua on their way to Whangaroa.

*Marianne gives an account of events from the beginning of the
year, leading up to 19 January and the possible evacuation of
Paihia aboard the* Sisters.

Friday, 5 January 1827. At eight o'clock in the morning a vessel was
in sight. It was not a whaler. We all thought her a brig from Port
Jackson, and as William, Henry, Jane and I stood, watching her as
she came to anchor, you would have been amused with our
conjecture, about the probability of Missionaries, letters, Mr Strong
or Mr White.

Her decks were crowded, we saw a boat lowered and loaded. But
instead of coming this way she moved towards the watering place at
Kororareka, and was discerned to be filled with casks. Mr Fairburn,
when he went down to shipping to fetch a cask of bread, brought word
she had a very suspicious appearance, and upon Henry and William's
going over they ascertained that she was the *Wellington* from Port
Jackson bound for Norfolk Island laden with convicts and stores.

The prisoners had risen upon the crew, whom, with the Captain,
guard and passengers, they had made prisoners, and the convict
Captain at the head of 60 desperadoes set the two vessels in the
Harbour, the *Harriet* and the *Sisters* at defiance. Henry did not think
the Captain of the whalers inclined to follow his advice, which was
to fire into and take her, and we all felt great dismay at having a nest
of pirates so near us. The natives of New Zealand appeared quite
amiable beings by comparison.

Saturday, 6 January 1827. The prayer meeting was at our house. Mr
Davis, who was returned from the Kawakawa, whither he had been
after his wheat, expressed with all the others great apprehension
from these horrible neighbours. Our natives were set to watch the
boat, lest they should cut it off in the night, as they had said they
were in want of one. The natives came to ask the opinion of the
Missionaries respecting the characters of these new white thieves. It
blew a gale of wind. She drove from her anchorage, and the natives
round about said they were going over to cut her cable and get her
on shore.

Sunday, 7 January 1827. At break of day we were awoke by a cannonading. The two whalers were firing into the brig. It was a awful sight, for as Henry said the guns were loaded with shot. I felt that every report might be a deathblow. Yet we could not help rejoicing that these wretches should be checked in their career of mischief, and the poor passengers, soldiers and crew escaped.

The winds and waves seemed to have given her up to the ends of justice, for in consequence of the gale she was anchored just where the other vessels could effect their purpose, which in her old station could not, and it now blew a gale into the harbour so that she had no chance of getting away.

In the midst of these feelings, before the guns had ceased, we commenced service. After service, a boat came for Henry to go over and control the natives at Kororareka while the prisoners were landed, which was part of the terms of capitulation. Just before our Evening Service, Henry and Mr Fairburn returned. Henry brought us a visitor, a Mr Buchanan, an ingenious passenger to Norfolk Island.

He was a gentlemanly man and an acquaintance of Mr Cunningham. We listened with much interest to the history of his capture and sufferings, rejoiced in the taking of the vessel, but were uneasy that part of these men should be loose on shore. The natives (we heard) had stripped and made slaves of them, and would sell them when a man of war came. Several were brought to the villages on each side of us, and they vowed vengeance and death against the Missionaries, especially Mr Williams.

Monday, 8 January 1827. Henry went to the shipping to take Mr Buchanan and to see if anything could be done towards securing the prisoners on shore.

Wednesday, 10 January 1827. Before 10 o'clock while they were all as usual at the study of the language, a messenger from Kerikeri arrived with a letter from Whangaroa. The news flew through the settlement. Hongi [now recovered] was carrying on a war near Whangaroa. The Missionaries there were in danger of being plundered. Every native in their valley had fled, even their domestics, and they were for want of natives unable to move and wished for assistance to bring away Mrs Turner and the other females. Marianne Davis was there on a visit.

Henry and Mr Davis immediately set off, with sixteen natives (almost all the strong men and boys we had living with us), up to Kerikeri, intending to go by night to Whangaroa. It was determined that, as there was danger to be apprehended when they were gone, from our own wicked countrymen, that William, Mr Fairburn and our two Englishmen should have loaded fowling pieces by them at night.

As they were starting, Captain Duke called and seemed to have serious thoughts of going to Port Jackson with the brig, which his men considered as their lawful prize. He said the brig dared not take the prisoners. He pitied, he said, the Missionaries whose lives were in danger from them. One man had pointed a loaded piece at him at the watering place, but a native had snatched it from him. And they had vowed to shoot any of the Missionaries, especially Mr Williams, whom they considered instrumental to their being taken, and in setting the natives against them.

Thursday, 11 January 1827. Imagining that our friends would be on their way from Whangaroa, we did not look out for any boat, but while we were at dinner one was discerned just on shore. Bonnets were seen in it. Jane went down while I set the dinner in order, and presently little Marianne came in leading Mrs Turner's little girl, which spoke volumes. I ran out and met Mrs Turner but cannot describe my feelings. They had been attacked, plundered and fled five hours after dispatching their express. And Henry and his party, who had proceeded most rapidly, had met them about six miles from Kerikeri on the road to Whangaroa. The natives at Kerikeri would not allow them to remain there, fearing they also should be stripped and the Missionaries of that place. They were very glad therefore to accept Henry and Mr Davis's invitation.

It is impossible to describe the effect this had upon us all. Our first anxiety was to comfort, alleviate and assist our poor friends.

Those friends whom I had visited in peace and security not two months since. The next was apprehension for our brethren at Kerikeri, and thus it was felt that everyone must immediately pack up all they could to send by the *Sisters*, which would sail immediately. News from every quarter showed that all the tribes were more or less involved in this horrible civil war, and the fate of Whangaroa opened our eyes to listen to reports we had before disregarded, and showed us we were all exposed to plundering parties.

Friday, 12 January 1827. The great boat was sent early for things to Kerikeri, in the evening an express arrived thence stating that Hongi was wounded, and the natives could give our brethren no protection. They were now in the same critical and alarming situation the others had been in at Whangaroa, and they requested a boat to arrive secretly at midnight to convey away some things.

Henry and Mr Davis again started, intending to bring down Mrs Clarke, who they thought ought to be removed, and returned home the next morning early, having called at Rangihoua.

Saturday, 13 January 1827. Mr and Mrs Turner's passage taken and many things taken to the *Sisters*.

Sunday, 14 January 1827. We had a quiet Sabbath. The services and Mr Turner's sermon peculiarly appropriate. The sacrament was administered. In the evening an express from Kerikeri, Hongi reported to be dead. The boat again went up in the night and brought down Mrs Clarke.

George Clarke [Mrs Clarke's son, recalling the night trip from Kerikeri to Paihia]

My father and Mr Kemp determined to hold to their post, but made an arrangement secretly to send off the wives and children to the Bay of Islands. I was not much over four years old, but I remember a time between midnight and morning, being lifted out of my cot and told to be very still. In the dim light of a lantern I saw my poor mother enveloped in a cloak, and quietly sobbing, then father wrapping me in a thick blanket, and taking me in his arms, they crept stealthily out of the house and made their way in the starlight to a boat, with muffled oars, under the rock. Mother, and I and baby Sam, were deposited in the stern sheets, and we glided silently to the entrance, and passed the sleeping pa [fortified village], beyond which I can say nothing of my own knowledge, though I have been told that we went to Paihia, in the Bay.

Monday, 15 January 1827. Rose at daylight, to pack box after box, and case after case, a great fatigue. In the morning William went up to Kerikeri.

Tuesday, 16 January 1827. Our old chief came to entreat us not to go away, as he was able and willing (he said) to protect us, and he wished all the other white people to come and live here. Hongi is said not to be dead. The colours on board the vessels half mast high. We feared Captain Duke was dead. But a mate of another vessel was drowned from intoxication.

Wednesday, 17 January 1827. Report of a fight coming to us!

Thursday, 18 January 1827. A messenger from the Kawakawa to say that Hongi and Rewa were coming with their army here, that all Kawakawa, and Waikare etc. were on the move to meet them and protect us, and that there would be a great conflict.

We determined to prepare. Henry buried his dollars, had a part of the floor taken up in his study to bury some linen, and laid our best clothes ready to put on, and he told me to put my baby linen in pillow cases. At night an express from Kerikeri. Hongi not dead but dangerously wounded, through the breast, and now at Whangaroa.

Friday, 19 January 1827. We slept in quiet, rose in quiet, I write in quiet. The vessel has moved but does not sail till tomorrow. The surgeon will take this. I have spent every moment while he was here in writing, for it was Jane's turn to cook dinner, therefore I could write and she could not. She much wished to have written. But with 16 in family and under present circumstances you may suppose how we are. And now let me conclude by telling you we are all strong in the Lord.

Jane and I cling to the hope of weathering the storm and being able to stay, and we have shipping in the harbour to flee to in case of necessity. Pray for us. They have secured nearly all the prisoners on board the *Sisters* and will sail in a day or two.

We have just heard overland from Captain Herd and the settlers at Hokianga. They are going to the Colony and offer assistance. All the tribes are rising there in war, some to revenge Hongi's supposed death, other to oppose his avengers. I make an effort to keep on writing while the ship remains fearing exaggerated accounts may get aboard. But you may have the latest assurance that your children are still in peace and safety. That they do not apprehend being driven from their station, that they are in health after a late period of sickness, and have had their spirits supported through much continued anxiety, excitement and fatigue as well as commiseration for our Whangaroa friends, namely Mr and Mrs Turner with their three children, Mr Hobbs, Mr Stack, Luke Wade and his wife, who have all taken their passage in the *Sisters* for the Colony, on board of which vessel we have sent all our property which we can possibly do without, in order that the natives may have less temptation to strip us, and that in case of being driven to Port Jackson we may find some necessaries there. The natives of the Bay of Islands are immersed in all the horrors of a civil war.

Jane

19 January 1827. Paihia. Hongi has lately become totally indifferent to the Missionaries and has given them to understand that he does not care whether they go or stay. He still continues to wage war against the various tribes in this northern part of the island, and a little time ago after committing various depredations at Rangihoua they went to attack the natives at Whangaroa, most of whom fled and left the Wesleyans quite unprotected.

In this defenseless state they were attacked by a party of strangers who broke into the house at daybreak, and having no one to protect them they were obliged to give up the house to be plundered and flee to Kerikeri, having scarcely time to dress themselves and snatch a morsel of breakfast. The house and store contained much, very much valuable property, of which they could preserve nothing, but what they could carry on their backs or in their pockets, and in this state they proceeded to Kerikeri and were thence conveyed to this station. Mr and Mrs Turner and eight children are our inmates.

The stations have all been threatened in consequence of Hongi's being dangerously wounded. Whether he lives or dies, we shall probably witness many and great commotions. We are in great perplexity scarcely knowing how to act, but there are vessels in the harbour which can convey us to the Colony if we are obliged to flee like our Wesleyan friends. Things must speedily come to a crisis, and it is the opinion of most, either that the Mission will be established more firmly than ever or that it must be abandoned.

Ours is the only station at all likely to stand, and it is probable all may congregate here. It is consoling to reflect that the hands of these poor heathen can no farther be lifted against us than is permitted by the great ruler of all things. To Him only can we look for protection and guidance, in full confidence that he will hold us in the hollow of his hand until the danger be overpassed.

HONGI WOUNDED

William

1 March 1827. Paihia. The last letters from New Zealand would give you a very gloomy picture of our affairs. The Mission settlement at Whangaroa had been destroyed by the natives and our Wesleyan friends were living with us until they should be able to sail to Port Jackson, whither they are since gone. We were at the same time placed in a very critical situation, being daily told by the natives that we might expect to be served in the same manner.

The ground of this alarm is a barbarous custom among this people of plundering a tribe when the chief dies. Hongi, who had been fighting with the people of Whangaroa, received a musket ball in his lungs, from which it was expected he would die, and the consequence was to be that his tribe and the Missionaries at Kerikeri as belonging to that tribe were to be plundered of everything.

Hongi is still alive and there is a prospect of his recovery, so that we now are relieved for the present. I went over to Whangaroa last week to see him, at his own request, when I passed over the spot where the Mission premises had stood. It was a mournful sight after having seen the place in a flourishing condition but a few weeks before. The house was burnt to the ground, and it would be impossible for a person who had not seen the premises before to know where the house stood.

23 March 1827. We continue to enjoy every blessing we can desire for ourselves, and the natives suffer us still to remain in quiet. The storm which fell upon Whangaroa seems to have blown over, and all things are apparently as peaceable as ever.

Their attention is now turned to a distant war at the River Thames, whither nearly every male native is gone for the purpose of revenging the death of Pomare, a chief who met with his death there a few months ago.

Henry
29 March 1827. Paihia. It is now a week since the *Herald* returned to us from Port Jackson, which brought us the greatest supply of letters we have yet had. It took up more than a week to read.

12 April 1827. It is a week today since Mr Marsden arrived in His Majesty's Ship *Rainbow*. He landed about 8 in the evening. William and myself went on board before sunset and conveyed him on shore. Friday, Saturday and Monday were engaged in considering the question relative to the children. Our conclusion did not meet the approval of Mr Marsden.

William
28 April 1827. Paihia. Mr Marsden paid a very short visit at the beginning of the month. He was anxious to see our real condition, and to talk with us about the education of our children....

Three months ago, when we were living in a state of so great uncertainty as not to know whether we could continue in the land, it was thought desirable in the event of our temporary removal to Port Jackson to endeavour to form a settlement there for New Zealanders, quite remote from any white settlement.

The idea was first suggested to us by an enquiry made by some of our chiefs whether there was no distant island to which they could be removed, out of the reach of the continual warfare which is carrying on here. Communication was made with Mr Marsden, who approved of the plan, but proposed to make the experiment on some land of his between Parramatta and Sydney.

Jane

23 May 1827. Marianne three weeks ago resumed her usual active part in domestic affairs. [Marianne had had her sixth child, John William Williams, born Paihia, 6 April 1827.] There were long discussions respecting the education of the Missionaries' children when Mr Marsden was here, and with respect to the females it was decided that Marianne and I should make an attempt to keep school.

We therefore began a fortnight ago, and at present we go on very swimmingly, though we can only devote two hours a day to them. Our pupils consist of Mr Davis's daughters, the three eldest from twelve to sixteen, the youngest five, Mr Fairburn's little girl about six, and little Marianne, who is a very quick intelligent child. Our plan is to dine all together, and Marianne and I cook alternately. The one who does not cook keeps school.

We endeavour to instruct the elder girls in history, geography, writing, sums, grammar and plain sewing, etc. I quite enjoy my day for keeping school. It appears in New Zealand such ladylike work. Should we succeed with these children, we shall take the girls from the other stations. We have our native school in an afternoon, and I am glad to say that is in a more promising state. We have now eleven native pupils, but they are so uncertain that next week they may be all gone.

Henry

18 June 1827. Paihia. Time flies swiftly. The language occupies a portion of it, subject, however, to a thousand interruptions. The increase to our family is materially felt, and it requires much forethought to keep matters straight, both as respects the children and the natives. Our house and household frequently remind me of a certain old woman 'who lived in a shoe. She had so many children she did not know what to do.'

We at times are at a loss to know which way to turn. Yet we hope we may improve in a little time. We have outgrown our little beehive and have in addition a raupo building into which we think of removing the greater portion of our stock as soon as a kitchen be erected, for as yet we have not had one. This is to be begun immediately, with which we shall have the formidable undertaking of two chimneys.

20 July 1827. We have been occupied in preparing letters for the colony, to go by the little *Herald*. It has been blowing a heavy gale ever since yesterday at noon from the south-east. Our thoughts have been much taken up for some time past in considering a question which is quite new. That of forming a settlement in New South Wales for those of the natives who are desirous to abstain from war but cannot under present circumstances.

Also to ameliorate the condition of the male and females who might retire thither and sit quiet. Here their situation is very bad. They cannot marry or possess property and are liable to be killed at any time. The murder of these poor creatures is not noticed by their masters. Should a slave be promoted, it is only on account of his great wickedness.

William and Mr Davis were to proceed to the Colony to lay the question before the corresponding committee, but we have lately learned that the governors will not grant land on the coast for that purpose. Consequently, William remains behind. Mr Davis is to proceed by himself.

16 August 1827. Your account of the clans of Scotland corresponds in many particulars with the customs of the people here, particularly in those resenting injured honour. But there is one peculiarity among us not practised in Europe. If a chief is injured or insulted, he is visited by parties of his friends, who strip his plantation or make free with any property he may possess.

If he meets with an accident it is the same thing, and the same thing when he dies. Then the whole tribe suffers. Hongi has been several times subject to this compliment within the last 2 years. Once he was severely hurt by the falling of a tree. The pillage commenced immediately, and he was visited by parties from all the northern part of the island. He was served the same on the death of his son, his wives, etc.

When Pomare was killed, his people were stripped by many parties. Te Koki on the return of the *Herald* from Port Jackson happened to go on board, and the end of a rope falling from aloft struck him on the head and drew a drop or two of blood, and in the course of the day two parties came upon him.

I believe they are well disposed to walk into our premises on the same account, and why did they not? This is a question we may frequently ask. We are here in the midst of combustible matter, sparks flying about on all sides, and yet we are not consumed. It is of the Lord's mercies. There is a circumstance respecting this people which I will mention in this place. They are noted for quickness of sight and hearing far beyond Europeans. But I consider them void of taste and smell, from what I know them to enjoy. They are *nasty* in the extreme.

October 1827. . . . . A party of about 100 men, headed by Koi-koi, a man of dreaded name, came against Henry, because on some occasion he had refused to make him a present. Some friendly chiefs travelled all night to warn us of this, and the savage leader was frustrated. Wharenui was the peacemaker raised up by the Lord to succour His people.

I do not think you have any idea of our improved circumstances. Instead of being surrounded by carpenters' shavings, benches and a blacksmith's shop, we are now living in the midst of a garden with green grass plots and monthly roses; and at the back we have a large kitchen garden, well stocked with vegetables. If we are permitted to remain, we may in a few years have oranges, peaches, lemons and grapes, also apples.

The native men and boys are now more faithful, industrious and trustworthy than formerly. At this station we have about sixty natives under daily instruction. Mr Davis when at Port Jackson got some of the chapters printed, they have all been so busy translating. It is quite delightful to hear the natives read these words of life in their own tongue.

1828

29 January 1828. Paihia, Bay of Islands. In gratitude to you all for the kind assistance you have given me in presenting us with so many *stitches*. I would willingly send you as many words in return. And Jane and I have determined that it is our duty to express our thanks by setting aside a portion of our Evenings, at least one a week, to write to you who have so kindly worked for us and in fact by so doing have given us the capability of doing so.

I had a list of work which it was most necessary for me to attempt, and by the arrival of the Southwell boxes last week which our invaluable little *Herald* brought us from the Colony, together with Mr Yate and your last letter by him, in reply to the sad news of last January. Thus I am enabled to strike off from my list two frocks for Marianne, a better dress for Thomas, and some common trousers for the hot weather, night caps for Marianne, shirts for the boys, caps for old mother to please her husband, by discarding some old ugly ones (although one of the new ones is rather too smart).

To add to all this I must not omit to thank you and dear Aunt Kate for the bonnet and hats which will relieve the children from many a perspiration beneath a Scotch woollen cap, and Lydia has kindly furnished me with gowns, and John shirts and pinafores. So many stitches have afforded me many half hours in which to indulge myself by holding communication with you, in the only way within our power, and it is a pleasure for which I cannot feel too thankful.

Saturday afternoon, 23 February 1828. Very much fatigued, tried and dispirited, I feel as if it would be a relief to sit down and tell some of the little troubles and cross incidents so peculiar to New

Zealand. For you cannot form a just idea of the different ways in which the wheels of our domestic machinery are clogged.

Three of my girls are very ill, one of my eldest dismissed for improper behaviour, together with three of our best boys. Most of the natives are ill with something like a feverish cold.

Jane is hard set as I am, though it happens to be my cooking day. I must go and bustle and stir, for though I am not well it is out of our power unless ill enough to lie in bed to relax till all is done, and though I have a good set of girls now, six as servants and two as schoolgirls, the rest in a time of sickness will lie like logs on the floor. My biggest girl, however, says she is very ill but will work till this day is over, and then lie down all day tomorrow, and perhaps for a week.

6 March 1828. Let me this evening bring to your mind's eyes, a quiet trio seated at the table in our raupo sitting room. Henry is penning his journal, while I take up my pen to converse with you, and Marianne Davis, who is for the present fortnight our inmate, is finishing a garment for one of Jane's little native girls, who are also just now our inmates.

This present Thursday has been quite calm, after the bustle of the week. It has been our committee week and I ought to preface by saying what my family consisted of. Poor Jane has been so unwell that I persuaded her off to Kerikeri on Saturday for a fortnight's change of air. She took her two little dears, Elizabeth Kemp and five native girls with her, leaving me, with her husband when he pleases to be at home, Marianne Davis, Jane Davis, Jane King and three native girls in addition to my own family.

Thus on Monday morning I had thirteen native girls (for my number is now increased to 10), eight children and a rainy morning. I had to coop them all indoors and in the midst to cook a dinner and spread a table for eighteen people. I had, however, a large commodious wooden kitchen with a spacious wooden fireplace, the first of my husband's labours, a large oven and a good sized raupo dining room, with a convenient pantry between both nearly filled with good things on the Saturday previous.

It is somewhat singular that when I had to cook out of doors, and beg one neighbour to bake a joint or a pie and another a pudding, as I never had a wet committee [day]. Past recollections made me thankful for present circumstances.

I marshalled my troops, penned all the children except little Jane (who went home for the day to her mother) in the sitting room with access to the boys' bedroom, carefully closing the door against mine beyond, in which were deposited all the knives and spoons and the last ripe peaches of our own fine tree, etc.

I then set four girls to wash in an outbuilding, got Marianne to fix work for all the supernumeraries, and what with nursing, scraping potatoes and cooking, found each a station. Marianne I found a valuable assistant, and though I was obliged to put off dinner half an hour because Henry was so long with Mr Charles Davis settling the preliminaries of marriage between his man Rape and my maid Fanny, that I could not get the boys in the yard time enough to cut wood for lighting the ovens or fetch water to set on the ham; all was accomplished.

My servants acquitted themselves exceedingly well except that my biggest girl Maria, and Henry's eldest boy Pouter, having been married only a few days, were too shamefaced to stay in the room, and left Fanny and Tahu sole waiters. The children were all sent away to William's house during dinner, all the native girls turned out of the kitchen and the door locked until the dishes were washed, when they were rewarded for their absence by a feast.

The guests adjourned to the Beehive for committee business, the female visitors went home, and I called my little ones together, gave them their supper, cleared away, had the knives and spoons counted in, the spare dishes and plates carried into the cellar, sandwiches cut and a tray set ready for supper, the children in bed, etc., just in time for the prayer meeting, without attempting to join the party at Mr Fairburn's to tea.

I was able to attend the prayer meeting in the Beehive by leaving my little steady Marianne to watch the baby, which was a great refreshment after so much toil; for toil it is for a missionary's wife to receive company in New Zealand. It is well the committee come only once in three months!

The following morning I got Marianne Davis to make breakfast in the kitchen for the children, whilst I made breakfast for Mr Yate, Mr Kemp, Mr King, William and Henry in the sitting room. We all met first in the kitchen for prayers, where, as all William's natives, except those with Jane, were with ours, we had nearly forty.

After this I set about the washing and folding, and gave the eight children their dinners, after which we went to meet the whole settlement at Mr Davis's to dinner, at Mr Mair's to tea, after which I came home to give my children their tea, put them to bed, fold the remainder of the clothes and set out supper for the committee, who were talking till late.

The following morning, Wednesday, I was told they would depart early. I nevertheless cooked dinner for our three inmates, who as it happened did not go till after they had dined. Thursday we resumed school as usual, and during the remainder of Jane's absence we had school morning and afternoon, and dinner every day at our house. Mary Ann taught on Jane's days and I took my own.

I have thus given you some idea of a committee week, and of my engagements during Jane's absence. But the numberless interruptions you must see and feel to know anything about.

12 March 1828. The report which has been for several days current, but which having been several times falsely raised was not now credited, was confirmed this day. Hongi, the renowned Hongi, is dead.

Henry immediately set off with the boat to fetch William, who, together with Mr Davis and William Puckey, have been at Kerikeri ever since the committee departed, bullock hunting, etc. Also Mr and Mrs Hobbs, who are there on a visit from Hokianga to the Bay of Islands. There is no danger in leaving this settlement alone, for all the chiefs are at Whangaroa, at which place Hongi expired, and if mischief be in prospect they are now hatching it.

Frederick Maning
Many years later Frederick Maning wrote about Hongi's death and the speech that was given by the chief about the time of his

death. The following extract comes from his 1862 The War in the North of New Zealand, *stories told to him by an old Chief of the Ngapuhi Tribe.*

Maning was known as 'A Pakeha Maori'. Born in Ireland, he moved to the Hokianga as a young man, where he married a sister of the chief Hauraki, and spent his life in New Zealand with Maori in Northland.

Many years ago, Hongi Hika, the great warrior chief of New Zealand, was dying: his relations, friends, and tribe, were collected around him, and he then spoke to them in these words: 'Children and friends, pay attention to my last words. After I am gone be kind to the missionaries, be kind also to the other Europeans; welcome them to the shore, trade with them, protect them, and live with them as one people; but if ever there should land on this shore a people who wear red garments, who do no work, who neither buy or sell, and who always have arms in their hands, then be aware that these are a people called soldiers, a dangerous people, whose only occupation is war. When you see them, make war against them. Then, O my children, be brave! Then, O my friends, be strong! Be brave that you may not be enslaved, and that your country may not become the possession of strangers.' And having said these words, he died.

15 March 1828. Everybody busy landing the goods from the brig *Haweis*, arrived yesterday. Jane's baby very cross. I nursed and fed it, as it was necessary to wean it. At night, just as they were assembling for prayer meeting, the news arrived from Hokianga of Warro Hume's fall [a chief of the Bay of Islands]. Mr Hobbs was immediately despatched on his way to Hokianga in our boat to Kerikeri, taking his two native girls with him, who would be here exposed to danger.

Sunday, 16 March 1828. The natives talking of nothing but the news. Things seemed to wear a fearful aspect. Pameka declared he must go, his brother a man of note having been killed and eaten. He left his wife behind. In the evening Captain and Mrs James from the *Haweis* came to the service.

Henry introduced the females to each other, and after all were gone the girls got up and mimicked us going through the same ceremony and contending whether a bow or a curtsy was the most proper.

Monday, 17 March 1828. Canoes passing, all consternation in consequence of the late news. The Kerikeri and Rangihoua boats busy landing the remainder of the goods from the *Haweis*. In the evening they were assembled in the whare padoo [whare-house, patu-weapon], settling what stores should be sent for from England, and determining whether they should comply with the request of some of our natives and go with the army here on their march to succour that at Hokianga, the news from which two days ago put us all in a consternation and hurried Mr Hobbs home and left his wife here in great anxiety.

The request our own natives have made is for the white people to go with them and endeavour to make peace. A late supper. Mr Kemp and Mr Yate quartered at our house.

This request for mediation was made by some Maori chiefs, as they believed the quarrel in the Hokianga could develop into a full-scale war. Traditionally, the role of peacemaker was carried out by the tohunga or priest, but, on this occasion, Henry and his missionary party accompanied the tribe to the Hokianga. From this point on, Henry continued to play an active part in negotiating peace and over the years made three trips to Tauranga and the Waikato as a peacemaker. As his reputation for courage grew, he earned great mana and respect among the Maori.

Thursday, 18 March 1828. Pameka Keri Keri's husband came back and after talking with the white people set off again requesting to take his wife with him and send her back on the morrow; accordingly I let her leave her washing and go. His brother it seemed though killed was not eaten as reported. From what Henry said in the morning I expected he would go and so it turned out, but it was not settled till the following morning.

Mr Shepherd went home to Rangihoua with the intention of meeting them in the morning at Kerikeri. Tohitapu had much to say about going with the thousands. He and Te Koki had been at Kororareka to hold a consultation with Tareha and Rewa, etc., chiefs lately full of animosity to Te Koki.

Henry mentioned his distress about his journal, I offered to copy it for him, 18 pages closely written. [One of Henry's jobs as leading Missionary was to write regular reports to the London CMS Headquarters. It would seem he had run out of time to accomplish this task. Hence Marianne's offer to assist.] I tried how much I could do in one hour in order to calculate how much time it would take. Mr Hobbs called. I was distressed for want of firewood in consequence of all the boys being employed in landing goods and could not set the girls to iron.

Wednesday, 19 March 1828. It is my turn to keep school this morning, but I have given a holiday that I may stick close at Henry's journal. They have taken with them a week's provisions. Henry providing bacon, sugar and spirits, Mr D. bread, flour and tea. Two candles were borrowed of Mr Fairburn to save carrying lamp oil, which Peter, who, being the eldest boy, ought to have known much better, broke in two to stuff into a little canister and then stuck it outside in the broiling sun till Henry should come.

But my heart is very full just now, and before I go on with my copying it will be some relief to tell you my trials and exercises. Henry is just departed taking with him in the boat for Kerikeri George and Peter the bridegroom, with Mr Davis. There they are to meet Mr Shepherd from Rangihoua, who went home last night from this place with that intention, and perhaps Mr Clarke may also join the party.

Some of the chiefs are for peace, others for war. If the majority is for peace, the Missionaries will proceed with this army to the place of conflict, or, to use Tohitapu's words, go with the thousands. There they are to be placed in the front of the battle to negotiate with the enemy's host. If war be irrevocably determined, they will pass on to Wyhoo [?] and stand by their Wesleyan brethren to endeavour to restrain our natives as they pass by.

Henry has thus left me for an unlimited time, to go with a little heroic band amidst a savage host, in the strength of the Lord, to endeavour to stay the slaughter of thousands. They have hitherto formed one warlike band against the Southern tribes with whom they have yearly gone to war; and now they are stirred up by the enemy of souls to butcher one another.

If a peace be not accomplished, a deadly hatred and the duty of revenge must be handed down to posterity, and the hitherto united friendly chiefs, supporters of the Wesleyan and our Missionaries, must be bitter foes. Henry is gone on an imperious duty, but I have a great struggle to quell anxieties. It certainly is very singular that at this season when nothing but confusion was expected in consequence of Hongi's death, all heads and hands are turned against a fresh cause of excitement and Hongi seems quite forgotten.

Thursday, 20 March 1828. I was hindered for want of boys but my girls were very useful. Mrs Hobbs called and staid to dinner and I went to Jane's to meet her at tea. Mrs Davis and Mrs Fairburn were there and a collection of babies. When I returned home Maria was crying because the news was come that ten of her tribe (which we believed a false report) were killed. The girls made my blood run cold with their description of fights and cannibalism.

Friday, 21 March 1828. I kept school in the morning and in the afternoon left my class to a deputy to sit at my copying.

Saturday, 22 March 1828. A violent thunderstorm at daybreak, and continued rain. A bustling day. I managed to do many of my sundry affairs in the morning and to write after dinner and after prayer meeting in the evening. Much disappointment, no news as promised by Peter from the Pukamai.

Monday, 24 March 1828. I felt very unwell all day, and scarcely able to see after the cooking and washing. A report in the morning that peace had been made by 'Rewa' Waru (or as he is often called)

'Wara Rue' signifying both great noise and negotiation, but as nothing further was heard we gave little credit to it.

In the evening William told me that he really believes it this time that peace had actually been made. That the Kawakawa natives were returned, and I might expect Henry tomorrow. After I had folded my clothes as I sat copying his journal, I could not help fancying every sound of the surf was the boat oars, and every native voice a shout from the boat!

Dear Thomas troubled with his cough, I finished the fourth sheet of the journal.

Tuesday, 25 March 1828. William determined to go up to the Kawakawa. I felt very unwilling that he should go. There were many flying reports that peace was not made, but that more canoes were going and that blood they would have. William, however, went.

William

Wednesday, 26 March 1828. Jane has not been very strong of late, which I attribute principally to her child, which is now weaned. Our two little girls are well, and our occupations as various as the changes of the weather. We preach, we talk, we keep school and translate. We fight, at least we stand on the defensive occasionally.

We lay bricks, we plaster, we plant, we salt pork and occasionally hunt cows in the bush. We take voyages in search of provisions for our schools. We have various hindrances which never occur to a person living in England. If we want a chimney we must make bricks and lime, and build also. We find, therefore, many essential secular matters to cut us off from direct missionary work.

But yet our intercourse with the natives increases; and we have increasing encouragement among them. Though there is nothing of a decided nature, there have been some very strong instances of the general inclination of the natives towards us. They begin to understand that we come not to seek our own good but theirs, and consequently they place confidence in us, to a greater degree than we have seen before.

28 March 1828. Henry's journal occupied every moment I could scrape till Tuesday afternoon when I completed it. The whole of that day we had been hearing flying reports. A man of Mr Davis's who was sent to relieve our anxieties told an inconsistent and false story.

You will imagine then how delightfully sounded the boat oars at nine o'clock at night, and the shouts of the natives, the well-known footsteps upon the pebble walk, and the vociferous delight of all the children upon hearing that papa was come.

You who live in favoured England, the land of roads and coaches and posts, know not what it is to say 'Good-bye!' or 'How d'you do!' and your post office preserves you from that feeling of separation which a week's absence in New Zealand occasions.

Had Samuel and Henry been in England, they would not have been told by mischievous boys, as these little things were on this day, that their papa and Mr Davis were killed by the warriors and thrown into the sea, and their joy would not have been so extravagant at his return in a whole skin.

The peace was as satisfactory as possible. The whole history a most gratifying exemplification of the influence of the Missionaries and the restraining hand of a prayer-hearing God. And the behaviour of all the chiefs was exceedingly good.

It has been a season of excitement and an occasion of joy, and it is a singular circumstance that just at this time some of the Missionaries should be called upon to meet every chief of note in the Bay of Islands, as friends and allies, with the exception of our own people at Kawakawa, who have excited great resentment for retreating home upon a false rumour of a peace, or rather of a peace made with an inferior chief who had no power to make it.

And now Henry and Mr Davis are going on Thursday in the little vessel to the East Cape among savages who have never seen white people, and expect to be absent a fortnight.

Mr Hobbs returned with Henry and took his wife to Rangihoua. She is to return here for her confinement, so that I have plenty before me added to plenty already on my hands. Jane continues unwell and it has been necessary to lighten her part in our joint business.

My girls still take pets and run away for nothing. But they do not resist authority so much as they used to do. They do not attempt to bathe without leave, or a bell ringing at half past one o'clock called the swimming bell, an intimation that no males must intrude. They do not now attempt to run outside of the fence when an English boat is on shore. If you desire a girl to do anything, she will not now as formerly tell a second, and the second a third, and all leave you to do it for yourself.

They are tractable at school, and have yielded to us to determine when they shall sit and when stand, and whether they shall write large hand or small. They will consent to wear their gowns over their shifts without sitting sulky about it, and though I have lost two of my best, I have two more who can and two more who soon will sew neatly, iron and fold all the week's linen except starched things, teach the others to wash when they like without trouble, but at other times I must see the copper cleaned and filled, send the boys and see them go for water and see them come back, cut wood, etc., see the clothes soaped in, and have various ill humours to contend with all the time, which sometimes especially on a school morning with crying babies, etc., try us to the uttermost.

Fanny made a beautiful light loaf for themselves on Saturday and baked it under an iron pot, turned bottom upward upon a hot hearth, with some hot ashes heaped over it, according to our practice before we had an oven. We cannot fancy their fingers in our bread or they might save us much time and trouble.

Pray, did you hear how we make yeast out of flour, sugar and water shaken in a bottle? The first time we made it we put a little bottled porter, or leaven, into the bottle, but afterwards what remains sticking to the sides of the bottle when all is poured out is sufficient to ferment it, and we mix one spoonful of sugar and 6 of flour with warm water and pour it into the bottle, about two-thirds full, to use on the following morning. Some of our missionary wives use only leaven, but we prefer yeast, and we have as light bread as you have.

Saturday, 29 March 1828. I endeavoured all day in vain to write to England. Towards noon Maria, lately married to Peter, went out in a huff because I reproved her for sitting out on the beach (a thing strictly forbidden) and doing nothing. She had a blister on her side a week ago and has been too much indulged. These poor creatures like children cannot bear a little extra kindness.

31 March 1828. Today I gave a holiday purposely to write letters to England. I rose late for New Zealand, having been walking about the room a great part of the night with little John, who is ill with his teeth.

I had some trouble in setting my girls to wash their different shares, one of the married ones being absent gathering in kumeras, and the other, Maria, having walked off in an ill humour on Sunday.

I was hindered after breakfast by a woman with a lot of children and a cross old man, who came to fetch away one of my girls. The girl did not wish to go and her companions urged her to stay, which she did, and when the people had sat till they were tired they departed. When the clothes were washed and boiling, a mob of natives came on shore, and the boys were all out to see and hear. And an hour was lost before water could be got to rinse and wring the clothes.

Jane is very poorly today, Mary Ann Davis complaining with head ache, my baby very cross and his favourite nurse gone away. Jane too has lost two or three of her best girls, and we have each some new ones, so that we have still 19 girls between us, ten with me and nine with Jane.

One result of the late campaign you will regret. Henry had written part of a letter to his mother and took it with him in his pocket book, but during the march or in the field it was stolen.

Henry and Mr Davis are in great haste and anxiety to be off to save the lives of the poor Rotorua natives who are flying for their lives in the little vessel and are daily in danger of being murdered here by parties of natives.

Tuesday, 1 April 1828. The girls were continually leaving their work and running out to buy new corn. I heard one native girl say the woman would not sell for fish hooks, she would have a comb. The old ones said they must not sell their combs. Another girl, the last taken in, said the woman wanted her apron. 'That', exclaimed Rebecca, 'would make the white people very angry, don't sell any of your clothes'. She and Fanny staid very steadily at their ironing.

I therefore got Henry to buy me a bucket of corn with which to reward the steady ones. They murmured but Fanny said it was the way she used to be served formerly, so they submitted.

Two of Jane's little girls were going away for nothing while Jane was engaged in the English school. Henry found them on the beach with mats over their heads and brought them into our yard till Jane was disengaged.

Teu brought the baby in crying violently. I asked her how he had been hurt but she said he cried for nothing. One girl exclaimed how white his cheeks are, another, that he must have tumbled out of his little waggon; finding he would not take his food or be quieted off to sleep, I went again to her begging she would tell me how and where he was hurt, but she would not speak and presently walked off.

At first I said she might go, but afterwards called to her to say if she did not come back directly and finish her washing, I would not receive her at all. In about a quarter of an hour I saw her standing at the tub with her mat over her head (a garment they seldom use except in rains, cold or ill humour). In due course all was right again. Pameka came back, I asked for his wife, one of my washerwomen. He said she had not finished working at the kumeras.

I had a violent headache, and with difficulty persevered in copying some more of the journal. Several muskets were fired. I trembled lest they should be the murderers of the poor men fighting for their lives in the Herald. Henry wished he was off and such was the interest these poor natives excited that I almost wished my husband gone.

Thursday, 3 April 1828. Marianne Davis came to help mix gingerbread for Mr C. Davis's and Henry's voyage. Henry made up all his despatches for England and I wrote a line to sister Betsy. As Henry determined, should there be any unpleasant appearances among the natives, to sail the next day although it was Good Friday, we collected his bedding, clothes and eatables together. I heard Maria was come and sent her word that she might go to her house and sit like a lady, and not come to work, for she did not like work, and I did not like obstinacy.

Good Friday, 4 April 1828. Service as usual on Sundays, but an hour later. At dinner they talked of these poor natives, four of whom had been killed inland. Te Koki, Rangituki and his wife came to see us. Keri Keri came to see me in the morning returned from getting in her harvest of kumera potatoes. She looked very sorrowful and said she thought she was come to sit still and work in her place. But she found that Pameka, her husband, had been like a crazy man, that he was greedy for payment, had quarrelled with Mr Williams and was going away.

She asked if she might not stay and let her husband go to the wicked spirit by himself, for she was full of love for me. I told her that though she was my servant she was Pameka's wife and must not make him angry with her. At first she arrayed herself in her Sunday clothes and said she would stop, but afterwards she brought them to me and said she would go with her husband, but added he will soon beat me and then I will run away and come back to you.

Poor thing, I pitied her as she went away crying. This man has many wives, and we believe his principal reason for going is because Henry will suffer none but Keri Keri to enter our house. Theirs was the first dwelling erected in Henry's new native village. They were very eager to come. The boys say he will soon come back again, but Henry told him to stay away unless he could behave like the rest of his men.

I heard that Maria was sitting outside and Henry saw her. After dinner she sent a message to desire I would come and speak to her, for her love to me had brought her there. I sent word she might go to her husband's house. About half an hour after, as I was rocking John to sleep, she appeared at the back window of the children's room. I never saw her so humble.

As I had heard that her husband treated her very coolly, I feared he would not let her stay unless he relented. I therefore asked her if I consented to take her in, whether she would consent to have her hair cut short. She said eagerly, yes, and I wanted not a greater concession, for ever since she had been married she had obstinately persisted in letting it grow long and had made a perfect fright of herself.

She was accordingly shorn, washed and dressed and appeared in her clean Sunday clothes at school. It was quite a transformation. In the evening my husband left me and sailed in the *Herald* to Tauranga about eleven o'clock at night, where he found that one third of the people had been lately cut off by the natives of the River Thames. At another place they landed and found several dead bodies of persons who had been killed about a fortnight before.

Monday, 7 April 1828. Heard that George had brought home a wife. He sent to beg his wife might have her hair cut and also be taught to wash. Maria therefore operated upon the anything but fair bride, and also upon a big new girl for Jane, in order to fit them for the wash tub.

HERALD LOST

11 May 1828. Henry arrived safe in the *Herald* from his voyage to the southward before she sailed for Hokianga. He gives a very indifferent account of the natives there, who are living in a worse state than in the Bay of Islands. They are not scattered in small parties but sitting together in fortified places for their mutual defence.

The *Herald* sailed to the Southward on the night of April 4th being Good Friday, anxious to save lives of the Rotorua natives on board who were flying for their lives. She returned into the bay on the night of the 17th. At 2 o'clock of the morning of the 18th, Henry tapped at his own window and at 6 the vessel was at anchor.

Saturday the 3rd of May she sailed for Hokianga, with Mr Fairburn on board for a cargo of potatoes, which there was every prospect of our wanting for the use of the schools, as we had just received news from the Colony of a distressing drought and expected scarcity of flour. Mr Clarke went overland to meet the vessel there.

On Thursday morning, the 8th, about ten, Mr Hobbs arrived and stunned us with the news of the *Herald* being lost on the bar of Hokianga, but that Messrs Fairburn and Mair, with all the crew, were saved though they had swam on shore at 4 o'clock in the morning, twelve hours after she struck, having been lashed to the vessel, and in imminent danger in a tremendous surf during the night.

That when they landed they were stripped and ill used by the natives. That a vessel of Captain Clarke's, built at Hokianga since ours, returning from the Colony laden with mission stores for Messrs Hobbs and Stack, was lost within a few miles of the *Herald* and all on board perished, some letters had been washed on shore.

Henry and William started immediately with all our most effective natives, taking poor Mr Hobbs, who had walked all night and intended to walk all night again. After they were gone Jane told me that it was on Mr Fairburn's account that William went, for he was very ill and exhausted, and had a great deal of salt water in him. This his poor wife knew nothing of.

Henry and I scarcely saw [each other] for five minutes after the news arrived. He rejoiced that all lives were saved and said he knew the place to be so terrific, he had not the slightest hope of saving any part of the vessel.

On Saturday morning Mr Yate came down to be our pastor and comfort us, which he did in a most delightful exhortation this morning, from the last verse of the 27th Chapter of the Acts – 'and they all came safe to the land'. On Saturday evening Mr Fairburn's boy came with a letter from him to Mrs Fairburn telling her how ill he had been, and as this boy was in the vessel with him all eagerly listened to his tale. Hope was entertained that the vessel might be got off, but the lad said that the natives had stripped and were going to set fire to her, but that Patuone was marching to prevent them.

This morning letters were delivered to Mr Davis from Hokianga, and I will copy Henry's as the most satisfactory intelligence I can give you.

Friday evening, Manguagu, the Wesleyan Settlement.

We have now been here about two hours after a tedious journey. Fairburn is better than I expected to see him. The treatment of the natives was most barbarous, and their conduct to the vessel very bad indeed. She has not sustained much damage from the weather, but they have cut away rope and sail, and her inside all to pieces.

I have not yet seen Mr Mair and have not ventured to ask Mr Fairburn any question as the subject is painful.

He is walking about but cannot yet walk to Kerikeri. Mr Clarke has sent for Mrs Hobbs' chair, as the wood is so tedious. We are going down at high water to see the exact position of our poor vessel. She could be got off with ease if the natives will let her alone.

But my anxiety respecting her has ceased since I know that all that were on board are safe. The crew of Clarke's vessel (I fear) are killed by the natives, from towards the North Cape little or nothing is saved from her.

Great is our cause for thankfulness!

In the conclusion he says, 'It is now high water.'

Therefore (it seems) they set off on Friday evening, to go down fifteen miles heads, and, as they took their tent with them, would I suppose encamp on the shore. Mr Kemp and a party of natives joined them at Kerikeri on their way, where they staid only 2 hours, and they would be a strong party.

William tells Jane, Mr Fairburn is better and that Mr Clarke had bled and blistered him before William arrived. From the account of the natives it appears poor Mr Fairburn was washed overboard in the night, and miraculously escaped. Mr Mair had given him up, and he being the last who left the vessel at low water in the morning was surprised to find him alive (though very ill) on shore.

William says, 'We had many surmises as to the reason for which this event was permitted. Whether it be viewed as a chastisement, or whether she has been cast away in our neighbourhood to prevent some greater evil which might have befallen her had she been wrecked at the Southward, there is doubtless much mercy in the event though we may not discuss it now.'

During her lifetime the Herald *had made three trips to Sydney, four to the Bay of Plenty and two to Hokianga. To replace her the small cutter* Karere *was built at Paihia in 1831.*

Jane

27 May 1828. Paihia. As far as regards civilized society I am this evening quite alone, my husband being out on an excursion among some of the neighbouring tribes. My two children are comfortably asleep and you must picture me to your imagination sitting with my desk upon a table around which are seated seven of my native girls sewing.

Our winter is just beginning. The evenings are of a tolerable length and it is my practice to allow these children to sit and sew with me. But their continuous 'Eh mother, give me some thread!' 'Eh mother, I have broke my needle!' 'Eh mother, fix my sewing!' etc. generally my doing much more than attend to them.

19 August 1828. Paihia. I have suffered so much from weakness during the last three or four months that I have been obliged to suspend my exertions in both English and native schools, and though I have but a small share of domestic duties to attend to, yet when evening has arrived I have generally been too much overcome with fatigue to think of writing.

I am now trying a salt water shower bath, constructed for me by Mr Hobbs and Mr Fairburn, and though I only began to use it last week I think I have derived benefit from it. In a few weeks I am again to visit Kerikeri for change of air. The weather at present is very unfavourable being our midwinter.

The inhabitants of New South Wales are at present suffering from a scarcity of wheat in consequence of one or two dry seasons. Should the want of rain continue we also may feel the effect of it in not being able to procure our usual supplies of flour from that quarter. We continually feel the loss of our *Herald*.

Both my children were vaccinated a short time since, and the effect of the operation was extremely satisfactory. I am considerably better and regaining my strength very rapidly.

22 September 1828. Kerikeri. I have been now nearly three weeks at this place together with my husband and children and find myself wonderfully benefited by the change of air and continued use of the shower bath.

I have been obliged to give up school for a season in consequence of the loss of health and strength, blessings which we know not how to appreciate while we possess them. I believe nothing but the loss of them can teach us their value. Dear Marianne's exertions have been really wonderful, particularly during the time Mrs Hobbs was with her. And since we left home her work and cares have again been increased by Mrs Fairburn's confinement a month sooner than she looked for.

The late winter has been marked by the deaths of several principal chiefs besides Hongi and Whareumu. The great men of the present day appear peaceably disposed, but apprehend an attack from their Southern neighbours, who at present neither know nor care much about the Missionaries, and as our settlement at Paihia might be exposed to danger in case of a sudden eruption, it was deemed advisable to construct a kind of fortress at the top of the hill overlooking our houses, which would be a place of refuge for all the inhabitants of the place, who amount now to 33 English and nearly 100 natives.

For a whole week all hands worked indefatigably that the fame of our Ports spread far and wide and created a small sensation. The threatened and much dreaded Armada, however, was turned into a number of trading parties who have successively arrived at different parts of the Bay in a very peaceful manner, and some of them have already returned as peaceably as they came.

Henry and William have taken their degrees as masters of the art of plastering, roofing, etc. and were you to see them in their master's robes you would scarcely recognise them. William's is a duck frock, and Henry's a kind of pinafore with a jacket similar to that of a butcher's apron. Both are unique. By their persevering assistance a very neat and substantial and roomy chapel has been erected, which was opened at the last monthly prayer meeting, when Henry read the principal part of the regular service for consecrating Churches, and Mr Yate preached from the words – 'I was glad when they said unto me, "Let us go up into the house of our God!"'

Henry
22 September 1828. Paihia. As our days pass swiftly along so does our work increase in interest. In considering the condition of this people we have only to

look back upon the ancient Britons. They are nearly in all respects alike, and when we look forward we can see those residing with us, who are the fathers and mothers of future dukes and earls, lords and ladies. And though they sometimes disturb the repose of our minds, I must say that it is impossible for any young ladies and gentlemen to show a stronger desire for knowledge.

We are at present experiencing a sad hindrance to the schools in want of food. They are now fed with corn which is not fit for them, as it is very mouldy. But such is their desire to continue with us that we do not hear the slightest complaint.

22 September 1828. My children are all in fine health and spirits. They are truly comforts, without which this land would indeed be a frightful wilderness.

Henry though not quite five years old is the little gallant of the family, so fond of playing with the little girls, and much an admirer of everything they do; that we have transplanted him into the boys' school and decreed that boys and girls must play separately and be wholly separated. Samuel is tall, thin and has not so much activity. In countenance he resembles Edward; he is always the spokesman, the one to talk all the news, announce all the fights, explain all questions either right or wrong and remember everything that happened and every promise that was made a long time ago.

Marianne is quite a little mother and teacher and is certainly a comfort to her mother, but mostly in the rectitude of her principles and service of propriety. Edward is not of so compliant a temper and not so tractable as assistant. But perhaps his energies and qualifications are more befitting his sex. He speaks the language like a native, gets on at school and is a boy of great activity and enquiry. We expect an addition in February.

Jane with her husband and children are at Kerikeri for a visit of five weeks, from the end of our committee to the end of theirs. I have had the inexpressible comfort of a better account of her. Her ill state of health has been a source of great uneasiness to us all.

We are at short allowance of flour and sugar, and have an increased scarcity of food for our increased numbers of natives and are threatened with invasion from the southward, to prepare against which a citadel is building, on the summit of the hill at the back of the settlement to flee into until the marauders shall have executed their hasty work of destruction. It is not expected they will ever make a stand, and all means will be sued for refuge and defence. We have none of us any fear that the Lord of Hosts will suffer us to fall into the hands of these ruthless savages. Last week I attended upon Mrs Fairburn, who had a fine little girl, and next month Mrs Mair expects to call for us.

Jane

5 November 1828. Paihia. Notwithstanding a violent and troublesome cough, I was so much recovered as to resume my share in the various departments of teaching, cooking and nursing Mrs Mair, who was confined the week after I came here, and I have not yet arrived at my usual health and strength and consequently feel not a little fatigued at the close of the day.

But I am enabled to go on, and I trust that every week I shall feel my burden lighter. About six weeks ago the children at every station became poorly with colds and coughs, which have since proved to be whooping cough. Some have it favourably, others suffer a great deal. Among the latter are Mrs Fairburn's baby, who was only a month old when she began, and Henry's youngest boy, Little John, whose coughing fits have been very alarming. He is now recovering, but Samuel, Henry and Thomas are still very poorly. My two children are among the former class.

14 November 1828. Poor Mrs Clarke has lost her baby, a sweet girl about four months old, who had been in considerable danger from the whooping cough and was apparently recovering, but was called home by the Heavenly Parent during the night, and you may perhaps imagine the distress of the mother on waking at day break to find her lying by her side, quite dead. From the sweetness and placidity of its countenance, it is supposed to have gone off without a struggle.

Just now we seem to have distress all around us. At Rangihoua, Mr and Mrs Shepherd are both ill with the whooping cough as well as their children, one of whom, their only girl, is in a very precarious state.

At this station every family has similar troubles, though somewhat less in degree, but we are all in fear respecting Mrs Mair's little girl, who was born the week after my return from Kerikeri. Every precaution was taken to avoid carrying the infection, but the poor little thing took it before she was three weeks old, and is now getting very bad.

Many of the natives have it also, and among others Tohitapu, who I think must be between fifty and sixty years of age. This priest and warrior of renown has lately become anxious to learn to read, and accordingly, as his abode is but a short distance from Paihia, he comes pretty regularly to school, but, whether from real desire of instruction or the hope of gaining food and clothing, it is difficult to determine.

20 November 1828. It has been a very busy day, but if my children will not cause too many interruptions, I will endeavour to relieve my fatigue by writing a few words. I must continue my story of distress by telling you that on Sunday last little Harriet Shepherd breathed her last, and to add to the affliction of her parents her little brother is scarcely expected to survive.

Death seems to be hovering around us and we know not how many more promising flowers he may be permitted to nip in the bud. We have reason to expect Mrs Clarke and some of her children next week. Her health and spirits have suffered much from the loss of her baby.

Friday, 21 November 1828. Our English school goes pretty well considering that the whooping cough has prevailed in every family. But I think the majority are now getting the better of it. And now Adieu! for I must ring the bell for school.

1829

THE EXAMINATION

Henry

29 January 1829. Paihia. I hope you have by this time received my spears. [Henry had sent back to family and friends in England a parcel of artefacts he had collected over the past few years, including weapons, a canoe and tools.] The stone tools (there is no doubt) were the ordinary tools before introduction of iron. Everything of native production comes now from the Southward, but these people furnish themselves by barter with muskets, axes, etc. The island two hundred miles to the south of the Bay of Islands is not known to us.

At Tauranga instruments of iron are finding their way, and every year they increase their prices for these commodities. The art of tattooing is in a measure lost to the natives about us. When a party from the River Thames comes up, they are occupied for a long time in carving the hides of men, small canoes, boxes, etc.

Jane

3 February 1829. Paihia. Tuesday night. I was roused before daybreak this morning by the report of several muskets. But knowing the New Zealanders never carry on hostilities in the night, I soon composed myself to sleep, again supposing that our own natives were amusing themselves. On rising, however, I found that Te Koki had been reduced to return to the Kawakawa in direct opposition to the advice of his English friends, and on occasion of his departure his friends had discharged all their muskets.

About three weeks ago he sent post haste for William, supposing that his life was in danger from a frightful sore on his arm, but William being from home on an expedition to the Hokianga, Henry went to see him and did all that lay in his power for him, and when William returned, which he did late on the Saturday night and heard the state he was in, he determined to go up the Kawakawa immediately after morning service on the Sunday.

This he did and found the poor old man really in great danger. He repeated his visit on the Tuesday, and finding that he required more attention than it was possible to give him at that distance, he had him conveyed down the river to this place, where he was comfortably fixed in one of the houses appropriated to Henry's boys. Here he had all the attention possible. William attended twice a day to dress his arm, and anything that he fancied in the way of food he had if the house could provide it.

At last the *Satellites*, a man of war, came into the Bay, and William requested the surgeon to come over to see him. His visits were repeated during the week and they had the satisfaction of seeing his arm begin to heal, with a very fair prospect of his recovery. Notwithstanding all this his wife and daughter, with their attendants, did all in their power to get him away, and would have succeeded had not William and Henry urgently withstood them.

When they left home yesterday for Rangihoua they considered him materially better and his appetite was very good. But last night it happened that he was very faint. They immediately said he was dying and insisted upon taking him to the native place, and in spite of Mr Fairburn's entreaties they carried him off. There is little doubt but his death will be the result, for his wound cannot have the requisite attention, neither can his sickly appetite relish the native food.

Many lives I believe are lost from similar inhuman conduct. It is only a month since a most promising little girl who had lived several months with us lost her life in the same way, being literally starved to death. She had been ill but was relieved by a little medicine and was getting better so long as the bread which accompanied it lasted. When that was gone the only food her friends offered her was fern root, which her stomach loathed, and as they would not send about six miles for better food her death was the consequence.

5 February 1829. . . . . It is no little business to provide sewing for my eight girls, and to find constant employment to keep them out of mischief, dirt and idleness. I keep twenty-four pieces of sewing ready fixed, which fill two large baskets. They have each a piece for school only: to provide in some measure for the neatness and cleanliness of this, they have each a school gown, to be worn in school only.

Then, in the evenings, their own garments must be cut out and fixed, for their employment, as the strongest inducement to domesticate quietly, and besides this, there must be a piece always at hand with which they may sit on the steps or in the garden, or on the top of the wash house, in the sun, or in the shade, provided they keep within the precincts of our gardens.

The two are laid out in one green, surrounded by a serpentine walk, and planted with shrubs and flowers, forming no inconsiderable space in which to wander in. Jane's girls and mine have taken a great desire to make us a native mat. They have been sitting in a circle today, preparing the flax, some the warp, some the woof, some the strings and fringe. Rino, a slave from the southward, is the only one who knows how to make those with coloured borders, and the others are quite surprised to see the superior way in which she dresses the flax.

This poor girl, only three days ago, came crying to me, and begging me to let her go to the Kawakawa, to be killed with her mother and some other slaves, on the expected death of Te Koki. She said it would be very good to die with her mother and her chief. I refused, and she has been since then perpetually asking to go and cry with a girl of Mrs Fairburn's, who is a sister or cousin.

Today I showed her a mat which Jane is going to send to her mother, when she said in a crying tone that, she liked to look at it, that it filled her with love for her old place, and instantly set to work to make one like it. Nor has she once asked to go and cry with Ripe, and seems inclined now to live, and weave a mat.

Henry

3 April 1829. Paihia. We have been in considerable bustle for several days past. ... Te Koki, our old chief, died about two months ago; and one of the [Maori] boys set fire to some rubbish which had constituted part of one of his houses. This, with them, is a high crime. Accordingly a large muster came upon us on Wednesday morning at daylight. Our boys had been up all night, expecting broken heads in the morning.

Our opponents were about four times our number; but Tohitapu, hearing of our expectation, came in the middle of the night, and made the hills resound with his vociferation, followed by two of his wives, bearing several muskets. He immediately called a council, and gave direction how our strength was to be disposed of, and went through several manœuvres, for the encouragement of our boys.

Soon after daylight the enemy arrived, but were exceedingly polite. After dancing a while, accompanied with, to an English ear, frightful yells, they sat down until two large iron pots of stirabout were prepared for them, and in a short time dispersed, asking if it was a very cruel fight.

Jane

24 April 1829. Paihia. I will venture to give you a little of the news. And first I must tell you of Marianne's confinement the latter end of February with her second daughter [Sarah], whose birth was attended with no small share of anxiety having nearly cost the mother her life, which was in imminent danger for several hours, in consequence of very violent haemorrhage and faintings, which came on about an hour after the baby was born. It was the wish of our Heavenly Father to restore her once more to her family and to preserve the life of so valuable a member of the Mission.

But her recovery has been very slow, and by almost imperceptible advances. I am thankful, however, to see her so well as she is. And now she takes her usual part in domestic as well as school concerns. The little girl is an exceedingly fine child and has done well from the first, notwithstanding the illness of her mother. The last few weeks have been far from tranquil, not that we have had any real cause for alarm, but on one pretext or another we have had a succession of fights and commotions which have tended to keep us in a continual state of excitement.

All the girls have also been very unsettled, and as the comfort of our houses and the regularity of our proceedings depend very much upon their good behaviour, it is not a little trying to the patience and temper when they do all in their power to vex and insult us. It is also a trying season to them being the time when they gather in their kumeras and potatoes, and at their native places they keep up a continual feast, while it very frequently happens that during the rest of the year they are half starved.

And for some few weeks back, in consequence of a scarcity of native food in the settlement, their daily allowance from us has been necessarily diminished. It is, therefore, no wonder that many of them are unable to resist the temptation to leave a place where they are obliged to do many things very contrary to their inclinations and return to their homes where they do nothing but eat and sleep, and sleep and eat.

But what grieves and mystifies us most is, when a girl has been some time with us and is making satisfactory progress at school and beginning to be useful in the house, to have her taken away by her nearest connections and carried on board the vessels which frequent the Bay, because the reward they received for their iniquity there is greater than we can afford for their services here. These things are really discouraging but I am glad to say they occur much less frequently than they used to do, and I think our encouragements exceed our discouragements, if we weigh them impartially.

You have often heard of the New Zealand fights, but I do not know whether your English notions can form a very just idea of what is here termed a fight, neither can I give you a very accurate description. But you may imagine one, two, or more canoes filled with natives, coming full speed towards the beach, upon the first glimpse of whom (whether they be friends or foes) the settlement rings again with the cry of 'He tana he tana' (a fight, a fight). All the natives assemble on the beach and on the landing of the strangers, rush down to the shore in order to receive them. Both parties then mingle together and have something like a wrestling match which ends with a grand 'Haka' or dance, in which they jump altogether an amazing height from the ground and make the air resound with their hideous yells.

They do not always, however, go through these ceremonies, for only last week a party came from Rangihoua in a very treacherous manner instigated by a man who had left Mr Davis's only the day before. They endeavoured to keep out of sight till they heard the bell ring for Evening prayers, and when all were safe in the chapel they made a rush upon the houses of some natives who live very near to Mr Davis's and succeeded in possessing themselves of clothes, saw, iron pots, etc., etc. before prayers were half over.

In consequence of the vociferations of a woman who was remaining at home with her children, they found out something was the matter and burst out of the chapel, some through the door, others through the windows. Some of the aggressors had reached their canoe but the others were overtaken, and one of the chiefs of the party detained prisoners by Henry and Mr Davis till the stolen articles were all brought back. A gun was also seized by one of our party as a payment for his child having been nearly thrown down on the fire.

The following day at the same hour they returned to demand the musket which being refused they were proceeding to cut down the fence and to load their guns, when Tohitapu's wives made their appearance in the crowd and immediately it became a war of tongues, all parties beginning to nag with the utmost vehemence. Tohi himself was gone with William and Mr Davis to Waikare, and by the time they arrived the contending parties had come to our agreement that an equivalent should be brought for the gun, which was accordingly given up to them, and the next day they brought a little female slave.

On Good Friday during the service we had another alarm which brought every individual out of the chapel in the middle of William's sermon, but it proved to be nothing and we were all enabled to return and have the service completed.

Dear little Mary has hindered me too. She has got the chicken pox and is very feverish and restless tonight. She and her cousin Thomas have ascertained that the complaint is the 'pocken chicken', after which she told me it was the 'pecken chicken'.

12 August 1829. Paihia. You will rejoice to hear of the birth of my little boy and of the many mercies which have been vouchsafed to his mother. I am so well and strong that I can hardly believe that anything has happened except when I look at the fine, fat, little babe upon my lap, now just 3 weeks old.

Last Sunday was a day of much interest to me, being marked by the baptism of our own little boy and four native children. Their father's name is Taiwanga, he has lived among the missionaries several years, first at Kerikeri and then here. Though he has still but little light, he is thoroughly convinced that God of the missionaries is the only true God. About 2 months ago he wrote a very pleasing letter requesting that his children might be baptized and brought up in the religion of Jesus.

As soon as the translation of the baptism service was completed, a day was appointed and Mrs Yate came over as one of the sponsors. Our child was the first to be baptised in the Maori language, and it really was a very touching sight to see the four little heathen children brought by their parents to be admitted into the visible church of Christ.

October 1829. Paihia. We have had a great succession of incident, excitement and anxiety, and now, although enjoying good health, comfort and (for New Zealand) peace, our occupations crowd out every writing moment.

At this you will not wonder when you consider that our double family consists of ten children, which with Elizabeth Kemp make eleven under eleven years of age, and the oldest of six out of that number is only just turned four, added to which our native girls are as much trouble as so many children, and as I have eight and a little motherless babe about two months old whom I have had in the house since within a few days of its birth.

I have for my share sixteen children, the washing and clothing of whom alone is no little concern. As my husband has seventeen men and boys under his care, he cannot give me much assistance as he used to do. Added to this Jane and I have greatly increased our school, and this half year we have added to our first two hours of morning school the little nursery dears, Thomas, John, Colman Davis and Mary, and as many of the native girls as can come from thirteen to twenty according to the employments of the several days.

The two elder Davises take these two classes, while we attend to the other English girls, and the last hour which is sweetly quiet by comparison is devoted to them. In the afternoon all meet at the native school at the chapel. I had today thirty-one native women and girls, which with a nurse left at each of the five houses, and allowing for some sick, will give you our number, forty girls in the school.

Jane and I, although incessantly tired and often dispirited, never felt so much encouragement. Yet this is the first half year we have had our full health and strength, and as yet no serious interruptions. We have advanced within seven weeks of the midsummer holidays, and anxiously looked for the general examination at Kerikeri. Our specimens of work and writing are in a great state of forwardness, and they so far surpass our expectation that we will make it a point of duty to refrain from using some of these valuable and needful pieces of apparel, to send home as proof of their great improvement.

But before I give you a hasty survey of the leading events of the past half year, let me draw up the curtain which absence has cast over us, that you may see us clearly, nay that you may spend an evening in the midst of us!

The Examination

As Jane and I stood for a few seconds on the grass after tea admiring the bloom of the roses and geraniums, the fresh verdure of our clover and grass, the calm serenity of the bay and the freshness of the mild evening breeze after a sunny day, and listening to a group of native men and boys saying the new catechism to your nephew Edward in the middle of the garden, we both said how much we wished we could have you with us.

Jane went in to ring the bell for English prayer meeting, and I to my little sitting room and now you see me? Can you imagine little Marianne at the end of a long table in the kitchen with her mother's copy of the catechism in her hand, and eight native girls sitting round her, the little girl gravely questioning them.

Friday, 24 December 1829. Kerikeri. The general examination is over, and here at the end of the week are the whole Paihia settlement set fast at Kerikeri in a heavy gale of wind without any probability of getting home before Monday. For, though the wind and rain may cease, the sea will not have sufficiently subsided for our propelled boats, or indeed any boats, to go across the bay in safety.

We amused ourselves this morning with counting the numbers in the different houses. Mr Clarke's family during this visitation consists of 96, Mr King's 64, Mr Hamlin's 63, Mr Baker's 46 and Mr Yate's 34. The total number of Europeans 71 and of natives 218. Of these more than half are from Paihia. I am comfortably seated at Mr Kemp's though with thirteen children buzzing around me.

On Sunday week last (at Paihia) a vessel was in sight just before evening service. All our expectations were raised. It might be Mr C. Davis, it might be Mr Brown, it might be Mr Marsden, but what was very droll, Edward said it must be Mr Brown because his uncle had dreamt that a vessel appeared at 4 o'clock with Mr Brown on board.

She appeared to be no whaler but a vessel from the Colony, even the *City of Edinburgh*, and though it was not the expected brig, the *Haweis*, a boat was sent to her after service. Long before the boat reached the beach on its return, the tuki or native boat song of the natives announced Mr Brown and his wife.

The former was ushered in in the midst of our supper. I can never give you half an idea of these seasons of excitement. Mrs Brown was left on board. Therefore our long expected fellow labourer could only give us a look and a little news and return. He informed us that Mr and Mrs C. Davis, and Mrs Hart had sailed from Sydney in the *Haweis* a fortnight before them. Mr C. Davis's anxiety to arrive amongst us again was so great he seized the first vessel though everybody knows her to be a dull sailor.

To Mr Charles Davis, Mr Brown had given every letter and packet under his charge for the Missionaries. This was a sad check, for as the winds had been contrary we might still wait.

Picture to yourself Mr Brown short in stature, almost overwhelmed by the domestic natives from the different houses crowding around him until at length we were compelled to lock the door; still as William and Jane and Mr Davis were admitted others crept in and we had scarcely room to look at one another. Our children were all eagerness to see if they liked their new schoolmaster. Mr Brown's manner was most prepossessing. All seemed eager to ask questions, at last he said, 'Mr C. Davis has brought out a cousin of yours.'

All looked to see to whom the eyes were directed.

'A cousin of mine?' said Jane with a start, 'What was her name?'

'Nelson.'

You may imagine how surprised we all were, and as letters we had none, much was left to conjecture, and much had conjecture to feed upon. Jane and I could not help going forward and backward to each other's houses after the boat was gone, exclaiming, 'I can think of nothing but this cousin.'

The next morning Mr and Mrs Brown came early. I was ill all the morning with something of the cholera, but a dose of laudanum enabled me to appear at the dinner which my girls had done wonders to prepare.

It so happened that Mr and Mrs Brown arrived, as Jane said, in the busiest week, for all was preparation for the examination to which we were to depart on the following Tuesday. Henry had much ado to clear out the bedroom which once was ours in the whare raupo [rush house] for Mr and Mrs Brown. In the afternoon Mr Yate arrived, and in his delight to meet Mr Brown some necessary arrangements were neglected about the classes and prizes for the examination.

Jane had her little Jane very unwell, a great trial for her, and we both of us found Mrs Brown a valuable assistant to plait the back of a girl's gown, set some buttons on a child's waistcoat, run a tuck in a frock or let one down, fix a bit of work here and there just exactly as we liked.

It was raining almost all the week, and washing and ironing was quite an exercise to everyone. On the important morning the day broke without a cloud. The whole settlement was in immediate action.

The husbands arranged their boats and crews, the wives had their children, their native girls, their boxes, their breakfast, etc., to look after, and although our breakfast was laid the night before we were obliged to enforce the necessity of staying to partake of it, and when done, how could I be so cruel as to insist upon the things being washed.

The boys, after they had taken my cloak and baby, seemed inclined to carry me. They scolded the poor girl who stayed to wash the cups, told me we were the only boat left behind and the day was all gone, though after I had locked up every door and arrived at the jetty, I was quite in time.

Mr Davis, who stayed to receive the *Haweis*, and Mr Mair to take charge of the settlement, helped me down into the boat, in which Henry had seated Mr and Mrs Brown and all the seven children. The smooth sea glistened in the early sun.

Mr Fairburn's white flag spread in the gentle breeze as they in the large canoe glided along first. All moved with native paddles, one youth standing as a kind of fugleman to Tuki, with all his native gestures, noise and animation.

Calm as was the bay our boats were so filled that I could not for some time get the better of a sensation of terror as our boat seemed to stagger and reel with her load. We were nearly forty individuals in her. The three others and the large canoe were proportionately full.

Each of our five little vessels had a white flag. On ours Henry had painted in gold leaf a dove.

The little fleet was a brilliant sight for this dark corner of the earth, so many English bonnets in the boats, and so many merry little English faces peeping up as we passed, repassed and closed in order, and so many cheerful little English voices mingling with the vociferous gabble of the natives. The excitement was quite too much for the strength, though not for the spirits of us matrons. We were all off by seven.

At Moturoa (Island) we overtook Mr King, with all Rangihoua, except Shepherd, in a boat and canoe, and before we went on shore at Kerikeri all the boys went on shore to dress. Peku and their gathering, in rank and file, delayed much time.

When we opened upon the settlement we were seven in number abreast and paddling in unison. The boys dressed in uniform, in white shirts and trousers and Scotch caps. The Kerikeri lads dressed in the same manner assembled on the landing place. All voices hushed and we seemed in the native fashion to steal gently along.

The song or chant of the native paddlers was first soft, then swelled and increased in volume to the very utmost. As we advanced it had a very pleasing effect, and then the loud English hurrahs of the boys on the landing place was instantly answered by a sudden burst of every voice in the boats, the boys standing up and waving their caps. The children were in ecstasies and were well nigh deafened.

Amongst other friends Mrs Hobbs of Hokianga gave me an affectionate welcome at the landing place. Mr and Mrs Brown accompanied us to Mr Kemp's, where we found Mrs Kemp still weak.

At two o'clock all the missionaries and their families met at the chapel. William preached and after the service Mr Yate administered the sacrament. We then all adjourned to our respective houses for tea, which was hurried over by the mothers and fathers that we might all go to see our children assembled by the frame of Mr Yate's new house. The sight was quite affecting.

Forty-eight (for Mr Shepherd's were not there) were regaled with tea and sweet cakes, that is each one who could hold a cake in its little hand, for eight were babes in their nurses' arms, and several others scarcely old enough to sit at the long table prepared for the purpose.

Amongst these, six native children intermingled their happy little faces who had been baptized and were neatly dressed by their proud mothers in English attire, two belonging to one of Mrs Kemp's domestics, and four to Taiwanga and his wife living with Mr Davis at Paihia.

These were plentifully regaled with sweet cakes and after the repast Mr Yate addressed the children as Mr Yate only can, for he has quite a talent for talking to little children, explained what that wise Solomon meant, when he said that children were like asses' colts, even the young donkeys at Kerikeri.

He told them that their friends in England thought much about them and prayed for them, that they might have new hearts and become good and wise, and how much they had considered what they do for them. And what had they done? Could any little girl tell him? Why, they had sent Mr Brown to teach them, etc. Mr Brown seemed affected with the sight of his future charges. After all was over the boys literally had a scamper like so many wild colts up and down the front of Mr Yate's house until bed time.

So much for the first day. Tired as Henry was, the natives came to ask him to hear their catechism before they slept, which he did on the grass plot although half asleep.

In the morning the chapel bell rang before all had breakfasted. After native prayers the natives were examined. And now I must invite you to go with me up the hill on which the chapel stands. Just outside the door upon the grass sat a group of girls being the third class waiting to be called, all arranged in clean blue gowns, white aprons and buff handkerchiefs.

Inside the chapel were the first class of boys and girls from the three settlements undergoing the first trial of examination by Mr Yate and Parata in the two catechisms.

After looking on some time and speaking to Mrs King, Hobbs, Fairburn, Mair, etc., I walked outside, where Henry, Mrs Clarke and Mrs Hamlin were examining a large circle of boys and girls of the second classes. And now the third were called up. Mr Fairburn, Mr

Puckey and Mr Baker took them. To these succeeded a trial for sums and writing from dictation. Specimens of writing were exhibited.

When all was concluded and we had all dined, the bell for the native dinner rang. Benches and planks had been erected, and now a troop of natives singing as they went brought a quantity of rush baskets from each house filled with bread, cakes, potatoes, pork and beef, and all the tables were spread in succession.

Every native had a basket before him, which they greatly admired, because they could take away with them what they could not eat. All seated themselves in great order and waited till grace was said at each table, four in number. Seventy girls sat at one table by themselves.

After dinner the English females adjourned to Mr Clarke's to examine the girls' work, which Jane had spread upon a long table, and as each article passed the scrutiny she hung them round the room.

Half of each settlement were to have been judges, but we put it all into the hands of Mrs Brown and Mr Hobbs, who made three lists. Those in the first were each to be rewarded with a gay new gown from Mr Yate. Those in the second with a bag or apron, etc., and the third nothing, and to judge was really an arduous task, for there were gowns, shirts, frocks, pinafores, trousers, flannels, nay even a boy's jacket. Indeed we were all astonished at the quantity of good work when we saw it all together.

Rain came on and the girls were obliged to have tea at their respective houses. But the boys drank tea under the frame of Mr Yate's house.

The following morning was wet and showery, we again adjourned to the chapel, where we saw a window sash, pannelled door, table, etc., for which prizes were adjudged as good specimens of carpenters' work. After all the prizes were distributed, William addressed the natives and all dispersed.

But the rain prevented our return to Paihia. Therefore the heads in council sat upon the important question where Mr Brown should be placed. Friday, Saturday and Sunday we had a most unusual quantity of rain for this time of year.

Monday was as fine for our return as the day on which we set out. We left our most hospitable friends and after a pleasant voyage reached home in perfect safety, and were welcomed by solitary Mr Davis and Mr Mair at Paihia. No *Haweis* had arrived.

Tomorrow is Christmas Day, how this sounds even now to my English ears, this very hot weather! Edward has just brought me with great delight 2 bunches of English currants out of his gardens, all his harvest, the only tree we have. We have each had one currant.

It has this week been determined at a committee at Kerikeri that Mr Brown shall be stationed at Paihia. Rejoice with me in the prospect of having my boys at the same settlement! It was found that William and Mr Brown must be together and some were for sending them both to Kerikeri, but Henry said if Jane and I were divided I could not take the girls at Paihia. That plan must fall and all are to stand at Paihia. All whose opinions are worth having are unanimous.

Our clock will be very useful, for our watches went to England in the *Sisters*, and we have neither watch nor clock in our house. We thirst after tidings of you.

FIRE

Jane

24 December 1829. Paihia. Mr and Mrs Brown have arrived, Mr and Mrs Charles Davis and Mrs Hart sailed a fortnight before them from the Colony but are not yet here, and it is supposed in consequence of the adverse winds they have put back to Port Jackson.

It is impossible to describe to you my astonishment on hearing from Mr Brown who this long expected Mrs Charles Davis was. We have been looking out eagerly for Mrs Hart, little thinking she was bringing out another sister for me. But the pleasure of anticipating their arrival has been mingled with many fears and apprehensions.

We know that all things ordered well and will work together for good to those who love God. We trust their arrival is only delayed.

After Marianne's confinement and illness we went on with tolerable regularity till our holidays, towards the close of which Henry took Marianne and his family up to Kerikeri to pay a visit to Mrs Clarke.

A week after their return my Little Leonard was born. When he was about two months old Mrs Shepherd was taken ill and both Marianne and myself went over to Rangihoua to see her, as she was considered in imminent danger. I was there two days and when I left her had no idea of seeing her again in the flesh. She was, however, happily restored to her family.

But other afflictions awaited us. We had seated ourselves at supper and were enjoying the quietness, children and domestics being all asleep, when suddenly a cry of fire from the other end of the settlement struck over our ears. William rushed out of the house followed by all the native girls, and when I could get to the door to see the sight it was truly awful.

All the native buildings beyond Mr Davis's were in a blaze, and the reflection of the flames on the surrounding hills was very grand. Every exertion was made to preserve Mr Davis's house by covering the thatch with wet blankets. The children we brought over, some dressed, some in blankets, and began to carry away books, linen and whatever was most valuable, as the sparks and burning raupo [bulrush] continued to fall around, the wind freshening from the very worst quarter.

By the time, however, that the garden fence was consumed, the fire was got under. Mrs Davis and her family were glad to remain in our two houses for the night, and we would have kept them the following day as so disastrous an occurrence in New Zealand cannot happen without a party coming to strip you as a consolation for your misfortune.

As soon as the fire was extinguished, a messenger was dispatched to our friends up the river to require their presence for fear any stripping should assail us. They accordingly came at daybreak, but a heavy rain, I think I may say (providentially), kept away all our enemies, and Mr Davis had to repair his fences, etc., before anybody could molest him.

Is it not almost a miracle that our raupo houses are preserved and we permitted to dwell in safety from day to day. Mr Davis and his family are now comfortably fixed in their new lath and plaster house, and we hope to have one in time.

The week after Mrs Fairburn was taken seriously ill, and for some time her life was despaired of. Her illness was similar to Marianne's, only it proceeded from a miscarriage instead of from a confinement. A few weeks subsequent to these two affairs Mrs Kemp was attacked with puerperal fever nine days after her accouchement [delivery], and for a week her life was in danger. Mrs King was ill at the time with a liver complaint. So that sickness and distress seem to have visited every family in its turn.

William was to and fro between the settlement continually. Mrs Kemp and Mrs Clarke were both confined at the same time, previous to which Mrs Hamlin's baby was so ill that we expected some of us would be called upon to perform the part of nurse. Our own little Jane was also poorly for three weeks before the examination, so much so that I had almost given up the idea of leaving home. She was, however, much benefited by the change of air and is now quite well.

We were detained several days at Kerikeri by wind and rain, during which I had a slight attack of cholera which prevented my taking any part in the distribution of the prizes which this year consisted of gowns, bags, aprons for the girls, supplied by the bounty of Mr Yate's friends in England. We begin to thirst for news from home.

26 December 1829. Paihia. We are full of anxiety for the arrival of the *Haweis*, in which we hear (to our great astonishment) that Mr C. Davis has sailed from Port Jackson with Jane's cousin.

Mrs Shepherd in the beginning of September had a severe fever which began with inflammatory cold. Henry and I went over to see her on the Friday. She was in a pleasing frame, and, on Saturday, Jane went with her husband the Doctor and stayed till Monday.

The next week, as I was one evening at supper, my eye caught from the opposite window a sudden glare as of a broad sheet of flame rising from behind several out buildings. The fire proceeded from several houses beyond Mr Davis's belonging to his men. Mr Davis's house was saved by covering it with wet blankets, and watching the blazing raupo that fell. A rush house belonging to Taiwanga, which it seemed impossible to save, and was expected to communicate the fire. They shovelled earth over till it was covered.

Jane fetched Mrs Davis to sleep at her house, and four of the children stayed all night with mine and the following day, till all things were put in their places, again at home. We had all to look back with gratitude for our long preservation in such paper houses, and all looked forward to the time when more substantial buildings shall be completed.

Mrs Fairburn overexerted herself in soaking and wringing blankets in their large water cask, and helping the natives to pass them through the fence. The following week she suffered a dangerous miscarriage attended with haemorrhage and similar symptoms to what I passed through. I spent a fearful night with her. Her mind was very happy. She too was safely brought through and strengthened.

Next, Mrs Kemp was taken with inflammation after her confinement. In October death was hovering around us, but as yet has not been permitted to take any individual. The young cousins are a very interesting little noisy merry set. My little native baby died when not quite three months old. Mrs Clarke has another little girl, and is very watchful not to make it an idol, as she seems to fear she might have done the one she lost last year.

The launching of the 55-ton *Herald* at the Paihia Mission Station, 24 January 1826. Many Maori came from around the area to witness this event. She was wrecked at the entrance to Hokianga harbour on 6 May 1828. Copy of the sketch by Marianne Williams. *(Auckland War Memorial Museum, NZ)*

The mission vessel *Karere*, accompanying a war party, 1832. Sketch by Henry Williams. *(Auckland War Memorial Museum, NZ)*

The Paihia Mission Station in 1845. Marianne and Henry's house is just to the right of the boathouse. View from south end of the beach. Sketch by Henry Williams. *(Auckland War Memorial Museum, NZ)*

Rangihoua, showing Maori pa, European settlement and farm. *(Auckland War Memorial Museum, NZ)*

Te Waimate, the first inland mission station and farm, established 1830. *(Auckland War Memorial Museum, NZ)*

Meeting of the artist and the wounded Chief Hongi (Hika) and his family, Bay of Islands, November 1827. By Augustus Earle (1793–1838). *(Alexander Turnbull Library, Wellington, NZ, G-707)*

The Busby Residence at Waitangi, 1934. Known today as Waitangi House. *(Photo: Crawford. Auckland War Memorial Museum, NZ)*

James Busby, first British Resident in New Zealand. *(Alexander Turnbull Library, Wellington, NZ)*

Etinou young girl and *Taiwhanga*. Copied in 1825 or 1826 by Antoine Chazal, from two 1824 ink drawings by Jules Louis Lejeune. *(Alexander Turnbull Library, Wellington, NZ, C-082-100)*

Inhabitants of New Zealand with a view of the fortified stronghold or Hippah (pa), Rangihoua, 1825–6. Copied in 1825 or 1826 by Antoine Chazal from an 1824 drawing by Jules Louis Lejeune. *(Alexander Turnbull Library, Wellington, NZ, C-082-098)*

The whaling ships anchored off Kororareka in 1837. Across the bay is the Paihia Mission Station. Drawing after the original by Louis le Breton, artist on Dumont d'Urville's expedition to New Zealand, 1837–40. *(Alexander Turnbull Library, Wellington, NZ, Publ. 0028-183)*

The Stone Store built 1833 (centre) and the Mission House built 1821 (right) at Kerikeri. Marianne Williams spent her first weeks in the Mission House, staying with the Revd and Mrs Butler. They are the oldest stone and wooden buildings in New Zealand. This photograph was taken *c.* 1915–16. *(Alexander Turnbull Library, Wellington, NZ)*

View of the church bell at the Paihia Mission Station, Bay of Islands, looking out towards the sea. Photograph taken c. 1900. (*Alexander Turnbull Library, Wellington, NZ*)

1830

7 February 1830. Paihia. This is the third vessel within the last nine months which only brings us word that our things are still detained in Salisbury Square [London]. At dinner today Jane apologized to Mrs Brown for not being able to boil her any barley water of a good colour, for we had had saucepans at the Church Missionary House since last November, twelve months without any prospect now of receiving them.

Our pork is now finished and no supply of trade to buy with. One of my girls' payments was due last week, I had kept it back a fortnight as a punishment, and when I did apply, Henry said he did not know anything was left in the store to give her. I dread now their going away to that place of iniquity where they at all times receive threefold what they do here.

It is now nine weeks since Mr and Mrs Brown arrived here to gladden and strengthen us and relieve our anxieties about our children. Mr and Mrs C. Davis had then sailed more than six weeks from the Colony. You will feel especially for poor Jane.

There is something peculiarly refreshing to us in converse with persons just fresh from the land of fond recollections. I hope I am thankful for the pleasures of this kind lately enjoyed. But yet it has been felt that these newly arrived Missionaries from England could not tell us anything of the friends we most wished to hear from.

Mr Fairburn is just recovering from a dangerous illness, as is Mrs King also. During the last year Mrs Shepherd, Mrs Fairburn, Mrs Kemp and myself have all been brought down to an apparently hopeless state, and the Lord has shown his care over this vineyard in bringing each one through their portion of trial. Poor William has been in perpetual call.

We have been again this morning tantalized by a vessel coming in from Tonga. Mr King met one of their boats and learned that a boat from Tonga with letters for New Zealand upset and the letters were all lost. There seems to be quite a fatality attending all our letters at the present time.

Kakunga has been fetched away by her mother (we are told) to the vessels of which there are six in the harbour and Pooheca could not persuade her husband to stay and was obliged very reluctantly to accompany him.

One letter has been received from Mr Turner at Tonga. A boat had arrived there with five men amongst whom was the master of the *Minerva* from Port Jackson ship-wrecked. She was taking supplies for the Wesleyan Mission at Tonga. They have not even saved the letters.

If you would like to cut out two or three little frills or a little shirt or two, we will get them made. But the materials here are very difficult to procure. Jane is well and her three children.

16 February 1830. Paihia. On Sunday week three natives were publicly baptized at the chapel in the middle of service. Three of those who had lived longest amongst us, and had been candidates for baptism for some months past. I have seen four native children brought to the font at the same time as our little nephew, and a short time since a very interesting youth living at Mr Mair's had given a most satisfactory testimony during the illness which proved to be his last.

But these were the first we had beheld in full health and in the pride of life, coming forward to renounce all to which we had seen them so warmly, so obstinately attached and dedicated themselves thus publicly to the Lord. I think I for one can say my feelings were never so powerfully excited.

Taiwanga with whom you are probably acquainted, a relation and once a follower of Hongi in his bloody triumphs, but who has for nearly five years turned his sword into a ploughshare, and though he has had from his rank and influence and naturally strong passions many and deep struggles, yet he has been wonderfully influenced.

I saw him advance from the other end of our crowded chapel with firm step but subdued countenance an object of interest to every native as well as every English eye, and meekly kneel where six months before we had at his own request stood sponsors for his four little children.

I deeply felt that it was the Lord's doing and wonderful in our eyes. Pita and his wife Meri's demeanour were far more strikingly pleasing, but he was always a quiet well-behaved man, and his wife had been enabled to overcome a violent and disagreeable temper, and live in peace with her neighbours, and all were sensible of her changed countenance. Pita was one of Henry's boats' crew when he first brought me home to Paihia, and ever since Mr Davis came has been employed in his service.

Amongst the strange natives present was the first chief I was introduced to in New Zealand, Uree Okuna, or as I was then taught to call him, Mr Gunner. But he appeared on the following day as dark and as cold on these subjects as when we first anchored in the Bay of Islands.

Henry

6 March 1830. About nine o'clock, much firing at Kororareka; by our glasses we could observe persons moving in all directions, and the canoes pulling off to the shipping, filled with people. Mr Davis and I immediately went over in the boat; and after communicating with Captain King, on board the *Royal Sovereign*, went on shore, to endeavour to stop the firing. Landed at the scene of action; but could not see any one of rank, as all were concealed by fences and screens. I made as much noise as I could, but to no immediate effect.

This was to be known as the great battle of Kororareka or 'The Girls' War'. It was the result of a jealous quarrel between two women of rank: one the daughter of Rewa, a Kerikeri chief, and the other the daughter of Morunga, of the Kawakawa. Both were rivals in the affections of the captain of a whaling ship. The result of a few heated insults lead both their tribes into war, which would eventually escalate to the Southwards.

Unable to be heard over the ferocious firing, Henry went to seek Tohitapu, who was camped out of harm's way at the far end of the beach. It was agreed to halt all hostilities immediately and the attackers left.

Richard Davis, the Paihia missionary

6 March 1830. Alas! What a day of horror and distress this has been! As the *Royal Sovereign*, Captain King, was lying not more than two hundred or three hundred yards from the scene of action, we went to his ship. I went on board, but Mr Williams went on shore, and landed. This was a hazardous attempt on the part of Mr Williams as he was in much danger of being shot.

The deck of the ship presented a woeful spectacle of horror and despair; many of the wounded men had been brought on board, and were lying on deck in a mangled state; the surgeon employed dressing their wounds, assisted by as many of the people as could be spared (some of the wounded had been carried over to Paihia, where their wounds were dressed by Mr William Williams). Besides the wounded there was a great number of women and children, who had fled on board from the village for protection.

I stayed on board at the request of the captain to assist him in the management of the natives . . . but I had not been long on board before the assailants gave way and fled in all directions. On seeing this I went ashore with Captains King and Dean. The sight was dreadful as nearly one hundred were killed and wounded. Soon after we had landed, the assailants were permitted to come and carry away their dead and wounded chiefs, but the bodies of the dead slaves they left behind. As one of the bodies left behind was that of a chief, but one of little note, a chief of the village ran out, and with a hatchet cut the body open, and took out a small piece of liver: this, they told me, was for the New Zealand God. After having visited both parties, and remained with them till midnight, we returned home.

20 March 1830. Paihia. We have all been in commotion, by efforts which the enraged adversary of souls was making aided by one of our unhappy countrymen [an English ship's captain] at Kororareka to stir up all the natives to engage in a civil war.

Every tribe has been in motion on one or the other side. Every individual in the schools has had a season of trial, either to go to fight, or to resist and stay to cry over or with relations, etc.

It is a fortnight today since the day of bloodshed at Kororareka, just on the opposite side of the Bay. All within hearing and in view from our settlement. The women and children fled in their canoes to this beach for refuge, the wounded came here to be dressed.

Magnified reports were brought of the really many slain, and to increase our agitation Henry started as soon as he discovered by his glass the state of things, and landed amidst the flying balls. We had with William, Mr Davis and Mr Browne, spent the whole of the preceding day persuading the parties to make peace and had (they thought) succeeded. On this occasion we all thought him rash, but Henry thought himself in the way of duty. He was preserved and certainly did stop the firing sooner than it would have been.

The natives thought that all the boats from eight ships in the harbour were coming and were discouraged. Since this day our beach has been a most busy scene. We have had no quiet, one tribe has lived here as our protectors and constant succeeding parties have gone to and fro. Both the contending armies sent messengers in every direction to assemble reinforcements for a great conflict, and if we had believed one quarter of what we heard, our being stripped and being driven away would have appeared a light thing in comparison. [Messengers had been sent inland. It was expected that, within a few days, some thousands of warriors would arrive and join the fighting.]

We did not, however, tremble for we rested in the strength of the Lord of Hosts. On the Sunday following, our service was carried through with the usual order notwithstanding incessant noise and uproar on the beach and a large part of strange natives, bustling out of chapel in the midst of it.

In the afternoon the native houses in Kororareka were all in flames, and the natives embarking to go to a fortified spot up the entrance of the Kawakawa. Yet in the midst of this I kept upwards of thirty native girls quietly seated at school. As I went to afternoon service I counted nineteen canoes on the beach, and there were parties in all directions. Five parties landed during service.

But notwithstanding all this uproar without, all was quietness and attention within. On Monday all was noise again. About noon a brig appeared in sight. Through the rain it resembled the *Elizabeth*, in which we had heard we might expect Mr Marsden and his daughter, and 'a ship and Mr Marsden,' was echoed with quite a tremendous shout!

A New Zealand warrior I heard was dancing to and fro in the midst of a harangue, when he suddenly stopped, and let fall the weapon which he had been flourishing. Henry was at Kororareka, but he and the other missionaries were speedily on board and brought the poor old gentleman and his daughter on shore to dinner, and much were our hearts gladdened by the sight of such a venerable and beloved friend.

I scarcely saw him the last time he was here, and felt quite overpowered. He, Henry and William were fully employed for ten days, going amongst the natives up to the port at Kawakawa – in which (they apprehend) was a thousand fighting men, and as many on the other side at Kororareka and Moturoa, talking to the natives and dressing wounds.

On Wednesday the fleet of canoes were in motion. The missionaries and Mr Marsden in two boats each bearing a white flag joined them amidst a great firing of musketry and persuaded them to return. Three principal chiefs went in a canoe between the two boats, the natives all saying that, if either of those chiefs were killed, the white people's lives should be the payment.

The negotiations we completed and ratified on the following day, but the armies are not yet disbanded, and it is said that all Hokianga are on the way to join one or the other army, and will be enraged that peace is made.

. . . The frightful gap in our correspondence seems of late to have cut us off from our friends. Nothing has been heard of the *Haweis*, Mr Hill writes from the Colony, he hopes almost against hope that she may be in Tahiti. She has all the letters. Mr Charles Davis brought all Mr Brown had and all he found waiting in the Colony, supplies for us, and private communications executed in the Colony.

Maria, my eldest servant, is just confined with a fine little girl. She and Ripeka and Toopoopo continue to give satisfactory evidence of a new heart and a new spirit. They with several of Henry and William's men and boys are candidates for baptism. They always wait about every night to be assembled; and this little evening assembly is a green spot in this barren wilderness.

This refreshing hope is not confined to this family of natives, it is the same at Mr Davis's. Though the number be yet few and it be but the beginning of things, it is ample comfort after a long dark night, to see but the dawning of this day; and surely the Lord has and is and will be with us; for not a hair of our heads has been touched, though Satan, war and slaughter have been all around us.

Pray for us that we may be supported in sorrow, and staid in joy! As Mr and Mrs Brown and Mr Marsden are at this house, and Miss Mary Marsden, our great favourite, at Jane's, we are no small family. We have, however, kept up school regularly through all. Miss Mary Marsden has been helping us to keep school.

25 March 1830. Though amidst uproar and confusion from the natives without, we are preserved by the hand of the Lord in much safety, you will, I am sure, sympathise in our long and painful anxiety respecting the *Haweis*, especially poor Jane, whom Mr Brown told to expect her cousin every day. Many a time have we watched in a vessel which appeared to be of the size expected, and many a disappointment have we experienced. Four months have now elapsed; and we have only a faint hope. Most of us give her up for lost.

We are in distress now for supplies both public and private. Let us beg you will all do your utmost to make up the frightful gap in our communications from England. It is a comfort to receive the assurance that you are acquainted with our joys and sorrows, trials and encouragements. We have now much promise of fruit in the Lord's harvest, as there is a great change in the conduct and deportment of many.

25 April 1830. Paihia. You will be so much interested with a conversation between my two sons, Samuel and little Thomas, as they lie in two cribs in their sister Marianne's room, during a violent thunderstorm; she being absent with Miss Marsden; that I am even moved to take up my pen and write it down, at least as much as I can catch.

Little Thomas attracted my attention by saying – 'God can step from here to all round the world, but I do not know how big the world is. He can see into the cows and into the bones.'

SAMUEL. 'Yes, he can do everything. If he said this bed should be made into a great lump of iron it would be done directly.'

THOMAS. 'I know how He would do, He would only say "Great big iron!" But He will not take care of the wicked people.'

SAMUEL. 'No, if we are wicked Satan will take us into the fire and kick us like the cows.'

THOMAS. 'Oh, how Nancy did do her legs (the nurse).'

SAMUEL. 'No, do not talk about Nancy on a Sunday! But Satan is not so strong as a man that believes and the Bible is Jesus Christ's bread.'

THOMAS. 'And what is the tea? Is there no tea in Heaven?'

SAMUEL. 'They are always singing there and so happy!'

THOMAS. 'Oh we must love God and be happy and we must not do one rude trick.'

SAMUEL. 'There is no thunder, no rain, no lightening, nor anything in Heaven.'

THOMAS. 'I know how God makes us believe the book. He says children, you must believe me and Jesus Christ.'

SAMUEL. 'Yes, I know what we must talk about on Sunday, we must talk about God, and not about any of the nasty things.'

THOMAS. 'Will you play with me, Samuel, on Monday?'

Edward and Henry (junior) who were much entertained with what they had overheard wanted to come and join in it, and I was obliged to silence them all. Henry has a large congregation of natives in the Raupo house. The storm is somewhat abated.

25 May 1830. After the many disappointments and delays Mr Marsden has had, a vessel is at length arrived to take him and his daughter home. They sail tomorrow. During the time they have been with us Jane and I have had, including Mr and Mrs Brown, nineteen in family to provide for, besides all our natives.

You will imagine that with our schools in addition we have not time for much writing. Mrs Brown has lately kept school two mornings in a week which has been a considerable relief. We like all her ways, and were in a great fright about a fortnight back on hearing that they might after all be removed to Kerikeri.

All the Paihia people and the three clergymen were for the school being at Paihia where the individuals are willing to assist in the charge, but all the other members of the committee, who are certain that a school will never answer in New Zealand at all, and intend, some of them, to send their children to Port Jackson, were for trying it at Kerikeri and nearly outvoted them.

Some very strange reasons, plans and propositions were made. We all here hope that the school may answer, that is, if it be at Paihia, for we imagine amongst ourselves that Mr B. is more likely to get on well amongst those who do know what school is than those who know nothing about it. Mr Davis and Henry have offered to receive the boys from the other settlements into our houses until Mr Brown's permanent house be erected in order that they may attend school.

I am to have for my share three of Mr King's sons and Henry Kemp, and Mr Clarke's and Shepherd's boys, that is if they like to send them, for that is doubtful. Mr Clarke has refused and is bent on the colonial education. Mr and Mrs King think education not necessary, and Mr Shepherd is in favour of the Colony.

But against the Colony I never before had so great an antipathy. We hear nothing but wickedness and they are now all put under martial law. Mr Yate is very anxious, he says, to get away from such an abominable place, and we are as anxious to have him home.

Williams (Wiremu), Pootoo (Mathew) and his wife Maria were publicly baptized at the chapel in the midst of the morning service on Easter Sunday and their infant Lydia, together with Mrs Davis's little girl, in the evening, all in native. It was a day of joy to our hearts. The little Lydia is a fine promising babe more than two months old. She sleeps in a light wooden cradle made by her father (who is one of our best carpenters) in the kitchen in the day time, and the little schoolgirls take it by turns to nurse her; and it is quite pretty to see the father come in to caress her when he leaves off work at dinner and carry her home to their cottage at night.

Maria washes her and all her clothes as carefully as she does Sarah's; for she has now been four years with me. Besides all this the work of the father and mother has been so consistent that there is every hope for the little one, that it will be brought up in the fear of the Lord. And here we feel the great advantage of sponsors.

I have lately had to attend Mrs Fairburn in a second disappointment, but she was not so ill as she was last September. Last week Jane visited poor Mrs King at Rangihoua.

It is uncertain how soon we shall remove into our new house. Mr Davis's family have been in theirs six months. You will think of me in my new house with seven boys more than my own to take care of. I have looked carefully to count the cost in undertaking them, and in order to keep them distinct from the girls, and not endanger upsetting the girls' school, they are always to dine at our house, and the little girls at Jane's.

Therefore, although we shall go on as we do, the two families dining together, I shall always give my seven boys their dinner when it is not my cooking week, and Jane will do the same with her girls. We intend also to have a fence down the middle of the garden. It will take from the beauty of our pretty lawn, but will divide the children and keep them in their place.

I have been telling you what we mean to do, but alas, how little do we know what of all this we may be permitted to do, or what even a day may bring forth. Pray for us that we may be strengthened to do the duty of the day in its day, even as the day requireth.

I have said nothing about our venerable Mr Marsden. Though he is a very old man, with all due deference, his opinion in some points is his own. I hope his heart has been gladdened here, where his patience has so often been tried. We have all very great regard for him, and his daughter Mary too, and shall part with mutual regret and affection.

Our seven dear children are all well. My two daughters, the eldest of whom has just turned ten, are quite a mother and daughter. Dear little Sarah is the pet and plaything of the whole family. Thomas has both observation and perseverance. Mr Brown always calls him Farmer Thomas, but he has quite the organ of preaching. I hope some of them may be useful as farmers. I had rather see them all follow the plough than go to be initiated in the arts of Port Jackson.

I trust we daily meet at a throne of Grace, and shall do so till we meet in our Father's house. Within these two months we have seen a comet and felt the shock of an earthquake.

Thomas Coldham Williams

When a little boy, some five years old, I strayed, contrary to orders, early one fine morning as far as a large pa not far from my father's house. I saw a number of warriors, who had finished their breakfast, outside the pa, all fully armed, lying prostrate on the ground praying to their god Whiro for strength to fight ('E Whiro e homai te kaha').

I peeped in at the corner of the pa – I there saw three Maori lads, about ten years of age, with a kit of hot steaming potatoes between them. They had each a small pointed stick, with which they were conveying the potatoes to their mouths; but before they ate them, they pointed them with a jeer at a fresh cut-off Maori head, fully tattooed, stuck up on a stick!

You may not quite believe all I tell you, but you may believe me when I tell you that, being myself then rather a fat little chap, I scampered home as fast as my then fat little legs could carry me.

Henry

27 August 1830. Paihia. My fingers are stiff after a day of hard labour in mixing mortar and looking after my boys at their respective works in the conclusion of my house, for certainly nothing that I yet have inhabited merits that title.

It is now 7 years since we landed on this beach, and until Saturday last I have never possessed a room to myself, where I would leave my papers or anything else without fear of some disaster. You will suppose therefore that I entered my study with delight. It is eleven by nine feet three, and has a small stove which will be exceedingly useful in the winter.

In this apartment I hope frequently to enjoy that retirement which I greatly need; and from which I have been wholly debarred since our departure from England. In some respects I wish my house to be furnished a little after the English fashion. It will be pleasing to the recollection and (I think) beneficial to the children, and will be attended with no disadvantage to the natives.

It will be plastered inside and out, and I intend in process of time to paper some of the rooms, which will be a novel thing in this region of the earth. Mr Marsden gave us a good scold for not having built our house sooner, as our late dwellings were not fit for cow houses.

We were some time before we learned the particulars of the organ. It has come without the slightest injury, and the first evening all were delighted with its sound. It was packed with great judgment, and the directions so simple, that we were not at a loss though entirely ignorant of such things. We have placed it at the end of the chapel, which to us Europeans gives a strong indication of the place we are in.

On Sunday last by the aid of a chandelier and a few sconces (the lamps we borrowed from every house in the parish) we had a third service at six past meridian, with the natives only. As our lamps were unfortunately of a very common kind a dim cloud ascended to the ceiling and almost obscured the lights. It was my turn to take the service, and I was rather apprehensive that we should be forced to come to a stand on a sudden as I could not swallow the smoke sufficiently fast, being somewhat out of practice. I think this might be remedied.

William

27 August 1830. Paihia. There has been a strong party in point of numbers [re: children's education] in favour of Port Jackson, along with whom were Mr Marsden and the corresponding committee in New South Wales. Henry, Mr Yate, Mr King, Mr Davis and myself were opposed to it, and the torrent of reasons urged by Mr Yate against the colony has now decided the question in favour of New Zealand.

For myself I have the utmost horror of that place. The best class of society is degraded in the extreme with very few exceptions, and even those families where religion is professed are so loose in their ideas of propriety that I could not on any account entrust a child in whom I had an interest even to visit any one of them for a single month.

But the children of many amongst us cannot be brought up as their parents have been before them, if dependent only on their resources. We all naturally wish that our children should be employed in missionary work, but of their fitness for it we cannot judge, until they arrive at years of maturity.

I will send you a practical illustration of wear and tear in New Zealand in a brown paper parcel. The boots and shoes were in good wearing condition the beginning of last week, their present state is the result of three days exercise in the bush while endeavouring to drive home some of the Society's wild bullocks.

A lay missionary's salary is twenty pounds, with which he is to provide for this wear and tear, all furniture beyond the bed and chest of drawers which he brings from England, pepper, mustard etc., wine or spirits which are needful for his stomach's sake, and crockery, saucepans, towels, etc. for household purposes, beyond what is supplied on his first departure from England.

7 September 1830. Paihia. I am going out to dinner at Mr Davis's, it being our quarterly Paihia prayer meeting and committee meeting, and am tired with the fatigue of yesterday when I had eighteen to dine and prepared for twenty-six. Last week was my cooking week.

The Saturday night that Mr Yate arrived, there was not one letter and we were tantalized by having a whole week to wait until the stores were landed and the vessel had been up to Kerikeri to unload.

The Saturday night following William and Mr Chapman returned from Kerikeri and brought in the boat a box from Hampstead, one from Southwell, and one from my sister Sarah.

On Sunday afternoon I gave Edward his uncle's sermons to employ him, and out of the books tumbled two of his letters. Henry was out amongst the natives. Therefore I opened the one for him, and ran to Jane with the discovery that the organ, the arrival of which had given such general satisfaction, was not, as supposed, the subscription one, but from their uncle to Henry and William. This discovery was a most unexpected and gratifying one to us all, and greatly enhanced the value of the organ.

In the middle of this week we received another package containing garments for the native girls. The last thing we received on shore was Henry's great sea chest from Southwell. Had these

187

been sent, as was intended by Mr Charles Davis, we should have been ignorant of much of your kindness, and have lost very many letters. Indeed the receipt of these old and, as we fancied, lost letters gave us more delight than those of earlier dates, which we received first.

I must no longer defer telling you how deeply the children have been interested in every circumstance related respecting their cousin Mary [Marsh]. I trust her blessed example may be blessed to them. I could well enter from experience into all your cares and anxieties during the dangerous illness of your sweet daughter, but your succeeding feelings I can only imagine, and imagination must fall short either of the poignancy of a mother's feelings, or of the power of such consolation as you must possess.

You will hear from many of us the cheering prospects of the mission. The work continues rapidly to advance. There have been for some time past several earnest candidates for baptism in almost every family. Those already admitted have walked steadily; and we feel driven to them by new ties of affection, as we listen to their Christian experience or witness their struggles on many occasions to use their own native expressions between their new head and their old one.

Mr Yate has brought the new [Testament] translation; to enhance the value of which they were not permitted to be given away, and are eagerly sought by some as wages. But I must not forget one little grandchild as we call Maria's daughter Lydia Williams. She is grown a fine fat, lively child more than five months old. Both Matthew and Maria tell us not to spare her when she grows older and is naughty, but to punish her as we do our own; which is quite foreign to all New Zealand ideas.

I am greatly relieved by this frightful question of sending the children to Port Jackson being for the present at rest. Mr Yate is returned from the Colony disgusted with it and shamed to his old opinion. Therefore the school will stand for the present in New Zealand, though not (I fear) on so firm a foundation, the point being conceded of moving Mr Brown up to Kerikeri, where he will have no assistance.

Mrs Brown, to whom Jane and I feel much attached, and who seems to have the girls' school as much at heart as we have, comforts herself with the idea that the parent committee may fix them at Paihia before Mr Clarke can be moved off to Waimate. The children here are all improving, though Messrs Kemp and King refuse any offers to take their children as boarders to share in the benefits and Messrs Clarke and Shepherd refuse all Mrs Davis's offers.

Poor Mrs Brown was taken ill on a visit to Rangihoua and prematurely confined of a stillborn daughter. She was graciously preserved; and they bore this severe trial with Christian grace. Jane went to nurse her.

Our holidays were spent in nursing; I had Mrs Mair in the commencement; and Mrs Fairburn had another long and dangerous illness. She is now recovered. Mrs Brown is at her pretty cottage, made out of the school rooms at the back of the chapel, and we are now reinforced by Mr and Mrs Chapman, who are to be stationed at Paihia because Mr Davis is going to Waimate; and seem to be sent by the Lord to labour in the place of Mr Charles Davis, by Him who taketh away one and giveth another.

They are Jane's visitors and we like all we have seen of them. Mrs Brown now teaches the English girls every afternoon with the little boys, who belong to the girls' school; which leaves Jane and me able to pay more undivided attention to the native girls, of whom we assemble thirty to forty in an afternoon, and from ten to twenty in a morning with our English school.

We have, including little Jane, eight English girls of ages from 3 to 17 and four English boys with Taiwanga's oldest boy, who is the age of Thomas, and comes cleanly dressed to learn his English alphabet, etc. There will shortly be a child from each house in the settlement old enough to be admitted; and it is not our fault that only the Paihia children come, and only the Paihia parents feel and acknowledge the benefit of the school.

We divided Mrs Macbride's present to the natives between us. The gowns came as fresh as new looking in the tin case as if just sent home from a shop in Hampstead. We might have received the cheese and all the sweet things our dear Mother and Kate intended to send us instead of mites and dust had they been soldered down in tin cases, for when I was ill Henry bought for me out of a vessel a box of London biscuits in as good preservation as those you used to buy out of tilted cart at Hampstead.

Marianne's merino frock will fit her next year which renders it doubly valuable. All the females as well as males met in the chapel to hear the new organ the first week it arrived, and I was glad the overpowering sensations which its full and melodious sounds produced and all the recollections it roused were a little moderated before the Sabbath.

The whooping cough was brought to Port Jackson for the first time by an English vessel, and, shortly after, a vessel which brought the news brought the disorder to New Zealand.

The Rotorua natives fled for their lives from chiefs, not only distant, but those in our immediate neighbourhood, who, though they were restrained by the Missionaries from murdering them, yet the poor things were not safe till they were embarked, and were threatened like the last, and when they did arrive safe, treated the missionaries with ingratitude.

Henry is hard at work plastering.

8 September 1830. Some packages and letters from Hampstead dated November 1828 Mr Yate found, lying in a corner of Mr Campbell's store in Port Jackson, under some heavy packages written upon them 'Too late for the *Anne*'.

Edward is fond of setting forth to his sister and brothers that he has been to Grandmamma and Aunt Catherine's house, but I do not fancy he remembers it. He certainly must remember Camden town, as there only he could have remembered seeing coaches going over a bridge, or a hearse standing at a door where was a funeral.

He often says he should like to go to England to be a doctor, like Uncle William, and as nothing can be done for the children after fifteen, we should like (that is, I could try to like) to send him home about that age, if the way and the means be made clear. He will be twelve in November.

Marianne thinks and talks of England as a distant Paradise, felicity beyond her reach, not that she would like to leave her father and mother, but her cousin Lydia has told her she would be happy at Grandmamma's school, and she should see this wonderful England. These two children always seem to think that they are entitled to think and know more about England, while the others listen with great attention.

When any stranger arrives from England, the native girls tell me to put my children born in New Zealand by themselves, that he may see that they are the stoutest, which, valuing them by their circumference, certainly they are, particularly Thomas, but not in a particular way to an English eye.

Marianne, Henry, John and Sarah are flowers. Edward, Samuel and Thomas are plainer but do not want intelligence. Thomas is quite a promising pupil in the girls' school and eager to be advanced to Mr Brown. John is very playful but very quick. Sarah and her cousin Leonard have been two such good-tempered sweet babies that they are general favourites.

I expect Sarah will be a musical genius, for she is always trying to sing. She is going out to tea tonight with all the little English girls in the settlement to Mr Brown's at the rural deanery, as we term his cottage, and the mothers are going to look at them.

Henry [senior], like his mother, will tell nobody he ails anything, till he can conceal it no longer. The other day I feared he was going to have an inflammation in the stomach like Mr Fairburn. He concealed his pain for four days. When I fetched William he administered the medicine as well as prescribed, and he, instead of letting him preach and then take medicine, made him stop at home and take three doses one day and one the next, and through much mercy after a few days he recovered.

The —— [supplies and treats in a newly arrived box from England] were entire and very good. The tin kept them better than any other sweet that came. Had you soldered them down in tin cases your cakes would have come well. I soaped a tub full of linen in water, and all the huge stains came out.

The toys and dolls were quite intoxicating. Anything coming as a present with a name written and affixed to it is delightful either to young or old. Mrs Chapman was present at this last opening and great entertainment. The trap and ball from Grandmamma, and one, a present from Uncle John, formed the afternoon's amusement at Mr Brown's last week when he assembled all the English boys to an entertainment at his house, and the English fathers to teach them how to play.

Henry is very hard at work plastering and looks a droll figure mounted upon a scaffolding, dressed up in William's dissecting dress and a red worsted cap.

18 September 1830. Our new house will bring us all to a focus and greatly to our comforts. The bricks were burnt here, and just when they were beginning to build chimneys a bricklayer came and begged for work. Another man who can make good chairs and tables has also been sent just in time to work for us. Thus are our needs supplied by Him who knoweth all things.

Now that there is a yard to cross between our bedroom and eating rooms, and in order to listen to our little ones, we often sit all evening in the bedroom. No one knows, where or in which house to find either Henry or me, and if I am in one house, I am sure to be called to get or attend to or see something in the other.

If I am looking after my girls, I am fidgety after my children, and if I sit with my children, I am fidgeting out after my girls, for a New Zealand wife and mother must have eyes like a spider and ears as many, though my having two girls now who are evidently actuated and restrained by Christian principles, and consequently are becoming daily trustworthy and capable of setting a better example to the others, is an inexpressible comfort as well as a great cause of rejoicing.

Monday, 20 September 1830. You must be in New Zealand to know the bustle and excitement and hindrances and extra work of an arrival of personages and packages. First there is all the anxiety and waiting before we get our letters and things. Then there are all the letters to read and the things to look at.

Then Jane and I have to talk about them, then the letters have to be exchanged and read soberly, then the things to be aired, etc., before being put away, besides our things from the Colony, cheese, sago, wine, etc. All these things added to cooking and school-keeping and visitors, and a committee dinner, which was in our raupo house this day week, drove us late.

Henry has been plastering, and William has been bullock hunting. I am so delighted with all the letters we have received. Henry and I had 25 for our share, and Jane and William about as many.

Henry

25 September 1830. Paihia. Last week we were concluding the interior of our house, and my presence was absolutely required, to keep about twenty native lads on the move.

We have had many seeds sent out lately, but I should like the buttercups and Sweet William of a dark kind. If they were packed in a bottle and sealed down they would come safely.

You will be much grieved at the news of poor Charles Davis's non-appearance. What a remarkable Providence that detained Mr and Mrs Brown from embarking in the same vessel! From accounts which have reached us there can be little doubt that she must have upset. Yet the Captain was an experienced man and very careful.

26 November 1830. Paihia. We have been thrown into considerable uneasiness for some days past by a report, brought us by Captain Clendon of the *City of Edinburgh*, which he received from Captain Brind, who stated that, when at Tongataboo [Tonga], he had seen some natives, who had come from all the Navigators islands, who stated that a brig had touched there and landed some people, that amongst them were two females, one of whom had died, and the second had been delivered of a son.

So seriously impressed were we that these were our friends from the *Haweis* that we immediately made a proposal to the captain of the *Bee*, a brig bound to the islands, to go in quest, and, should he succeed, and convey them to the missionaries at Tongataboo, that he should be paid the sum of 500 pounds. At first he appeared to like the proposal, but since has declined, unless we would pay him 250 pounds, whether he found them or not. The *Active* is expected every hour and will proceed.

8 December 1830. The *Active* arrived on Friday last. No English letters except one from yourself. Our Hebrew books were in the *Haweis*. The translation has gone on. The press is in use as far as it can be employed, but the types are very indifferent. Mr Yate has the charge of it. A younker [youngster] from the colony assists, who acts also as clerk.

Our children we expect to cultivate the land, and attend their flocks and herds. We have written to the Society respecting the propriety of purchasing land on their account; we do not wish to commence anything of the kind without their approbation. At the same time, I do not see what else can be done.

9 December 1830. By letters which Marianne has received, it appears that Maria Coldham has not been treated in the most handsome manner by Mr and Mrs Roberds, who have signified that they have no room for her. Consequently she is without a home. The thought has occurred to Marianne that she might be exceedingly useful here, should her mind be well disposed for this important duty. [Maria, one of Marianne's sisters, had been living with their uncle and aunt in England. Before Marianne had left England, Maria had not been permitted by her uncle to visit and say goodbye. Maria arrived in Paihia in April 1832 and helped in the school. She later married John Morgan, a missionary, and had eleven children.]

We actually grew out of our last dwelling. We could not move. Our present one is very convenient; and the swing of the doors and throwing up of the windows is quite music to our ears. We are free from smoke and all things are beginning to wear a more civilized aspect; our fences are after the English order.

1831

27 January 1831. Paihia. I know that I ought to go to bed and try to get what I very seldom do now, a good night's rest; but the roaring of the wind and sea during a heavy gale, and the pouring of the rain sounds so new during an unusually long, dry summer, have such an awakening influence, especially with the fidgeting idea that my husband is sleeping out in the bush in the midst of it all, at a place inland two days' journey from any civilized spot whither he is gone with Messrs Fairburn, Shepherd and Baker as negotiators for peace to a savage camp, that I prefer taking up my pen to write a line.

Jane and I have had such a succession of failures, excitements and hindrances, that we have had many interruptions, and we are doing our utmost amidst school business, that we may be prepared for our expectations.

After our excessive fatigue in removing and preparing immediately upon it for our examination which proved the largest and most satisfactory of any we have yet had, it was planned that Henry should stay at home and let me rest a little. But this was not to be done. [Held in December 1830, it was the third general examination of the schools. Invitations had been sent out to 178 men and boys, and 92 girls, but about one thousand additional Maori, all armed, but peaceful, came as spectators.]

When Mrs Hobbs and her children left us, which was not till after Christmas Day, in consequence of the unsettled state of the natives who were fighting in the neighbourhood of Hokianga, Henry accompanied them as far as Kerikeri on his way to the quarterly committee held earlier than usual previous to Mr Yate's sailing in the *Active* in search of Mrs Charles Davis.

195

8 February 1831. The Captain, of the *Leydes*, is returned after a month's cruise, to take up his passengers for Tongataboo, who are to-day expected from Hokianga where they have been all visiting. Our good neighbours have, however, determined that the three couples are to be received at the houses of Messrs Chapman, Brown and Fairburn. . . . Henry was quite unsuccessful in his embassy [he had gone off to the Hokianga]. They were I believe well received at the first pa or fortified place, but met Mr Shepherd and Mr Baker returning from that to this opposite party, where their lives had been providentially spared, for the natives had fired upon them on their approach, calling out, 'Do not spare the white people', and would not listen to anything like peace.

Thus it was not all imaginary distress I experienced the previous Tuesday in preparing the provisions for Henry's departure in the midst of the natives, persuading him not to go, Tohitapu urging that no native chief would go, his wives saying 'I only half loved my husband' or 'I should go to die with him', and the girls telling me this was his last journey.

This day he did give up going, and if he had not done so would have been with Messrs Shepherd and Baker, and he and Mr Fairburn [would] have been two more to be shot at, and Henry you know presents a broad front. Ever since his rashness in landing alone amidst the firing of the contending parties at Kororareka, we have been more anxious when he steps forward. All these various matters have been a trial to me, and whenever excitements arise indisposition and bad nights have been my lot.

Wednesday, 9 February 1831. This morning Jane had been unwell since five o'clock. She was busy folding up her week's wash and putting all things away, when in came Mr Clarke, Mr Davis, Mr Brown, etc., on a committee. Mrs Brown came very appropriately and staid all morning to help Jane, and I came away to assemble the morning school in our front sitting room, which is not yet painted and furnished.

Just as we all assembled Henry came in to turn us out for the committee to meet here. I, however, persuaded him to assemble in the back room. I went on regularly with school, after which I fetched dinner over here. William took his children to Mrs Chapman's, who lives in William's old rush cottage, leaving me only Mr King to entertain.

Before four o'clock Mrs Brown called me out to tell me my sister had a fine boy and to beg I would keep all the girls longer than usual. Mrs Brown came to help me to make tea for the committee, and I had all the gentlemen. It was not till after I had given the children their tea, and sent Mary and Jane home, that I could go and see my sweet little nephew. Mr Hobbs is arrived with his brethren, the Wesleyan missionaries for Tongataboo, and I must go and make up his bed.

Henry

17 February 1831. Paihia. In my last expedition inland a short time since, I got so completely soddened with the rain and flood, that an ugly place broke out on my leg which I am obliged to nurse.

Friday, 25 February 1831. Yesterday afternoon I had to run in a great hurry to fetch Mrs Mair and despatch a message for Mrs Davis and William, and before the latter was at hand the little squeaker gave notice of her arrival in good health. [This was the birth of Catherine, Marianne and Henry's eighth child.]

While I was sitting on watch, who should enter but Aunt Jane with her son in her arms, who is sixteen days old. Mr and Mrs Brown have taken charge of Leonard and Sarah during this interval.

The last time I was out we had to swim a good part of the way home and I am now laid up with an unpleasant leg. We had all much to do to keep from serious illness. Travelling here is a serious matter, as we have to foot it over hills and dales, through swamps and rivers, and to sleep how we can, that is, to run the chance of wet and dry, for we always carry a tent and have a clean carpet of fern tops, though it may be wet. We are getting into the way of using horses, which will greatly relieve our legs. We have thought seriously of a settlement about the river Thames. There are vast numbers of natives there in proportion to this neighbourhood.

William

25 February 1831. Paihia. I herewith announce the arrival of Thomas Sydney Williams in New Zealand. He came on the ninth of this month and has ever since been actively employed in eating, sleeping and growing fat.

Our dear friend Mr Marsden would I think have no objection to end his days in New Zealand. He says on his return to Port Jackson, 'New Zealand is the land of Goshen, but I am now returned to the darkest part of the land of Egypt.'

Henry

26 February 1831. Marianne and her little one are doing well. Little Miss gives a squawk now and then, as significant of her not being satisfied. We think of her being called after Aunt Kate. It really makes my hair stand up when I think of our prodigious families. Our good friends in Salisbury Square may well hang the lip at such a generation pending, the natives are not sparing in their remarks and tell us we shall soon take the land.

Monday, 28 February 1831. Respecting my eldest boy: some good while ago it was our desire that he should have the advantage of going to England, and be put as apprentice to a surgeon. The expense of a passage home by a whaler is not much. But it is of great moment to ensure a good opportunity. We do not attempt to think of his being a minister at his tender age. Yet, were he to be educated, as a surgeon, he would always be a useful member of the Society; and should it please the Lord to call him to His work, there would be no loss of time and expense.

William is busy erecting a stone building, which will be a very good one when finished. The children are all in good health, and attending close to school.

At our last examination we were at a loss for some prizes for the girls. Mr Yate has furnished us hitherto from the bounty of his friends. If you could send something of the gown kind, it would be a great assistance, something rather gay and a washing material, large size, or some neat handkerchiefs, good size, and quality, to wear as shawls, a few aprons of good print, gay colours. The schools have gone on well, and deserve patronage. Few females stand exposed, as these.

2 March 1831. Jane's boy was born February 9th, and our girl on the 24th. Mrs Brown expects confinement before midwinter. They will not leave Paihia till after that I think, even if our provoking majority of the New Zealand committee drag them up to Kerikeri.

Thursday, 3 March 1831. The mercies that have been vouchsafed to us are manifold. Little Catherine will be a week old at two o'clock this afternoon; and I am through infinite mercy as strong as I was last time at the end of the month, having been spared any repetition of what then brought me to the lowest ebb.

Perhaps it has been a useful and necessary lesson for me to have gone through the previous expectation and preparation; and certainly I never enjoy as sweet and more tranquil reliance upon the Saviour than when awaiting His will concerning me during the previous hours of illness, when from choice I was principally alone. My eyes are weaker than my head; or I wished to tell you how much our oldest boy has occupied my thoughts during my confinement. It is my fervent prayer that the Lord may go with him, or suffer him not to go.

Henry

3 May 1831. This is now the third day of rain; and I feel tired of out and indoor duty. Our gales of wind are somewhat singular here. They generally commence with very fine weather, calm. The wind springs up from the northward, and gradually thickens sometimes two or three days before it affects us on shore. Then comes the rain, and lasts for three more days.

We then come forth like Noah from the ark, and enter with fresh vigour on our respective employments. The wind in any degree, east or north, or south, brings dirty weather. We are now better prepared for enduring these perplexing seasons since we have entered our dwelling.

Last winter we had to paddle about like ducks, between house and house with one or two children clinging to the back. But now we are more civilized, and have only to amuse the little ones, and separate them when they become too noisy. But this is no easy matter when there are eleven in our house and we have no servant to whom we can entrust any one of them. But upon the whole they behave very well. Our little ones appear to possess very fine abilities and are fond of school.

We heard from poor old Mr Marsden the other day. He writes under great depression of spirits, and says he should like to lay his bones amongst us. The colony is in a dreadful state and he has lost a good deal of money by lending to one and another, principally amongst his brethren the clergy. His own son has gambled and his son-in-law is over head and ears in debt.

We have recently had a visit from three Wesleyan missionaries and their wives on their way to Tonga. One of them was a printer and had a press with him of considerable value. We have made application from time to time, and have been very considerably delayed for want of a press. But these men carry with them the means for immediate work. Perhaps these men are more clever.

Your blankets for Tohitapu have not arrived. He is a very important person in his way, though our good folks generally cannot manage him.

28 July 1831. Occupied fishing.

31 August 1831. Captain Deans arrived on the 18th and brought two letters from you to me. We were happy to hear that all were well. As our good Mother is now advancing towards the close of life, our thoughts are more particularly directed to her.

About three weeks since I was at Aruru, which is to the North of Whangaroa. It is an important station in a missionary view, and all were particularly importunate that someone might live with them; and they would gladly have received Edward, who was with me at the time. I intend to bring their case forward at our meeting.

But within this last week we have had an application from another quarter, from Rotorua, to the southward of Tauranga in the Bay of Plenty. We have had considerable connection with these people. Many lads have been living with us. They have therefore seen the advantage both spiritual and temporal of our residing amongst them.

We feel it a call demanding our attention, and it is probable that William and I may take a run down there to have an interview with the people in our little cutter (*Karere*) previous to the general meeting of the natives in the summer at Tauranga, as all will then be under arms, either to fight or make peace.

[Three years before, in 1828,] Pango, a chief from Rotorua, was paying a friendly visit at the Bay of Islands. During his stay, mysterious reports were circulated, threatening his safety. It was hinted that Pango by witchcraft had directed the course of balls by which Hongi Hika and Whareumu had fallen. Pango, with several of his followers, applied for a passage by the *Herald*; but she was undergoing repair, and could not quickly be ready for sea. Happily, there was another vessel [*Haweis*] in the bay about to sail to the southward, and in her they made their escape under cover of night. The rest of the party were shortly afterwards conveyed in the *Herald*.

Tohitapu came to Paihia, and inquired if Pango had gone on board by the sanction of the missionaries, and being told it was so, he said it was very wrong. He declared he could not eat unless he were to kill someone, and that, as he was restrained by the missionaries, he must die.

The next morning he again went to Paihia, and holding up a hatchet in his hand said, 'Sixteen persons have been sent by this to the shades below, and unless I can kill and eat some one I shall have no rest.' I reasoned with him on his madness and wickedness and how greatly Satan desired to have him. After some little time he cast away the deadly instrument, saying he would use it no more.

9, 10 September 1831. At work at Mr Brown's house. It may be considered by some to be out of place thus to be toiling at bricks and mortar, etc., but be it remembered that family men here have a great weight and responsibility to endure: they are dependent upon one another; and as they constantly require the assistance of their neighbours, so they must give in return; thus are we, therefore, without distinction, required to assist ourselves, and all who may stand in need; and I trust that our children and grandchildren will behold, the years to come, with pleasure and admiration, those exquisite pieces of work which their forefathers accomplished in the infant state of things in this land.

3 October 1831. Paihia. . . . Last night I heard nothing but the infant school; this morning, nothing but the French man-of-war, now working into the bay.

La Favourite, *commanded by Captain Laplace, was a French discovery vessel. Much excitement was caused by the expectation of this visit because of the rumour that the French were planning to annex New Zealand. The news was alarming enough to cause the New South Wales Government to order Captain de Saumarez of the ship* Zebra *to investigate, and, if he found the French to have taken possession, to lodge a protest on the grounds of prior possession by Britain. When he arrived, he found that Laplace had stayed only for a few days to rest his crew.*

David Taiwanga came running in to tell me that the ship was now come, about which we had heard so much by our own vessel, and from Rewa, who had visited New South Wales – that they were the enemies of King William, come to spy out the land, and had four hundred men on board; that, as Mr Williams was at the Kerikeri at the Committee, I must give him the flag of our nation to hoist upon the flagstaff on the hill. I told him the line was broken, which was the reason no flag had been hoisted for several Sundays. Oh! He would send a boy up; would I not give him a rope? I should have it again in a few days. Did I not wish to shew the flag of my country? Then, if they tore it down, Mr Williams would write to the rulers of our land to fight for us. Of course I had a great heart to unfold the banner of my country, for which David (pronounced Rawiri) gave me full credit when I gave him my new clothesline for the purpose. . . .

I should like to give you an account of the French captain and two of his lieutenants coming on shore to tea with us. Our room presented quite a new picture, in the various characters and features that presented themselves. An interesting English boy, about twelve years of age, who is going home from the Derwent [a river in Tasmania] to be educated, accompanied them.

Little John crept in, and edged close up to him with playful delight. Rawiri went down upon his knees at the tea-table, and put in his dark, expressive, good-humoured countenance between the two children; which the French captain observing, shrugged up his shoulders, exclaiming, at a view of his countenance, 'Diable' [Devil].

The foreigners were very polite; the contempt they express of these people, and the New Zealanders' dread of them, is quite amusing. The conversation was in English, with a strong French accent, and a little French. They had read Captain Dillon's book, and all his abuse of us, which they seemed to treat with its merited contempt. Henry dined on board.

*The captain also informed Marianne that he was to have
brought out, by direction of the French Government, a Roman
Catholic bishop to New Zealand; but that the revolution in
Paris had caused the abandonment of their plans. In November
1831, a petition by several chiefs was sent to King William IV,
by way of the Colonial Secretary of New South Wales. It asked
that the King should become the 'friend and guardian of these
Islands' to protect them from the unscrupulous Europeans and
from the 'tribe of Marion' – i.e. the French, who were so called
after the visit in 1772 of Marion du Fresne, which resulted in
disastrous consequences for both Maori and French.*

Henry

1 October 1831. Employed in the garden. The providing vegetables an
important consideration. But two potatoes each the allowance. Titore [a chief
of Waimate] came over to speak upon the projected letter to the King. Engaged
two hours and a half with him and his friends, talking upon the state of affairs.
He approves of our going to Maketu [Bay of Plenty] to speak to natives in that
quarter. He appears well disposed.

HENRY MISSING

21 November 1831. Paihia. Now that joy and gladness have
succeeded, anxiety the most distressing, and grief the most poignant
I ever endured, I wish, before the vivid scenes of the last fortnight
fade, to picture some of them to you. To look back, it seems like a
dream or a romance, the incidents have been so many, and the
feelings have been wrought up to such extremes.

If you have received a letter from me, by the French man-of-war,
about a month ago, you will know that Henry was purposing a visit
down to the southward. He did sail in the little cutter *Karere*,
accompanied by Mr Chapman, and several of our most valuable
natives, all husbands, and most of them fathers, on an expedition of
twofold interest, the preparatory steps towards establishing a
Mission amongst an enquiring and seeking people, and the making
peace between them and the people around us, called Ngapuhi.

They sailed October 18. Three weeks, Henry said, would be the full time of his absence, and as he came home from Tauranga, the last time he went in the *Herald*, at the end of a fortnight, my mind, unhappily for me, was prepared for a fortnight.

On the day three weeks, the day that Henry was to have returned, I sat up with Mrs Fairburn; at one o'clock, to oblige her, I laid down to take a nap, and as I was dozing off she told me she thought she heard the bugle horn, and then a distant gun: effectual medicine this, to cause sleep; but I told her, I was becoming acquainted with the noises, and had been several times out in the garden to listen in vain.

Many were the nights that succeeded this; many suppositions; fair winds, that I was told would bring them home in thirty-six hours; foul winds succeeding fair, and foul, and fair again. Friends would find me out, and come to see me, and blame me because I could not look happy. I fatigued myself all day, doing anything and everything, that I might not sit still and think, and at night my baby kept me awake.

A month and two days had elapsed on Thursday, November 17. I had been living upon hope, and two days fair wind, after a strong adverse gale; everybody told me to expect my husband this afternoon. The *Active* was to sail in the morning, as the wind and my hopes died away altogether, I searched some boxes, to provide a supply of linen for Henry and Mr Chapman, to go in the *Active*. Everything reminded me of her unsuccessful search for the *Haweis*. Mr Fairburn called upon me, and told me to hope even against hope; it was indeed, as Mr Fairburn afterwards remarked, man's extremity, and God's opportunity.

After dinner, Jane came in with the glass, saying, it was better to look at something, even if it were nothing, and there was a dark spec upon the water. I accompanied her into the front room. It was too large for a boat, but had no topmast, and was certainly not the *Karere*. Scarcely had she left, when a little boy burst in, out of breath, exclaiming: 'Mata!! Mata!! Te Wiremu!! Te Wiremu!!'

Henry was known by the Maori as Te Wiremu, *which means* 'Williams', *and* Karu Wha, *meaning* 'Four Eyes', *because of his round spectacles.*

'Where, where?' I almost screamed, 'I dare not believe you; call my sister to hear!' As the boy repeated, 'It is indeed, I saw him round the point; Matthew is with him, coming overland from Whangaruru.'

There was a shout, to confirm the story of this little breathless harbinger. Jane ran down to the beach, where the crew of the man-of-war stood all astonishment staring at her, and listening to the shouts, as people appeared coming round the point. She saw someone coming, and asked him to question some of the boys for her, and ascertain the truth of the report; but he, on her telling him, ran away from her, and back as fast as he could to Mr Brown's, to carry the news, and left her standing at the gate.

I, trembling, strained my eyes and ears at the front-window till I DID see my husband; his children all came flocking in after him. The instantaneously spread intelligence had broken up all schools, and all was wild New Zealand delight, and trembling English gratitude!!!

And now, my dear mother, for I write all these particulars only to a mother, and one who likes as dearly as I do to hear all the *hows* and *whens* – you must imagine a great deal; how baby sprang out of my arms into her father's; how the little children clung round his knees, and the bigger ones expressed their joy; how afraid I was that I should wake, and find it a dream; how at length we found out it was three o'clock, and Henry had been travelling ever since eleven o'clock the preceding night, and had taken no refreshment during that time, but a cup of chocolate.

How happy all were to wait upon him, and to hear the news. We learnt that he had been fifteen days at sea, struggling with strong adverse gales; that on one occasion, the very night I sat up with Mrs Fairburn, they were out of sight of land, without chart or quadrant, and very little water on board; or they had, when the wind was fair, so little that, setting every stitch of sail, they could scarcely creep on.

They attempted to get round Cape Brett the previous afternoon, and expected to have been with us at sunset; but there was such a tremendous swell that she dipped her bowsprit in the water, and, fearing to carry something away, Henry thought it better to put back into Whangaruru, leave the *Karere* there, and come overland, and get a canoe down the river.

Henry looked jaded, as well he might, he had not had his clothes off, except once, for fifteen nights, and had stood at the helm ten hours at a stretch. Mr Chapman was passed forward as soon as possible, in a boat to Kerikeri, to his distressed wife; he looked wretchedly ill, and had been very ill, quite laid aside on board.

December 1831. Paihia. I shall endeavour to give you as many particulars as the few days previous to the *Thetis* sailing for England will allow, just upon the eve of Henry's second, longer and more important voyage in his own boat, amidst the fleet of warriors who have at length been induced to listen to the voice of peace, to lay aside their murderous intentions, and be even willing, nay, request the Missionaries to go with them as mediators, to bring about a peace, instead of carrying death and destruction, and going for the purpose of annihilating a whole people – the very people from whom Henry and Mr Chapman had lately received so flattering a reception.

If I could entirely lay self aside, and all the trials which this anxious and eventful period have occasioned, I could only rejoice that Henry has not so long wrestled and struggled and preached and persuaded in vain. Never was a more remarkable answer seen to the prayers of our little church than the change in this people within one month, from a resolute determination to pursue their own wicked intentions to a willingness to take advice; even requesting that the schooner and the little cutter may go down, and that Henry should accompany them in his open boat.

The vessel going is an inexpressible comfort to me, for the *Active* will carry supplies, and meet with them wherever she can anchor, while the fleet of canoes are creeping down the coast. The *Karere* will be sent back to bring us news, and convey intelligence from us, thus breaking that total separation which renders absence so painful in this land, so postless and trying.

We all hope she will not again be fifteen days accomplishing a voyage of three. We try to hope everything – that is, Mrs Fairburn and myself; for it was not till last night we heard Mr Kemp had offered to go in the *Active*, setting Mr Fairburn at liberty to accompany Henry in the boat. Every hour may bring a summons to move. Tomorrow was intended, but our preparations are urged forward or retarded as news arrives from the armament assembled at Kororareka.

The features of the whole affair wear an infinitely brighter appearance as it advances, and my dreads and terrors are lessening every day; yet still Henry was away nearly five weeks, was delayed and buffeted about by foul winds, till I for one had feared the worst, and is now about to leave his family for several months on a fatiguing, if not a hazardous expedition.

1832

DEATH OF HENRY'S MOTHER

11 July 1832. Paihia. Henry's expeditions to Tauranga have occupied nearly the whole summer. On the last occasion he narrowly escaped shipwreck on some frightful rocks. It was the 8th of April. The manner in which the missionaries were received and listened to, by all as messengers of peace, the earnest desire expressed by people to the Southward on all occasions for Missionaries was most gratifying.

They entered camp or fort unmolested, and Henry spent several days alone in a savage camp, before the *Active* joined him.

All the following letters written by Marianne are to Henry's sister, Lydia Marsh. She and her husband, the Revd Edward Garrard Marsh, became the main Williams link and correspondents in England.

11 July 1832. Paihia. You must have lived in a far distant country to understand the craving which is felt for letters as the only means of intercourse and the nervous excitement which it occasions. We hail the approach of letters with the earnest prayer to be staid in joy and supported in sorrow.

And we have lately needed this support for an incidental mention in a stray letter from Maria Nelson [relation of Jane's] tells us of the death of our dear Mother [Mrs Mary Williams]. All our letters, we suppose, were sent to the Colony, and this came direct. We have the inexpressible happiness of knowing that we could hear nothing but what would give consolation to the Christian, and as our earthly ties loosen, we may frequently hope heavenly desires may grow and strengthen.

I believe neither Jane nor I loved our own mothers better. She dwells with delight upon her residence at Southwell, and I turn with equal pleasure to the long intercourse in childhood at Nottingham, and here I cannot dress a child or open a drawer without being reminded of her considerate attention to our wants, or converse upon any passing event but her letters, and something she has said, or would say, is brought to mind.

She was a constant correspondent, though her letters generally came long after date, and two or three together. Your dear husband [Revd Edward Marsh] is now the only one to whom we look for regular communication.

24 September 1832. Paihia. I wish I could just picture to you a most interesting scene, the baptism of Catherine Wokaweho, in our sitting room when 14 natives were present. This girl who is related to several principal chiefs has been with us eleven months; she came petitioning to be allowed to die here, and to have food for her body and her soul. She revived and we once hoped would recover, but now seems fast sinking.

Eight years ago Catherine enticed a younger sister out of our house and led her into sin, now she is the instructress of that very sister who lives with us. They were both daughters of an old blind chief whom Henry and Mr Fairburn used to visit every Sunday at Waitangi.

But this sick girl has led me away from the subject which is now nearest my heart, our eldest boy. Perhaps when you receive this, dear Edward may be on your shores. It has been a subject of anxious prayer for Divine direction.

I have very much before me in the next two months to set Henry off to the southward, hoping that he may return in time to arrange for his boy. I almost hoped that, in the peculiar situation of our family, Henry might on this occasion be excused, but all say he is indispensable. I must submit if duty calls. Edward is much favoured; he has a kind uncle here who instructs him in the holidays as well as in school, and if he goes to England, he has another equally kind, nay more than one in the neighbourhood of London.

There is a talk about dividing the strength of Henry and William, sending one to the southward, sweeping away the English girls' school, and if an insurmountable obstacle, the boys' also. . . .

Thank you again and again for your letter, I received more this year than on any former year.

1833

BUSBY AS BRITISH RESIDENT

On 5 May 1833, James Busby arrived at the Bay of Islands as the first British Resident Agent in New Zealand. His appointment came from England and he was sent across from Sydney with clear instructions to 'apprehend escaped convicts, encourage trade, assist settlers, keep on good terms with the missionaries and Maoris, and to urge the chiefs to keep law and order'. He arrived with no magisterial powers nor an armed force to fulfil his task, and became known as the 'Man-o'-War without Guns'.

His arrival was unexpected and on 17 May the residents of Paihia held a delayed welcoming ceremony, beginning with a seven-gun salute. On landing, the Maori set up a haka, brandishing their muskets on the beach before delivering their welcoming speeches. When he had been appointed, he was not provided with a house or land, but was allowed enough material to erect two rooms and was 'accredited' to the missionaries. Mr Busby stayed with Henry and Marianne for some time before building his home, now called the Treaty House, on his newly acquired farm at Waitangi. He was a keen winemaker, having studied viticulture in France as a young man. His daughter Sarah later married Marianne and Henry's son John.

Henry
Sunday, 14 July 1833. Paihia. Alas! Poor Tohitapu is no more; not long since, he was brought from the interior very ill, and remained at the place above a month, when he died. He expressed for some days a desire for religious

211

conversation and instruction; but finding that he did not gain strength, but rather grew worse, he requested that no one should speak to him on these subjects. His old superstition was too strong, though he did not submit to be karakia'd [to perform a religious rite; to worship] previous to dissolution. This last rite may be considered as 'extreme unction', and he died in comparative silence for so great a man.

He was at last taken away to some snug retreat, and the last I heard of him was that the dogs had found him, and eaten a good portion of the flesh off his bones. Thus died and was buried the renowned Tohitapu, in total ignorance of a Redeemer's love. Often have I spoken to him and others, but it universally brought on a sleepy fit.

23 September 1833. Paihia. The great question of the future prospects of our children has occupied a good deal of our thoughts. We feel that it is impossible to look to the Society, and therefore must use our utmost efforts to ensure them meat and drink; and as I know not how soon I must depart hence, I have been looking at a piece of land belonging to our friend Te Morenga of Taiamai, which will most probably form the basis of a 'Family Estate' for my children, and a township for the natives.

It is situated in a populous district, and I hope that, while it may afford a home for my young ones in time of need, it will also afford a light in the wilderness to the inhabitants around. They have been long desiring that a Missionary should reside amongst them, but this could not be done. We have therefore nominated a Missionary's son [Edward]. The natives appear well pleased and so also am I. I returned from viewing the place on Friday last.

After all that preliminary matter you may be a little surprised when I tell you that we have made up our minds to send Edward to England, and we have heard that Captain King, a southern whaler, a man of considerable respectability, may be in the Bay in two months for England.

1834

BUSBY ATTACKED

Jane

1 January 1834. Paihia. A brig came into the bay yesterday afternoon, and the captain offered to take charge of letters for England, but added that he intended sailing early this morning. Fortunately for us a heavy gale of wind came on which has detained him at anchor, and, though the weather is now fast clearing and it is 5 p.m., I hope I shall have time to give you some little portion of NZ news.

Henry returned from the southward, on the 4th of last month, having made choice of a favourable situation for a missionary station and set the natives to work to erect the raupo dwellings. Immediately on his return, Captain Clendon's schooner the *Fortitude* was taken up for the double purpose of conveying the necessary stores to the new station of Puriri, and of visiting the East Cape to restore some Ngatiporo natives to their families.

Mr and Mrs Preece and Mrs Morgan [Marianne's sister Maria] went to Puriri. Mr Yate and William accompanied them, and William intended to go to Tauranga while the vessel discharged her cargo at Puriri before proceeding to the East Cape.

Henry is now absent at Whangaroa, whither he is gone to render some assistance to the captain of the *Buffalo*. It is not improbable that Edward may be sent by that ship. Mr Yate also talks of taking advantage of that opportunity, and as he appears to take great interest in Edward, it would be very desirable to send him under such protection.

Edwin Fairburn

The missionary William Fairburn's youngest son, Edwin, recalled his memories of the first game of cricket played in New Zealand on the Paihia beach during the summer of 1833–4, when he was about six years old.

Mr William Williams had sent home for cricket balls and bats and there was a great excitement about the new game to be played. I know I thought it had some connection with green insects with long legs which my sister had told me were 'crickets'.

So one bright calm afternoon about 2 p.m., the whole settlement of Paihia, men, women and children, also the inhabitants from all round the Bay, went to the northern end of Horotutu Beach.

It wasn't a match of eleven each side but of forty or fifty at least. All the church mission school boys were there; the establishment at that time was at Paihia, a year or two afterwards it was removed to Waimate.

I was allowed to join in, but they drew the line at me and John Williams, who was just three weeks my elder. I remember when my turn came Mr William Williams, who bowled to me, saying, 'we must not be too hard on the youngsters' – delivered me a very nice ball, which I hit over the bank, about eleven yards off, on to the beach, where it rolled down some distance on to the sand, and I got a run, at which our side applauded, while the other side grumbled and called out for short work to be made of me. The ball was thrown up to the opposite end bowler, who straightaway bowled me out, but I got a run in the first game of cricket played in New Zealand.

I may observe here that there were no 'overs' in bowling at cricket in those days but the ball was generally thrown up to the bowler nearest the fielder, or to whichever end the fielder chose – also the fielders pleased themselves as to the positions they took in fielding and things were generally carried out in a very independent manner all round.

30 April 1834. Paihia. On Monday Henry went to his farm at the Waimate intending to be absent two nights, and I was beginning to expect the return of the *Fortitude* from the southward with William and our boy Edward, who had been with Mr and Mrs Fairburn and Mr and Mrs Colenso and their children to their new station. It was a fine calm night.

About two in the morning I was roused by a call at the window. It was a summons to Mrs Busby. In the absence of William, the surgeon of the *Eliza Francis* was sent for. Mr Chapman conducted me in the boat and I left Marianne in charge. All went on well, and at 10 o'clock Mrs Busby was safely delivered of a son.

I stayed all day, trying in vain to get a messenger to hurry Henry home to his bairns, and I took late watch at night in order to allow Mr Busby and their maid a night's rest that they might be fresh when I was gone.

On Wednesday afternoon Henry fetched me home. That very night we were roused by an Englishman calling at the window to say that Mr Busby's store had been attacked; the window was smashed, the manservants' apartment broken into and stripped, muskets fired, Mr Busby aimed at, and he was come to call Mr Williams and the doctor.

Henry hastily dressed and obeyed the summons, and with his permission I did the same, fearing the effects of the fright on Mrs Busby.

It was a beautiful quiet night, and the boat glided over the bay as over the still waters of a lake. I thought of the tremendous storm and hurricane, which one month previous would have made all communication with Mr Busby for several days totally impossible and felt how beautifully times and seasons were ordered, perhaps Mrs Busby's affair being over before this fright may have saved her life.

We found the attack had been worse that we imagined; poor Mrs Busby was greatly agitated, but no alarming symptoms, and happily she was ignorant that her husband had been fired at and narrowly escaped being killed, the ball which passed close by his head lodged in a door post, and his cheek grazed by a splinter.

The store is a detached building with the servants' apartments; native or Englishmen, it is a very black affair. All the chiefs are greatly roused and express themselves well, but the depredators are not yet brought to light.

Our arrival seemed to have given great comfort and composed matters and our natives had made no noise. Boats came from 3 ships with armed sailors, and Henry and Mr Chapman had to persuade them to return. Mr Chapman accompanied them in his boat.

He said afterwards it was quite a romantic moonlight scene, the boats and the sailors in groups on the beach priming and loading and urging each other to bravery.

Jane came the next day in Mr Mair's boat and I went home. They had a false alarm, though Henry was there with his boat's crew to keep watch at night and let the agitated sleep.

Last night Te Koki arrived from Whangaroa and staid with them. This great chief takes the matter up well.

I must return to my preparations for my dear boy. Mr Yate has taken by the *Buffalo* to be ready at the end of June. Such an opportunity for Edward could only occur once in his life. Perhaps it is well I have no room to touch upon this all engrossing subject. Oh may the Lord guide him, keep him, call him, and use him in His service.

Henry

20 June 1834. Paihia. The time is fast advancing when I must close my scribbling. Two more days, and our boy [Edward] leaves us. But how thankful I feel that he is not 'going to fight the French upon the sea'. I would rather follow them one by one to the grave than expose them to the severe trials and temptations of a sailor's life, especially on board a man-of-war.

Jane

June 1834. The general stir throughout the island and the want of volunteers for distant service, together with the anxiety felt by both Henry and William that those distant tribes should have the gospel preached to them, has led me for many months to consider our separation as probable – consequently I was somewhat prepared for what has been to Marianne a great shock and will be a trial to both of us.

I must leave my two eldest children behind – and the other two must come as soon as they are old enough for school, as the duties of a new station will quite preclude the possibility of our attending properly to their education. This separation from my children will be the greatest sacrifice I have been called on to make. May it be made in the true spirit of love to Him with whom neither brethren nor sisters nor children may be brought into competition.

I dread these approaching trials more than I did leaving England nine years ago, but perhaps that may be because I know better what it is to be separated from those we love, besides which there will be no kind brothers and sisters to receive us at Waiapu with open arms.

Henry

1 December 1834. Paihia. . . . I am happy in the expectation that the children may soon be beyond the reach of want, humanly speaking, as I have been enabled to procure for the benefit of the children a good piece of land as a farm, upon which I have put some stock, which seem in a thriving way. This method we have adopted rather than suffer them to fall upon the hands of the Society.

We had the means, and felt it needful to avail ourselves of it. And as the lad [Edward, who had been sent to England to obtain a degree in Medicine] in all probability will be called upon to exercise his abilities in the management of a farm in its various parts, should he not be a fit person to join the Mission, perhaps the knowledge of this would be most beneficial to him, should our first idea be beyond reach. However, let the worst come to the worst, I consider it will be money well spent, were he to return in a year or two, as it was needful to give him some idea that the world is not confined to the shores of New Zealand.

1835

TE WAIMATE

Henry

12 May 1835. I am glad you approve of my purchase of a piece of land for the children. I think also that you would be pleased with its situation. The stock upon it is doing very well, and in a little time we hope to have butter, cheese, poultry, eggs, etc.

Jane

29 May 1835. Waimate. Our transplantation to this rural place took place a fortnight ago in the interval between tremendous rains which almost deluged us for three weeks, and, having only just recovered from a rather severe though short illness, I have reason to be very thankful for being permitted to establish myself in my new domicile (which is a very airy one) without taking cold.

We bade adieu to the dear inhabitants of Paihia which had been our happy home for nine years with some feelings of regret you may be sure, but when I remember what our destination was to have been, and the distance which would have separated us from our children and other dear relatives, I feel that I can hardly consider it a separation to be placed within less than half a day's journey, opposed to which Mr and Mrs Hamlin, who are appointed to Waikato in our stead, will have 9 or 10 days travelling after quitting the ship and many privations to endure.

Both Mr and Mrs Hamlin are valuable characters, indefatigable missionaries with an excellent knowledge of the language; he will I am sure supply William's place well, while she will more than supply mine, and I trust they will be honoured as the means of effecting much good in that dark region.

The place (Waimate) is in many respects most interesting. There are many Christians in the neighbouring [Maori] villages, with above 50 of whom we were privileged to commemorate the Supper of our Lord on Sunday last.

This *will be* a capital house, but it is not likely to be finished for many months. An effort is being made to make the lower rooms habitable, which will we hope enable us to receive all the older boys, by the middle of July. We have got a respectable Irish couple attached to our household, but whether the wife will prove an efficient assistant remains to be seen; she appears very clean and well disposed.

My two neighbours here are very kind and attentive, Mr Clarke especially, but I miss Marianne greatly and Maria Coldham [Marianne's sister] almost equally so. She is a dear kind hearted creature, who would go through fire and water to serve those she loves.

30 October 1835. It is nearly six months since we left Paihia and removed to this place, but only as many weeks have elapsed since the boys assembled and William began school in earnest. Our family amounts to twenty-one, but in the fatiguing parts of my occupations I am greatly relieved by an Irishman and his wife, who with their two children form a part of our household though they inhabit a small adjoining cottage.

CHARLES DARWIN VISITS THE BAY AND WAIMATE

The following is an extract from Darwin's Journal of a Voyage Round the World, 1831–1836, *describing Charles Darwin's visit to the Bay of Islands, New Zealand. It had taken the HMS* Beagle *just over three weeks to cross the Pacific Ocean after leaving Tahiti. Darwin was the naturalist aboard the* Beagle, *which had been sent by the British Admiralty on a surveying expedition around the world. The voyage took five years in all, in which time they also visited South America, the Galapagos Islands and Australia. They were now on their homeward bound leg and Darwin was nearly twenty-six years old. Aboard was Captain FitzRoy, who would later return to New Zealand in 1843 as Governor FitzRoy.*

Charles Darwin

19 December 1835. In the evening we saw in the distance New Zealand. We may now consider that we have nearly crossed the Pacific. It is necessary to sail over this great ocean to comprehend its immensity.

21 December 1835. Early in the morning we entered the Bay of Islands, and, being becalmed for some hours near the mouth, we did not reach the anchorage till the middle of the day. Only a single canoe came alongside. This, and the aspect of the whole scene, afforded a remarkable and not very pleasing contrast with our joyful and boisterous welcome at Tahiti.

In the afternoon we went on shore to one of the larger groups of houses, which yet hardly deserves the title of a village. Its name is Pahia [Paihia]: it is the residence of the missionaries; and there are no native residents except servants and labourers.

In the vicinity of the Bay of Islands, the number of Englishmen, including their families, amounts to between two and three hundred. All the cottages, many of which are whitewashed and look very neat, are the property of the English. The hovels of the natives are so diminutive and paltry that they can scarcely be perceived from a distance.

At Pahia it was quite pleasing to behold the English flowers in the gardens before the houses; there were roses of several kinds, honeysuckle, jasmine, stocks and whole hedges of sweetbriar.

22 December 1835. In the morning I went out walking; but I soon found that the country was very impracticable. All the hills are thickly covered with tall fern, together with a low bush which grows like a cypress; and very little ground has been cleared or cultivated.

I then tried the sea-beach; but proceeding towards either hand, my walk was soon stopped by salt-water creeks and deep brooks. The communication between the inhabitants of the different parts of the bay, is (as in Chile) almost entirely kept up by boats. I was surprised to find that almost every hill which I ascended had been at some former time more or less fortified. The summits were cut into steps or successive terraces, and frequently they had been protected by deep trenches. I afterwards observed that the principal hills inland in like manner showed an artificial outline.

These are the pas, so frequently mentioned by Captain Cook under the name of 'hippah'; the difference of sound being owing to the prefixed article.

That the pas had formerly been much used was evident from the piles of shells, and the pits in which, as I was informed, sweet potatoes used to be kept as a reserve. As there was no water on these hills, the defenders could never have anticipated a long siege, but only a hurried attack for plunder, against which the successive terraces would have afforded good protection.

The general introduction of firearms has changed the whole system of warfare; and an exposed situation on the top of a hill is now worse than useless. The pas in consequence are, at the present day, always built on a level piece of ground. They consist of a double stockade of thick and tall posts, placed in a zigzag line, so that every part can be flanked.

Within the stockade a mound of earth is thrown up, behind which the defenders can rest in safety or use their fire-arms over it. On the level of the ground little archways sometimes pass through this breastwork, by which means the defenders can crawl out to the stockade to reconnoitre their enemies.

The Revd W. Williams, who gave me this account, added that in one pa he had noticed spurs or buttresses projecting on the inner and protected side of the mound of earth. On asking the chief the use of them, he replied that, if two or three of his men were shot, their neighbours would not see the bodies, and so be discouraged.

These pas are considered by the New Zealanders as a very perfect means of defence; for the attacking force is never so well disciplined as to rush in a body to the stockade, cut it down and effect their entry. When a tribe goes to war, the chief cannot order one party to go here and another there, but every man fights in the manner which best pleases himself; and for each separate individual to approach a stockade defended by fire-arms must appear certain death.

I should think a more warlike race of inhabitants could not be found in any part of the world than the New Zealanders. Their conduct on first seeing a ship, as described by Captain Cook, strongly illustrates this: the act of throwing volleys of stones at so great and novel an object, and their defiance of 'Come on shore, and we will kill and eat you all', shows uncommon boldness. This warlike spirit is evident in many of their customs, and even in their smallest actions. If a New Zealander is struck, although but in joke, the blow must be returned; and of this I saw an instance with one of our officers.

At the present day, from the progress of civilization, there is much less warfare, except among some of the southern tribes. I heard a characteristic anecdote of what took place some time ago in the south. A missionary found a chief and his tribe in preparation for war – their muskets clean and bright, and their ammunition ready. He reasoned long on the inutility of the war, and the little provocation which had been given for it.

The chief was much shaken in his resolution, and seemed in doubt; but at length it occurred to him that a barrel of his gunpowder was in a bad state, and that it would not keep much longer. This was brought forward as an unanswerable argument for the necessity of immediately declaring war: the idea of allowing so much good gunpowder to spoil was not to be thought of; and this settled the point.

I was told by the missionaries that in the life of Hongi, the chief who visited England, the love of war was the one and lasting spring of every action. The tribe in which he was a principal chief had at one time been much oppressed by another tribe, from the Thames River. A solemn oath was taken by the men, that when their boys should grow up, and they should be powerful enough, they would never forget or forgive these injuries.

To fulfil this oath appears to have been Hongi's chief motive for going to England; and when there it was his sole object. Presents were valued only as they could be converted into arms; of the arts, those alone interested him which were connected with the manufacture of arms.

When at Sydney, Hongi, by a strange coincidence, met the hostile chief of the Thames River at the house of Mr Marsden. Their conduct was civil to each other, but Hongi told him that when again in New Zealand he would never cease to carry war into his country. The challenge was accepted; and Hongi on his return fulfilled the threat to the utmost letter.

The tribe on the Thames River was utterly overthrown, and the chief to whom the challenge had been given was himself killed. Hongi, although harbouring such deep feelings of hatred and revenge, is described as having been a good-natured person.

In the evening I went with Captain FitzRoy and Mr Baker, one of the missionaries, to pay a visit to Kororareka. We wandered about the village, and saw and conversed with many of the people, both men, women and children. Looking at the New Zealander, one naturally compares him with the Tahitian, both belonging to the same family of mankind.

The comparison, however, tells heavily against the New Zealander. He may, perhaps, be superior in energy, but in every other respect his character is of a much lower order. One glance at their respective expressions brings conviction to the mind that one is a savage, the other a civilized man.

Both their persons and houses are filthily dirty and offensive: the idea of washing either their bodies or their clothes never seems to enter their heads.

I saw a chief who was wearing a shirt black and matted with filth; and when asked how it came to be so dirty, he replied, with surprise, 'Do not you see it is an old one?'

Some of the men have shirts, but the common dress is one or two large blankets generally black with dirt, which are thrown over their shoulders in a very inconvenient and awkward fashion. A few of the principal chiefs have decent suits of English clothes; but these are only worn on great occasions.

23 December 1835. At the place called Waimate, about fifteen miles from the Bay of Islands, and midway between the eastern and western coasts, the missionaries have purchased some land for agricultural purposes.

I have been introduced to the Revd W. Williams, who, upon my expressing a wish, invited me to pay him a visit there. Mr Busby, the British Resident, offered to take me in his boat by a creek, where I should see a pretty waterfall, and by which means my walk should be shortened. He likewise procured for me a guide.

Upon asking a neighbouring chief to recommend a man, the chief himself offered to go; but his ignorance of the value of money was so complete that at first he asked how many pounds I would give him, but afterwards was well contented with two dollars. When I showed the chief a very small bundle, which I wanted carried, it became absolutely necessary for him to take a slave.

These feelings of pride are beginning to wear away; but formerly a leading man would sooner have died than undergone the indignity of carrying the smallest burden. My companion was a light active man, dressed in a dirty blanket, and with his face completely tattooed. He had formerly been a great warrior. He appeared to be on very cordial terms with Mr Busby; but at various times they had quarrelled violently.

Some time ago, Mr Busby suffered a far more serious attack. A chief and a party of men tried to break into his house in the middle of the night, and, not finding this so easy, commenced a brisk firing with their muskets. Mr Busby was slightly wounded; but the party was at length driven away. Shortly afterwards it was discovered who was the aggressor; and a general meeting of the chiefs was convened to consider the case.

It was considered by the New Zealanders as very atrocious, inasmuch as it was a night attack, and that Mrs Busby was lying ill in the house – these latter circumstances, much to their honour, being considered in all cases as a protection. The chiefs agreed to confiscate the land of the aggressor to the King of England.

The whole proceeding, however, in this trying and punishing a chief was entirely without precedent. The aggressor, moreover, lost caste in the estimation of his equals; and this was considered by the British as of more consequence than the confiscation of his land.

As the boat was shoving off, a second chief stepped into her, who only wanted the amusement of the passage up and down the creek. I never saw a more horrid and ferocious expression than this man had.

At the point where the boat landed, Mr Busby accompanied me a few hundred yards on the road. I could not help admiring the cool impudence of the hoary old villain, whom we left lying in the boat, when he shouted to Mr Busby, 'Do not you stay long; I shall be tired of waiting here.'

We now commenced our walk. The road lay along a well beaten path, bordered on each side by the tall fern, which covers the whole country. After travelling some miles, we came to a little country village, where a few hovels were collected together, and some patches of ground cultivated with potatoes. The introduction of the potato has been the most essential benefit to the island; it is now much more used than any native vegetable.

New Zealand is favoured by one great natural advantage – namely, that the inhabitants can never perish from famine. The whole country abounds with fern; and the roots of this plant, if not very palatable, yet contain much nutriment. A native can always subsist on these, and on the shell-fish, which are abundant on all parts of the sea-coast.

The villages are chiefly conspicuous by the platforms which are raised on four posts ten or twelve feet above the ground, on which the produce of the fields is kept secure from all accidents. . . . The soil is volcanic; in several parts we passed over slaggy lavas, and craters could clearly be distinguished on several of the neighbouring hills. Although the scenery is nowhere beautiful, and only occasionally pretty, I enjoyed my walk. I should have enjoyed it more if my companion, the chief, had not possessed extraordinary conversational powers.

I knew only three words, 'good', 'bad' and 'yes'; and with these I answered all his remarks, without of course having understood one word he said! This, however, was quite sufficient: I was a good listener, an agreeable person, and he never ceased talking to me.

At length we reached Waimate. After having passed over so many miles of an uninhabited useless country, the sudden appearance of an English farm-house and its welldressed fields, placed there as if by an enchanter's wand, was exceedingly pleasant. Mr Williams not being at home, I received in Mr Davies's house a cordial welcome.

After drinking tea with his family party, we took a stroll about the farm. At Waimate there are three large houses, where the missionary gentlemen, Messrs Williams, Davies and Clarke, reside; and near them are the huts of the native labourers. On the adjoining slope, fine crops of barley and wheat were standing in full ear; and in another part, fields of potatoes and clover.

But I cannot attempt to describe all I saw. There were large gardens, with every fruit and vegetable which England produces, and many belonging to a warmer clime. I may instance asparagus, kidney beans, cucumbers, rhubarb, apples, pears, figs, peaches, apricots, grapes, olives, gooseberries, currants, hops, gorse for fences and English oaks; also many kinds of flowers.

Around the farm-yard there were stables, a thrashing-barn with its winnowing machine, a blacksmith's forge, and on the ground ploughshares and other tools: in the middle was that happy mixture of pigs and poultry, lying comfortably together, as in every English farm-yard. At the distance of a few hundred yards, where the water of a little rill had been dammed up into a pool, there was a large and substantial water-mill.

All this is very surprising, when it is considered that five years ago nothing but the fern flourished here. Moreover, native workmanship, taught by the missionaries, has effected this change; – the lesson of the missionary is the enchanter's wand.

The house had been built, the windows framed, the fields ploughed, and even the trees grafted, by the New Zealander. At the mill, a New Zealander was seen powdered white with flour, like his brother miller in England. When I look at this whole scene, I thought it admirable. It was not merely that England was brought vividly before my mind; yet, as the evening drew to a close, the domestic sounds, the fields of corn, the distant undulating country with its trees, might well have been mistaken for our fatherland: nor was it the triumphant feeling at seeing what Englishmen could effect; but rather the high hopes thus inspired for the future progress of this fine island.

Several young men, redeemed by the missionaries from slavery, were employed on the farm. They were dressed in a shirt, jacket and trousers, and had a respectable appearance. Judging from one trifling anecdote, I should think they must be honest.

When walking in the fields, a young labourer came up to Mr Davies and gave him a knife and gimlet, saying that he had found them on the road, and did not know to whom they belonged! These young men and boys appeared very merry and good-humoured.

In the evening I saw a party of them at cricket: when I thought of the austerity of which the missionaries have been accused, I was amused by observing one of their own sons taking an active part in the game.

A more decided and pleasing change was manifested in the young women, who acted as servants within the houses. Their clean, tidy and healthy appearance, like that of dairy-maids in England, formed a wonderful contrast with the women of the filthy hovels in Kororareka.

The wives of the missionaries tried to persuade them not to be tattooed; but a famous operator having arrived from the south, they said, 'We really must just have a few lines on our lips; else when we grow old our lips will shrivel, and we shall be so very ugly.' There is not nearly so much tattooing as formerly; but it is a badge of distinction between chief and the slave, it will probably long be practised. So soon does any train of ideas become habitual that the missionaries told me that even in their eyes a plain face looked mean, and not that of a New Zealand gentleman.

Late in the evening I went to Mr Williams's house, where I passed the night. I found there a large party of children collected together for Christmas-day, and all sitting round a table at tea. I never saw a nicer or more merry group, and to think this was in the centre of the land of cannibalism, murder and all atrocious crime! The cordiality and happiness so plainly pictured in the faces of the little circle appeared equally felt by the older persons of the mission.

24 December 1835. In the morning, prayers were read in the native tongue to the whole family. After breakfast I rambled about the garden and farm. This was a market day, when the natives of the surrounding hamlets bring their potatoes, Indian corn or pigs, to exchange for blankets, tobacco, and sometimes through the persuasions of the missionaries, for soap.

Mr Davies's eldest son, who manages a farm of his own, is the man of business in the market. The children of the missionaries, who came while young to the island, understand the language better than their parents, and can get anything more readily done by the natives.

Charles Darwin Visits the Bay and Waimate

A little before noon Messrs Williams and Davies walked with me to part of a neighbouring forest, to show me the famous kauri pine. I measured one of these noble trees, and found it thirty-one feet in circumference above the roots. There is another one close by which I did not see, thirty-three feet; and I heard of one no less than forty feet.

These trees are remarkable for their smooth cylindrical boles, which run up to a height of sixty and even ninety feet, with a nearly equal diameter, and without a single branch. The crown of branches at the summit is out of all proportion small to the trunk; and the leaves are likewise small compared with the branches.

The forest was here almost composed of the kauri; and the largest trees, from the parallelism of their sides, stood up like gigantic columns of wood. The timber of the kauri is the most valuable production of the island; moreover, a quantity of resin oozes from the bark, which is sold at a penny a pound to the Americans, but its use was then unknown.

Some of the New Zealand forests must be impenetrable to an extraordinary degree. Mr Matthews informed me that one forest, only thirty-four miles in width, and separating two inhabited districts, had only lately for the first time been crossed. He and another missionary, each with a party of about fifty men, undertook to open a road; but it cost them more than a fortnight's labour!

In the wood I saw very few birds. With regards to animals, it is a most remarkable fact that so large an island, extending over more than seven hundred miles in latitude, and in many parts ninety broad, with varied stations, a fine climate, and land of all heights, from fourteen thousand feet downwards, with the exception of a small rat, did not possess one indigenous animal.

It is said that the common Norway rat, in the short space of two years, annihilated in this northern end of the island the New Zealand species. In many places I noticed several sorts of weeds, which, like the rats, I was forced to own as countrymen. A leek has overrun whole districts, and will prove very troublesome, but it was imported as a favour by a French vessel. The common dock is also widely disseminated, and will, I fear, for ever remain a proof of the rascality of an Englishman, who sold the seeds for those of the tobacco plant.

On returning from our pleasant walk to the house, I dined with Mr Williams; and then, a horse being lent me, I returned to the Bay of Islands. I took leave of the missionaries with thankfulness for their kind welcome, and with feelings of high respect for their gentlemanlike, useful and upright characters. I think it would be difficult to find a body of men better adapted for the high office which they fulfil.

Christmas Day, 1835. In a few more days the fourth year of our absence from England will be completed. Our first Christmas was spent at Plymouth; the second at St Martin's Cove, near Cape Horn; the third at Port Desire, in Patagonia; the fourth at anchor in a wild harbour in the peninsula of Tres Montes; the fifth here; and the next, I trust in Providence, will be in England.

We attended divine service in the chapel in Paihia; part of the service being read in English, and part in the native language.

Whilst at New Zealand we did not hear of any recent acts of cannibalism: but Mr Stokes found burned human bones strewed round a fire-place on a small island near the anchorage; but these remains of a comfortable banquet might have been lying there for several years. It is probable that the moral state of the people will rapidly improve.

Mr Busby mentioned one pleasing anecdote as a proof of the sincerity of some, at least, of those who profess Christianity. One of his young men left him, who had been accustomed to read prayers to the rest of the servants. Some weeks afterwards, happening to pass late in the evening by an outhouse, he saw and heard one of his men reading the Bible with difficulty by the light of the fire to the others.

After this the party knelt and prayed: in their prayers they mentioned Mr Busby and his family, and the missionaries, each separately in his respective district.

26 December 1835. Mr Busby offered to take Mr Sullivan and myself in his boat some miles up the river to Kawakawa; and proposed afterwards to walk on to the village of Waiomio, where there are some curious rocks.

Following one of the arms of the bay, we enjoyed a pleasant row, and passed through pretty scenery, until we came to a village, beyond which the boat could not pass. From this place a chief and a party of men volunteered to walk with us to Waiomio, a distance of four miles.

The chief was at this time rather notorious from having lately hanged one of his wives and a slave for adultery. When one of the missionaries remonstrated with him he seemed surprised, and said he thought he was exactly following the English method. Old Hongi, who happened to be in England during the queen's trial, expressed great disapprobation at the whole proceeding: he said he had five wives, and he would rather cut off all their heads than be so much troubled about one.

Leaving this village, we crossed over to another, seated on a hill-side at a little distance. The daughter of a chief who was still a heathen had died there five days before. The hovel in which she had expired had been burned to the ground. Her body, being enclosed between two small canoes, was placed upright on the ground, and protected by an enclosure bearing wooden images of their gods, and the whole was painted bright red, so as to be conspicuous from afar.

Her gown was fastened to the coffin, and her hair being cut off was cast at its foot. The relatives of the family had torn the flesh of their arms, bodies and faces, so that they were covered with clotted blood; and the old women looked most filthy, disgusting objects. On the following day some of the officers visited this place and found the women still howling and cutting themselves.

We continued our walk and soon reached Waiomio. Here there are some singular masses of limestone, resembling ruined castles. These rocks have long served for burial places, and in consequence are held too sacred to be approached. One of the young men, however, cried, 'Let us all be brave', and ran on ahead; but when within a hundred yards, the whole party thought better of it, and stopped short. With perfect indifference, however, they allowed us to examine the whole place.

At this village we rested some hours, during which time there was a long discussion with Mr Busby, concerning the right of sale of certain lands. One old man, who appeared a perfect genealogist, illustrated the successive possessors by bits of stick driven into the ground. Before leaving the houses, a little basketful of roasted sweet potatoes was given to each of our party; and we all, according to the custom, carried them away to eat on the road.

I noticed that, among the women employed in cooking, there was a man-slave; it must be a humiliating thing for a man in this warlike country to be employed in doing that which is considered as the lowest women's work.

Slaves are not allowed to go to war; but this perhaps can hardly be considered as a hardship. I heard of one poor wretch who, during hostilities, ran away to the opposite party. Being met by two men, he was immediately seized; but, as they could not agree to whom he should belong, each stood over him with a stone hatchet, and seemed determined that the other at least should not take him away alive. The poor man, almost dead with fright, was only saved by the address of a chief's wife.

We afterwards enjoyed a pleasant walk back to the boat, but did not reach the ship till late in the evening.

30 December 1835. In the afternoon we stood out of the Bay of Islands, on our course to Sydney. I believe we were all glad to leave New Zealand. It is not a pleasant place. Amongst the natives there is absent that charming simplicity which is found at Tahiti; and the greater part of the English are the very refuse of society. Neither is the country itself attractive. I look back but to one bright spot, and that is Waimate, with its Christian inhabitants.

1836

Marianne's third child Samuel was at school at Waimate under his uncle William from 1835 to 1838. During this time a Sports Day was arranged for the Waimate boys of which an account is given in Samuel's biography, Pioneering in New Zealand, *written by his son, William Temple Williams, in 1929.*

William Williams

The sports were held in what was known as the Oak Tree Paddock at Pakaraka. The Maoris from far and wide attended to witness the novel spectacle. Samuel arranged an event on the spot for the Maoris. It was to be a test of horsemanship. Competitors were to gallop down 'Long Lane', and take the sharp corner round the oak tree.

A number of Maori youths clamoured to take part in what seemed such an easy feat. They were soon mounted, and at a given signal away they galloped, but in rounding the corner they all dropped off like ninepins.

The Maori onlookers thoroughly enjoyed the joke, and chaffed the youths unmercifully, as with rueful faces and bruised limbs they made their way back to the starting point.

Finally, Samuel mounted a horse, and in the midst of tense excitement rode down the lane at a hand-gallop, and swooped round the corner in such a graceful manner that Maori and Pakeha alike roared approval.

Sunday, 8 May 1836. Paihia. A bright morning, but a piercing cold wind. I sent for Hera, to put my infant school into her charge and Mrs Ashwell's during my absence; went down to the boat with my husband; we got in at the rocks and rowed against a strong wind, and were off to the Kawakawa before the bell had rung for morning service.

Our row up the river was slow, the wind piercingly cold; I almost repented my undertaking. We landed a little before twelve on the Church Mission Society's land; twice I had landed there before, the first time ten years ago. The river and all its banks looked the same; but time had advanced and made many changes in us and in the state of the natives since then.

We walked some little distance through low brushwood to the new pa on the opposite banks of the stream; we were carried across. We saw the men and boys standing in front of the new chapel, and concluded that morning service was over, and that they were at school.

The old lady, widow of our chief, came to welcome us at the top of the steep bank, with several others: she conducted me to the verandah of a new kumera house, where she invited me to sit down upon a bundle of clean raupo. The number of women and children soon increased around me to a crowd.

With most of them I was well acquainted, and first one and then another exclaimed, '*Mata Wiremu* [Mother Williams] is sitting at the Kawakawa!! *Mata Wiremu* is sitting amongst us!! Sitting warming herself in the sun at the Kawakawa!!'

It was not long before their bell rang for the female school, and I accompanied Ana, Hera, Meri, Katerina, Riripeti (Elizabeth), Mariana, etc. The roof was finished of the new chapel; it is wider than ours at Paihia, and entirely their own performance; but it was only boarded up about six or seven boards from the ground.

A blanket was fastened up to keep the wind from my shoulders, the only chair at the Kawakawa placed for me, and fresh green fern spread under my feet; sixty-four women and girls were arranged in much order in different classes round the chapel, and twenty-four children.

Katerina has the women's school, and Meri Makarini the children's. Ana exclaimed, '*Mata Wiremu* will teach the first class!' I consequently heard the catechism, but upon concluding walked round all the others, and looked at the children. Katerina had the book and pencil I gave her. They then gave an account of the morning sermon, which Moses had that morning addressed to them, but Ana gave such a prolonged account of *Te Wiremu*'s at Paihia, a fortnight ago, the parable of the seed and the sower, that Henry called me to close before some who were waiting had said anything.

Meri ran away and wrote a long slateful, which she brought me while I was seated in the verandah. The bell then rang for church; I counted about a hundred and fifty, possibly more, who were assembled for divine worship, at least half decently dressed in English clothing.

Henry addressed them from Matt. VII, 24–27. As the floods had been at the Kawakawa, it was very applicable. It was a sight and a scene to stir up feelings of joy and gratitude to the Lord of the Harvest to be permitted this refreshing view of what God had wrought in the wilderness.

Jane

23 September 1836. Waimate. Within the last ten days we have had letters from our friends at the southward giving a deplorable account of the native proceedings. War is still raging between Rotorua and Waikato, and the settlement at the former place is given up for the present. Mr Chapman's house, after being plundered by one party, was set on fire by the others and burned to the ground to prevent old Waharoa making it his headquarters for the winter, and Mrs Pilley and Mr Knight were very roughly handled by the natives and stripped of their clothes, etc.

When this intelligence reached Matamata, Mr Brown considering that place no longer safe, immediately conducted Mrs B. and Mrs Chapman, and Maria Morgan (Marianne's sister, now married to Mr Morgan) to Puriri, leaving Mr Morgan in charge of the deserted houses. From thence he went to join Mr Chapman at Rotorua and with Messrs Fairburn and Wilson to do what they could towards promoting peace.

Our letters from Mrs Brown, Mrs Chapman and Mrs Wilson state that their husbands had been absent for a month and that they had not heard a syllable of or from them; no trifling source of anxiety, added to the distress of having to forsake their homes and so much that had already become dear to them.

Henry is wishing himself among them. Many of his old friends among the chiefs have been cut off in the attacks upon the Tauranga Pah. The country is indeed in a sad state, and our friends in a very critical situation just now.

1837

Queen Victoria came to the throne, aged eighteen years.

Henry

13 February 1837. I am paying more attention than heretofore to the children, a duty which I think has been too much overlooked, in a too ardent desire to carry on the public duties of the Mission.

You are aware that I purchased a piece of land as a farm, yet the general opinion of its qualities was bad. I therefore laboured under considerable disadvantage, and ploughed and sowed without hope, as the farmers told me I might get a crop of straw, and no wheat.

After my seed was in the ground, I paid a visit to the Thames and Tauranga, and on my return was thankful to learn that my wheat looked surprisingly well, and indeed it surpassed my utmost expectations. I pay an occasional visit to my native farmers, for I have no one else.

The last week we concluded our harvest. Our Waimate friends tell me it is remarkably good, far exceeding their own crop. My boys are now preparing land for the next crops, and are extending their borders.

I have a small native-built house for myself, and a large barn built by the natives. I have now to estimate in the year's expenses a blacksmith's shop of wood, cowshed, a shed for the sheep and fresh stock yards. We are obliged to proceed slowly, but, I hope, surely.

I wish to have things brought a little to hand by the time Samuel shall have done school, which will be January next, if all be spared. Samuel and Henry have taken the lead this year, and feel their importance. I hope I may not be led away by these things; but it is needful to attend to the children, and put them in the way to do something for themselves, and not be turned on the parish.

Mr Davis' land, Mr Clarke's and William's join mine. In this respect it is well situated.

28 March 1837. Paihia. By this opportunity I forward to your care a petition, which has been prepared here, and signed by several British subjects, though there are several who have not been able to put their names to it.

The one to the King is forwarded by Mr Busby, and we thought that you would be able, by the aid of Mr Hoare, to have it presented to the House of Commons by Mr Buxton, or some one else. It is high time that something be done to check the progress of iniquity committed by a lawless band daringly advancing in wickedness and outrage, under the assurance that 'there is no law in New Zealand'.

Without some immediate interposition on the part of the Government for our protection, our position will become very desperate, as we may expect to be surrounded ere long by a swarm of rogues and vagabonds, who indeed carry all before them, both as respects the respectable Europeans and also the natives.

Mr Marsden

March 1837. It is upwards of seven years since my last visit. On my arrival here, I find two of the principal chiefs at open war – Pomare and Titore; in consequence of which, the whole island was in the greatest commotion.

The chiefs from all parts have assembled, with their men, to support either Pomare or Titore. I have repeatedly visited both parties, with a view of bringing them to terms of peace; but have not succeeded.

The Revd Henry Williams has used every means in his power, but as yet without effect. There were one hundred and thirty-one Europeans in Pomare's pa, and a great number in Titore's camp. These are generally men of the most infamous character; runaway convicts, and sailors, and publicans, who have opened grogshops in the pas, where riot, drunkenness and prostitution are carried on daily.

What will be the issue of the contest cannot be foreseen. Pomare's pa is very strong. It appears to be impossible for Titore to take it. A few days ago, Titore sent eight hundred men, in forty-two war canoes, to attack Pomare's pa, but they returned, after much firing on both sides without effect. Two war canoes met and engaged, when three men belonging to Titore were killed; two of them were brothers and men of high rank.

3 April 1837. A fight at the pa (Otuihu, Pomare's place), or rather a squabble, which we fear will bring on trouble. A woman shot.

5 April 1837. Mr Brown has written to Henry, urging his return, on account of the disturbed state of the natives.

8 April 1837. Henry, Mr and Miss Marsden surprised us. The *Columbine*, when in sight, had been mistaken for the *Jessie*. A happy return. The dear old gentleman was delighted with his visit to Kaitaia.

9 April 1837. Henry went up through Kawakawa. He heard of the fight, and saw the canoes. No settlers at church. Heard of Mr Greenway's alarm, from the war party. Henry had called on Captain Clendon, and brought a box from them to be in a place of safety.

10 April 1837. Henry went to Kororareka, to see the army, and talk with leaders, to sound their disposition towards peace.

11 April 1837. Mr Marsden went with Henry and Mr Brown to the pa.

Henry

12 April 1837. I have returned from Kaitaia since Saturday last, and we found the natives here in great confusion, and know not what to say to them. However, on Saturday morning the parties met, and, after firing at each other for about three hours, the list of sufferers were one Englishman wounded in the foot, and one pig in the shoulder. Things look black around, but we shall be better able to judge in a few days.

Mr Marsden seems very much recovered since his landing; he is so very infirm that he is obliged frequently to rest when out for a walk, and requires much nursing and care. He has been very much delighted with all he has seen since his arrival; he says, nothing which we could have written could have conveyed to him the true state of the Mission.

William

13 April 1837. Waimate. It is now more than a year that the operations of the southern district have been suspended in consequence of war. Matamata where Mr Brown and Mr Morgan laboured is entirely given up. Rotorua for the present is suspended, and at Tauranga, one of the missionaries belonging to the three stations resides. This is all that can be done until peace shall be established. But a good work has commenced and at Matakiate about 140, and at Rotorua about 100 persons keep up regular worship among themselves in the absence of a missionary.

The remainder of Marianne's entries come from her journals.

14 April 1837. Mr Marsden and Henry went to Kororareka.

15 April 1837. A fearful day of excitement. Just as I went to the infant school, with Mr and Miss Marsden, Henry saw a movement among the canoes; was off, and up the river in his dressing-gown before we knew he was gone. Mrs Clendon and her children were brought over for refuge. She came weeping, and made me shudder with the account she gave of their skirmishing and fighting, and dropping down as fast, and my dear husband among them in the very thick of it. My husband returned safe. The poor natives had made a sad affair of it.

20 April 1837. Henry, Mr Brown and Mr Baker went to Kororareka, to see the captains of the vessels, who had a meeting on the occasion of the fight. Mr Busby went also. Mr Marsden went to see Captain Dillon, of the 'Jessie'. Rongo came, and her husband John (Hone) Heke. Rewharewha at Waimate. Our men at the farm, Matiu and Puriri, in great fear. The storm of war seems gathering, and fears increasing. But the Lord reigneth: we need not be dismayed.

22 April 1837. A volley of musketry at daylight. Papahia arrived at Waimate.

23 April 1837. Henry went up the Kawakawa.

24 April 1837. Henry went to see Papahia, at the camp at Waimate.

Jane

24 April 1837. Dear Marianne's sixth son [Joseph, her eleventh child] was baptised on Sunday week by our dear old friend Mr Marsden himself, who has now been some weeks in the land. He has grown very infirm, and his memory fails him a good deal, but he seems recreated by the little time he has been here.

The changes which have taken place since he was here seven years ago are very striking, and repay him for all the toils and trouble he has undertaken for the sake of New Zealand.

The school is going on very steadily under William and Mr Wade, and if nothing occurs to interrupt present plans, I hope the boys are likely to improve, but in this land we cannot calculate on anything or anybody, and all we can do is to make use of the present.

26 April 1837. Henry went inland.

27 April 1837. Mr Kemp breakfasted with us. The canoes were passing and firing; many sights and sounds of war.

29 April 1837. All was commotion. The fleet of canoes moved up the river, from Kororareka and Waitangi, to the attack of the pa. Henry was off before the breakfast bell rang: I had terror and anxiety to endure again.

2 May 1837. The natives firing and fighting behind the hills, near the Haumi. All the natives in the settlement up the hill, to see one man wounded.

3 May 1837. Henry went to Kororareka; thence to Whauwhauroa to meet Mr Davis.

4 May 1837. Mr Davis and Henry went up the river, and returned in good time.

5 May 1837. Henry and Mr Davis went over to Kororareka.

7 May 1837. Mr Davis and Henry went to Kawakawa. It seems now to be established that the Europeans should be unmolested.

9 May 1837. Henry set off directly after breakfast, to go and visit the Kawakawa; but the canoes passed from Waitangi before he started, and the firing soon began, and continued till three o'clock. The canoes were seen going from Kororareka. The firing had been heard at Waimate.

10 May 1837. Mr Marsden, Henry and Mr Clarke went to Kororareka, after there had been much firing, and playing, like children, at Bo-peep. The canoes from the pa, and those from Waitangi, coming out in a body, and daring each other to follow.

11 May 1837. Mr Marsden and Mr Clarke to Kerikeri.

12 May 1837. Henry did not return from Kororareka, where he had been toiling among the natives, till four o'clock.

16 May 1837. We heard of John Heke's near escape, being chased in a canoe from Wahapu. How sad that this Christian native should in any way mix in these civil wars.

22 May 1837. The canoes fired all day. Reports of killed and wounded.

23 May 1837. Henry and Mr Brown went up the river, and to Kororareka. Mr Marsden went with Mr Baker.

26 May 1837. Two vessels coming in; one expected to be the *Buffalo* or *Rattlesnake*.

27 May 1837. Mr Mair came with the letters just as we were dropping off to sleep. It was HMS *Rattlesnake*. Mr Marsden and Henry went aboard the *Rattlesnake*, and returned; the former in high spirits at having secured his passage to Sydney.

29 May 1837. Captain Hobson [of the *Rattlesnake*] and the first lieutenant called, with Mr Busby. The captain is a thin, pleasing man, said to be the original of 'Tom Cringle', of 'The Log'.

Tom Cringle's Log by Michael Scott told the story of a young midshipman's experiences fighting pirates in the West Indies. It was first published in a serial form in Blackwood's Edinburgh Magazine in 1829–33. Captain Hobson would return to New Zealand in 1840 with the Treaty of Waitangi and become the country's first Governor.

4 June 1837. Henry off at day-dawn to the Kawakawa. Heard news of peace at the southward.

6 June 1837. Mrs Clendon and children to dine, and spend the day. Captain Clendon [the American consul], after landing Mrs Clendon, picked up two captains, and saved their lives, from a boat upset, round which they were struggling; but he was near endangering the lives of his boat's crew, from the Waitangi mob, who ran along beach to fire at the boat, natives being of the opposite party.

14 June 1837. The canoes went up, a formidable show. News arrived of the slaughter of Pi; a chief of Hokianga killed. This mischief was done when we least expected.

17 June 1837. Henry returned unsuccessfully from his attempt among the natives to procure peace.

18 June 1837. Henry went up before it was well light to the Kawakawa.

19 June 1837. To our surprise, hear that Captain Wright's place had been stripped, and their inmates half murdered by three Europeans.

28 June 1837. Henry informed us that the Committee would be here next week, on account of the natives assembling, and the prospect of making peace.

4 July 1837. Mr and Miss Marsden embarked on board the *Alligator*, for Sydney, taking with them our eldest daughter, Marianne.

8 July 1837. Henry up the river, peace-making.

11 July 1837. Pi's son (Adam Clarke) arrived from Waimate. A grand haka of natives on the beach.

12 July 1837. Henry went up with natives, and had a fatiguing day; Wharerahi and Tamati Waka called. Noise of guns, and natives dancing on the beach.

14 July 1837. Henry returned with news of peace having been made; he had taken four individuals up to the pa. Rewa and Wharerahi came over in the evening to say that Kororareka were angry with the arrangements for peace.

15 July 1837. Rewa's great gun went off at Kororareka, as a sign they were angry. Henry had ordered *Maroro* (*Flying Fish*), the large boat, then ordered the little boat; and Wharerahi seemed inclined to give up all hope. All seemed gloomy again. However, Wharerahi came to beg the great boat might go, and he and Henry went to the pa, taking a red flag and a white one, for peace or war. We had the happiness of seeing Henry's boat return with his white flag flying to Kororareka, two canoes with him. A white flag was hoisted on shore. We knew that Henry had brought the Kororareka people back from the pa with a chief of the pa.

Two and a half years later the Treaty of Waitangi, known to the Maori as Te Tiriti O Waitangi, was signed on the front lawn of the Busby family home at Waitangi on 6 February 1840. This document signalled the arrival of British Rule in New Zealand and was translated and presented to the Maori chiefs by Marianne's husband, the Revd Henry Williams. There are no surviving letters of Marianne's written during 1838 and 1839, nor of her thoughts on the events surrounding the arrival of the Governor Hobson representing Queen Victoria and the British Government. During the early months of 1840, Marianne remained at Paihia while Henry and other missionaries travelled the North and South Islands collecting more signatures of Maori chiefs.

At the time that the Treaty was signed Marianne had just turned forty-six, her youngest child Joseph was almost three years old and her eldest son Edward was twenty-one; she had had, in all, eleven children. Life under British rule brought many changes for everyone in New Zealand, but Marianne continued running the girls' schools, nursing, cooking and entertaining the never-ending stream of visitors arriving at her home at Paihia, now affectionately known as the 'Williams' Hotel'.

Her husband, family and the welfare of the Maori people were always foremost in her heart. As the European population grew, she found herself in the impossible position of being torn between the Maoris' rights, new Government orders and the settlers' demands.

It has been said that in later years Marianne had very little patience with newly arrived missionary wives if she heard them complaining about the hardships they faced. Compared to the real dangers and genuine hardship she had first experienced, New Zealand life in the 1840s was for her 'almost sinful luxury'.

The historian Alison Drummond wrote, 'When most women of her class in England tended to subside gracefully onto a sofa, Marianne Williams was putting on her boots to cross the waters to Waitangi in the dark.'

Marianne has been described as belonging to an age and class that produced women tough and resilient enough to offer all the necessary practical pioneering qualities without jettisoning intellectual and social graces. A visitor to her home once commented on the fact that, regardless of their daily tasks, without failure everyone dressed for the evening meal.

Perhaps the final words are best left to the Revd Piripi Patiki, one of the first ordained Maori priests to work alongside Henry. He could well have been describing the successful and loving partnership of Marianne and Henry, when, in 1878,

*using some of Henry's naval metaphors, he described the role of
the wives of the clergymen:*

> A man is like the mast of a ship, and his wife is the rigging; if
> they left their husbands to stand alone, a sudden gust of wind
> might come and snap it off; but if the ship had its proper
> rigging, it would carry its sail and weather every gale.

Afterword

Henry's records for 1838 and 1839 show New Zealand was rapidly gaining international attention in regards to land investments and European settlement. On 28 April 1838, the French Roman Catholic bishop had arrived in the Bay of Islands and established a mission station on the shores at Kororareka (known today as Russell). Previous to the arrival of the French mission, Henry had written to the CMS committee in London with his concerns about the planned colonisation of the country by the New Zealand Company (referred to below as the New Zealand Association). While the CMS had links with the Whig government, the New Zealand Company had strong connections with the opposition, with a number of company directors and shareholders being Tory Members of Parliament. On 11 January 1838 Henry wrote the following letter from the Bay of Islands to the CMS in London.

The pamphlet relative to the New Zealand Association, and your remarks, we have now under consideration. I have read them with interest, and do not hesitate to say that unless some protection be given by the British Government, the country will be bought up, and the people pass into a kind of slavery, or be utterly destroyed.

The European Settlers are making rapid advances and are beginning to hold out threats. Should any encouragement be given to the Association, thousands would immediately come and overrun the country, and the natives must give way.

The only protection I can propose is that the English Government should take charge of the country, as the Guardians of New Zealand; and that the Chiefs should be incorporated into a General Assembly, under the guidance of certain officers, with an English Governor at their head, and protected by a military force; which would be the only means of giving weight to any laws which might be established, and preserve that order and peace so much required. The natives have many years since proposed this should be done, and have repeated their desire from time to time.

Added to this, news arrived that the Revd Samuel Marsden had died in Sydney on 12 May. He was in his 73rd year. Henry wrote at the time: 'Of our friend Mr Marsden we have had but one opinion – He was the Father of the Mission and we [were] glad to hear and receive his opinions, but he is gone and his fellow will not be found.'

In the winter of 1838 Henry mentions the early return of Marianne and Henry's eldest son, Edward, from England. After four years of studying medicine, he had become seriously ill and was 'invalided home by consequence of brain fever'. His uncle, Hugh Carleton, gives a dramatic account of Edward's arrival back in New Zealand in the wintry month of June:

Unable to bear the greater severity of the English climate, he [Edward] had been ordered to return home, and so came to an end his hope of a professional career. He came by way of Hokianga, a bar-harbour on the west coast. Signals were made on shore that the bar could not be taken, the sea being too high; but the master of the vessel decided to chance it. Probably he had no choice but to do so, for it was blowing hard onto a lee shore. . . . He gave his passengers the option of being battened down under the hatches, or lashed on deck; Mr Edward naturally preferring the latter alternative. The ship had been under double-reefed topsails; but the master now set every stitch he could, lashed two hands to the wheel, himself to the rigging and put her right before the wind.

They eventually landed safely and Edward returned to Pakaraka, where he joined his brother Samuel in the management of the farm. He was twenty years old.

During October 1839, Henry set sail for the southernmost point of the North Island at the request of the warrior chief, Te Rauparaha, who had been promised a missionary for his tribe. As soon as the anchor had been dropped, Henry discovered the New Zealand Company had already visited Port Nicholson (Wellington) and bought the entire harbour before leaving for the Middle Island (South Island) to buy land in Queen Charlotte Sound. Within four months the New Zealand Company had bought over twenty million acres in Wellington, Taranaki and Nelson from various Maori tribes.

The reason for Henry's journey was to deliver the young Revd Octavius Hadfield to the warrior chief Te Rauparaha at Waikanae, north of Wellington, before returning home, overland by foot, reaching the Bay of Islands in January 1840. Upon his return he went inland to Waimate, taking his family on a summer holiday.

Later Henry wrote his account of the events over the following days that led to the signing of the Treaty of Waitangi in 1840.

I was at the Waimate, after my journey from Wellington, having gone thither with the son and nephew of Rauparaha, to conduct Mr Hadfield, who had not been long in the country, to reside as the Missionary in that district; returning over land by Taupo, Whanganui, Rotorua and Tauranga, the first European who had undertaken that journey, bringing with me Iwikau, one of the leading chiefs from Taupo, and several others, on a visit to Ngapuhi.

On the night of the 29th of January, I was called up by a messenger from the Bay, to say that Captain Hobson had arrived in the Bay as Governor of New Zealand, and that he wished to see me as early as possible.

In the afternoon, I went on board HMS *Herald*, and was met by Captain Hobson, to whom I expressed my gratification that he had arrived to put an end to the great excitement then existing in the purchase of lands, caused by the sudden influx of Europeans arriving by every vessel from the Colonies [Australia].

At this date we had not received any intimation that the Government were contemplating any movement towards New

Zealand, though much correspondence had transpired, in consequence of the proceedings of the New Zealand Company. Captain Hobson had not been twelve hours at anchor before the Europeans commenced using most infamous and exciting language to the natives – that the country was gone to the Queen, and that the Maori were *taurekareka* (slaves).

On the 4th of February, about 4 o'clock p.m., Captain Hobson came to me with the Treaty of Waitangi in English, for me to translate into Maori, saying that he would meet me in the morning at the house of the British Resident, Mr Busby; when it must be read to the chiefs assembled at 10 o'clock. In this translation it was necessary to avoid all expressions of the English for which there was no expressive term in the Maori, preserving entire the spirit and tenor of the treaty.

The Treaty of Waitangi was translated into Maori with the help of his son Edward. Initially five drafts were prepared in English and one (only) was given to Henry. It guaranteed the Maori chiefs exclusive possession of their lands and estates, forests and fisheries, in return for ceding sovereignty to Queen Victoria. In all, forty-three chiefs signed Te Tiriti O Waitangi on 6 February, and, after shaking hands, Governor Hobson left to the sound of three thundering cheers for the Governor and Queen 'Wikitoria'. The 7th was wet, so celebrations were held on Saturday, 8th, when the Union Jack was unfurled at Waitangi, the *Herald* fired a royal salute and the ships in the harbour brought out their most colourful buntings. The next day the Paihia church was filled by the Governor and his entourage for a special service taken by Henry.

The following comes from a local Bay of Islands history guide regarding the life of Henry Williams after 1840:

Under the first two governors, Hobson and Fitzroy, the assistance, expertise with the language, and the experience of the missionaries had been appreciated. By his long association, and his genuine care for Maori welfare, Henry Williams had become one of the most influential persons in the country. But in standing up for what he believed was in the best interests of the Maori, Williams had made enemies in high places, particularly with directors of the New Zealand Company whom, he believed, were exploiting Maori. And he was out of favour with Governor Grey who regarded him as a rival to his own mana [respect], a situation which the autocratic Grey would not tolerate. Deviously he set about denouncing Williams and wrote to the Church Missionary Society with an accusation that he had acted traitorously, the evidence according to Grey being his continued relationship with [the chiefs] Heke and Kawiti during the 1845 war. He was also accused of unwarranted aggregation of land.

The CMS authorities in London, having this report from such an impeccable source, had no option but to believe it. Word reached Paihia in May 1850 that Henry Williams had been dismissed from the mission. The following Sunday he preached in the church as usual, and the next day announced that they were leaving Paihia.

So ended the Paihia mission.

Henry, Marianne and their family went to live at Pakaraka where their sons had farms. They built a house, which they called The Retreat.

A few years after Henry's dismissal, Governor Grey was in London and informed the CMS headquarters that the allegations against Henry were not entirely accurate. Henry was reinstated into the CMS fold in 1855. However, he spent the rest of his life living in The Retreat at Pakaraka with the Maori people until his death in 1867.

Marianne also continued to live at The Retreat and, when news spread that *Mata Wiremu* was dying, hundreds of Maori arrived and camped around the house. She died on 16 December 1879, just four days after her eighty-sixth birthday. She is buried beside Henry in the Pakaraka churchyard.

The Auckland newspaper *Southern Cross* published a tribute to Marianne shortly after her death:

From time to time we have to notice the death of those . . . identified with the early settlement and colonization of this country.

On this occasion we have to record the passing of a veritable pioneer in the person of Mrs Williams, widow of the late Archdeacon Henry Williams. She landed with her husband and three children at the Bay of Islands . . . 56 years ago. . . .

We regard with feelings of admiration the courage of the men who in those early days, in bands of two or three, came to this country for no other purpose than that of bringing the blessings of Christianity and civilization to its benighted and blood-thirsty inhabitants. If the courage of the men excited our admiration, with what feelings should we regard the women who with undaunted devotion accompanied their husbands on their mission of mercy. Conspicuous among these heroines was the venerable Lady whose death we now chronicle. . . .

Those must have been wonderfully courageous women who, without hesitation, parted with their husbands – we might say sent them forth to encounter unknown dangers at the hands of ruthless savages. Confident in the righteousness of their object, they were willing to be separated for six or more months at a time during which they underwent many hardships and not a few hair-raising escapes. It is hard to say who displayed the greater courage, the men who fearlessly went out at the call of duty, or their wives, who, with their helpless little ones, stayed behind at the mercy of excitable savages. The influence of the wives on the heathen was in some cases more effective than that of the missionaries. . . . At every station were schools for girls and women taught by the wives of missionaries . . . in all this work as well as in everything that had for its object the promotion of the causes for which she left her home, Mrs Williams proved herself an efficient and zealous fellow labourer worthy of her distinguished husband. . . . After the death of the Archdeacon . . . she was the object of devoted attention of children, grandchildren and great-grandchildren, whose delight it was to minister to her every want. Her faculties were unimpaired to the very last and she passed away after a brief illness, to the rest for which she had long prepared.

Appendix A

THE CHILDREN OF MARIANNE AND HENRY WILLIAMS

Edward Marsh. Born England, 2 November 1818. Died 1909. Farmer, linguist, director, magistrate, judge. Married Jane Davis, 9 February 1843. 13 children.

Marianne. Born England, 28 April 1820. Died 1919. Teacher. Married Christopher Pearson Davies, 9 February 1843. Medical missionary. 8 children.

Samuel. Born England, 17 January 1822. Died 1907. Teacher, farmer, missionary. Married Mary Williams, 30 September 1846. 7 children.

Henry. Born Paihia, 10 November 1823. Died 1904. Farmer, county councillor, legislative councillor. Married Jane Williams, 15 February 1849. 1 child.

Thomas Coldham. Born Paihia, 18 July 1825. Died 1912. Farmer and businessman. Married Annie Palmer Beetham, 20 October 1858. 13 children including Hilda and Algar Williams.

John William. Born Paihia, 6 April 1827. Died 1904. Farmer, provincial councillor, MP. Married Sarah Busby, 3 May 1854. 11 children.

Sarah. Born Paihia, 26 February 1829. Died 1866. Married Thomas Bidulph Hutton, 26 April 1849. Teacher, priest, artist. 5 children.

Catherine. Born Paihia, 24 February 1831. Died 1902. Married Octavius Hadfield, 19 May 1852. Bishop Primate. 10 children.

Caroline Elizabeth. Born Paihia, 13 November 1832. Died 1916. Married Samuel Bloomfield Ludbrook, 15 December 1858. Builder, farmer. 7 children.

Lydia Jane. Born Paihia, 2 December 1834. Died 1891. Married Hugh Francis Carleton, 30 November 1859. Trader, politician, educator. No children.

Joseph Marsden. Born Paihia, 5 March 1837. Died 1892. Farmer. Never married.

Appendix B

LIST OF MISSIONARY PERSONNEL, NEW ZEALAND, 3 AUGUST 1823

Passengers on the Brampton *under the command of Captain Moore*

Revd Henry and Mrs Marianne Williams and children Edward, Marianne and Samuel

Revd Samuel Marsden, Senior Chaplain to the Colony of New South Wales and Founder of the CMS Mission in New Zealand
William Fairburn, carpenter, and his wife

Revd Nathaniel Turner, Wesleyan missionary, and his wife, destined for the Wesleyan mission at Whangaroa
Revd John Hobbs, Wesleyan missionary
Betsy, English-born convict, engaged at Port Jackson to look after the Williams children
Te Puhi (Bushy), Maori relative of Hongi Hika returning from residence with Samuel Marsden at Parramatta
Watu, young Maori returning from residence with Samuel Marsden

Resident Missionary Personnel

At Rangihoua
William Hall, CMS catechist and carpenter
John King, CMS catechist, shoemaker and flax dresser, and his wife Hannah
James Shepherd, CMS missionary, and wife

At Kerikeri
Revd John Butler, CMS missionary, and his wife
James Kemp, CMS catechist and blacksmith, and his wife
Revd Thomas Kendall, CMS missionary, and his wife
John Cowell, twine-spinner, and his wife
William Puckey, CMS layman and accomplished linguist, and his wife

At Whangaroa
Revd Samuel Leigh, Wesleyan Missionary
Revd William White, Wesleyan Missionary
James Stack, Wesleyan probationer arrived 1823, transferred to CMS in 1831 after period in England

Appendix C

TWO RECIPES OF MARIANNE WILLIAMS

Marianne's Pound Ginger Cake

Taken from Marianne's handwritten recipe book with the kind permission of Mrs
Mary Jefford, Gisborne, New Zealand

2 cups of sugar	2 cups of butter
4 eggs	2 cups of molasses
5 cups of flour	

Rubbed together.

1 teaspoon Saleratus [aerated salt, an impure bicarbonate of potash, much used as
baking powder] dissolved in 1 cup sour milk

Ginger and fruit to taste.

Marianne's receipt for pound ginger
cake. *(Mrs Mary Jefford, Gisborne,
NZ)*

Marianne's receipt for hastening the vegetation of seeds

Take a cubic inch of water, a teaspoonful of common muriatic acid [hydrochloric
acid or seawater], two teaspoonfuls of oxyd [oxide] of manganese, mix them, and
place the seeds in them.

Allow the whole to digest with a heat of 18–20 Reaum [Réaumur's thermometric
scale where water freezes at 0 degrees and boils at 80 under standard conditions].
The seeds must be taken out as soon as the corkle [corcule = the embryo in a plant
seed] appears.

Bibliography

Unpublished and Primary Sources

Letters and journals of Henry and Marianne Williams; William and Jane Williams; notes of Miss Hilda Temple Williams, 1937; from the private collection of Mrs Belinda Fitzgerald

Letters and Journals of Henry and Marianne Williams held in the Library of the Auckland War Memorial Museum

Davies, George, 'The Shield of Faith: The Life and Times of Henry and Marianne Williams' (unpublished)

Video interviews with the late Mrs Sybil Woods, Waikanae, New Zealand, 1995

Published Sources

Bawden, Patricia, *The Years before Waitangi* (Self-published. Printed by Institute Press Ltd, Auckland, 1987)

Burns, Patricia, *Fatal Success: A History of the New Zealand Company* (Heinemann Reed, Auckland, 1989)

Carleton, Hugh, *Life of Henry Williams. Volume One* (Upton, Auckland, New Zealand, 1874)

—— *Life of Henry Williams. Volume Two* (Wilson & Horton, Auckland, New Zealand, 1877)

—— *A Page from History. By Metoikos* (Williamson & Wilson, Auckland, 1854)

Clarke, George, *Notes on Early Life in New Zealand* (J. Walch & Sons, Hobart, Australia, 1903)

Darwin, Charles, *Journal of Researches into the Natural History and Geology of the Countries visited during the Voyage of the HMS Beagle Round the World* (Nelson & Sons, London, 1893)

Drummond, Alison, *Married and Gone to New Zealand* (Paul Ltd., Auckland, and Oxford University Press, Oxford, 1960)

—— and Drummond, L.R., *At Home in New Zealand: An Illustrated History of Everyday Things before 1865* (Blackwood & Janet Paul Ltd., Auckland, New Zealand, 1967)

Egan, Jack, *Buried Alive: Sydney 1788–1792* (Allen & Unwin, NSW, Australia, 1999)

Glen, Robert (ed.), *Mission and Moko: The Church Missionary Society in New Zealand 1814–1882* (for the Latimer Fellowship (NZ), Christchurch. Printed by the Olive Tree, Christchurch, 1992)

Levin, Stephen, and Vasil, Raj, *Maori Political Perspectives* (Hutchinson Group

(NZ) Ltd, Auckland, 1985)

Maning, Frederick, *History of the War in the North of New Zealand against the Chief Heke in the Year 1845, Told by an old Chief of the Ngapuhi Tribe*, trans. A Pakeha Maori (George Chapman, Queen Street, Auckland, n.d.)

Nicholas, John Liddiard Esq., *Nicholas's New Zealand*, vols i and ii. *Narrative of a Voyage to New Zealand, 1814 & 1815* (James Black & Son., London, 1817)

Discovering Northland's Past: Route One. Prepared by members of the Northland Branch Committee of the New Zealand Historic Places Trust (Pukepuriri Publications, Kaikohe, 1999)

Orange, Claudia, *The Treaty of Waitangi* (Allen & Unwin, Port Nicholson Press, 1987)

Pickmere, Nancy, *The Story of Paihia* (Self published. Printed by Calder Design and Print Company Ltd, Whangarei, 2000)

Porter, Francis, *The Turanga Journals: Letters and Journals of William and Jane Williams, New Zealand 1840–1850* (Price Milburn & Co. Ltd, for Victoria Universtiy Press, Wellington 1974)

Rees, Sian, *The Floating Brothel* (Hodder Headline, Australia Pty Ltd, Sydney, 2001)

Ritchie, Rayma, *Cargoes: An Introduction to the History of the Bay of Islands* (Pukepuriri Publications, Kaikohe, 1999)

Rogers, Lawrence (ed.), *The Early Journals of Henry Williams, 1826–1840* (Pegasus Press, Christchurch, New Zealand, 1961)

—— *Te Wiremu: A Biography of Henry Williams* (Pegasus Press, Christchurch, New Zealand, 1973)

Salmond, Anne, *Between Worlds: Early Exchanges between Maori and Europeans 1773–1815* (Viking, Penguin Press (NZ) Ltd, 1997)

Williams, T.C., *A Page from the History of a Record Reign* (McKee & Co., Wellington, 1899)

Williams, William, *Dictionary of the New Zealand Language* (Williams & Norgate, London, 1852)

Williams, William Temple, *Pioneering in New Zealand: The Life of the Venerable Archdeacon Samuel Williams* (Published privately, 1929)

Woods, Sybil, *Marianne Williams: A Study of Life in the Bay of Islands New Zealand 1823–1879* (Self-published, Christchurch, New Zealand, 1977)

—— *Samuel Williams of Te Aute* (Pegasus Press, Christchurch, New Zealand, 1981)

Index

Notes
1. Most entries relate in some way to Marianne and Henry Williams. Entries under their names, therefore, reflect major incidents only. The *chronology* entry elaborates this.
2. The abbreviation M&H refers to Marianne and Henry Williams.
3. Sub-entries are in *chronological order*, where relevant.
4. Entries in *italics* with bracketed translations (mainly inserted by Marianne) are Maori words

Index

Index

Index

Index

Index

Index